PLURALISM, JUSTICE, AND EQUALITY

Pluralism, Justice, and Equality

Edited by
DAVID MILLER
and
MICHAEL WALZER

OXFORD UNIVERSITY PRESS

Oxford University Press, Great Clarendon Street, Oxford OX2 6DP

Oxford New York

Athens Auckland Bangkok Bogota Bombay
Buenos Aires Calcutta Cape Town Dar es Salaam
Delhi Florence Hong Kong Istanbul Karachi
Kuala Lumpur Madras Madrid Melbourne
Mexico City Nairobi Paris Singapore
Taipei Tokyo Toronto

and associated companies in
Berlin Ibadan

Oxford is a trade mark of Oxford University Press

Published in the United States by
Oxford University Press Inc., New York

© the several contributors 1995

Published as hardback and paperback 1995
Reprinted in paperback 1996

British Library Cataloguing in Publication Data
Data available

Library of Congress Cataloging in Publication Data
Data available
ISBN 0-19-827937-X
ISBN 0-19-828008-4 (Pbk.)

Printed in Great Britain
on acid-free paper by
Bookcraft (Bath) Ltd.
Midsomer Norton, Avon

PREFACE

———◻◆◻———

THE idea for this book emerged from some discussions between the two editors about issues arising from Michael Walzer's book *Spheres of Justice*, first published in 1983. A decade later the book was still being widely debated, and a fairly substantial body of critical literature had emerged concerning its central theses, the plurality of spheres of justice and the idea of complex equality. We thought it might be valuable to assemble a series of appraisals by political theorists and philosophers, including some who were quite sceptical about the general programme of *Spheres of Justice*, and others who were more sympathetic, but who might wish to modify or extend some of its arguments. David Miller would begin by circulating a general overview of the book's arguments, and Michael Walzer would conclude by defending, developing, or modifying (as the case might be) the ideas he had expressed there in the light of the appraisals being offered.

This explains the plan of the book. The contributors were chosen by the two editors together, but David Miller alone was responsible for commenting on draft versions of the papers. We should like to record our thanks to Trude Hickey of Nuffield College for her help in co-ordinating the project.

D.M.
M.W.

CONTENTS

NOTES ON CONTRIBUTORS

JUDITH ANDRE is an associate professor at Michigan State University where she holds a joint appointment in the philosophy department and in the Center for Ethics and Humanities in the Life Sciences. Her recent publications have addressed embodiment ('Respect for Bodies') and the moral/psychological relationships between professionals and those they serve ('My Client, My Enemy'). She is working on a paper about the paradoxes within preventive medicine.

RICHARD J. ARNESON is Professor of Philosophy and Chair of the Department of Philosophy at the University of California, San Diego. Since 1986 he has been an associate editor of the journal *Ethics*. Among his essays in social and political philosophy are papers on democracy, equality, and the meaning of work. He is currently writing a book on distributive justice and responsibility.

BRIAN BARRY is Professor of Political Science at the London School of Economics. He is former editor of the *British Journal of Political Science* and *Ethics*. His books include *Political Argument* (1965, reissued 1990): two volumes of essays, *Democracy and Power* and *Liberty and Justice* (1989); and *A Treatise on Social Justice*, i. *Theories of Justice* (1989), ii. *Justice as Impartiality* (1995). He is a Fellow of the American Academy of Arts and Sciences and of the British Academy.

JOSEPH .H. CARENS is Professor of Political Science at the University of Toronto. He is the author of *Equality, Moral Incentives, and the Market* (1981) and editor of *Democracy and Possessive Individualism* (1993). He is currently working on a book on immigration and political community.

JON ELSTER is Professor of Political Science at the University of Chicago. Among his recent publications are *Local Justice* (1992) and *Political Psychology* (1993). He is also the editor of *Local Justice in America* (forthcoming).

AMY GUTMANN, Laurance S. Rockefeller University Professor of Politics at Princeton University, is director of the University Center for Human Values and the Program in Ethics and Public Affairs. She is the author of *Liberal Equality* (1980) and *Democratic Education* (1987), and editor of *Multiculturalism: Examining the Politics of Recognition* (expanded edition 1994), *Ethics and Politics* (2nd edition, with Dennis Thompson, 1990), and *Democracy and the Welfare State* (1988). She is currently developing a theory of deliberative democracy and addressing various moral and political issues associated with multiculturalism.

DAVID MILLER is Official Fellow in Social and Political Theory at Nuffield College, Oxford. Among his books are *Social Justice* (1976) and *Market, State and Community* (1989). He is currently finishing a book on the idea of nationality, and working on a set of essays exploring different aspects of the idea of social justice from both empirical and normative perspectives.

SUSAN MOLLER OKIN is Professor of Political Science and Director of the Program in Ethics in Society at Stanford University. The author of *Women in Western Political Thought* (1979) and *Justice, Gender and the Family* (1989), she is at present working primarily on questions about gender and relativism.

MICHAEL RUSTIN is Professor of Sociology at the University of East London, and a Visiting Professor at the Tavistock Clinic. He is the author of *For a Pluralist Socialism* (1985), *Narratives of Love and Loss: Studies in Modern Children's Fiction* (with Margaret Rustin, 1987), and *The Good Society and the Inner World: Psychoanalysis, Politics, and Culture* (1991).

ADAM SWIFT is Fellow in Politics and Sociology at Balliol College, Oxford. He is co-author (with Stephen Mulhall) of *Liberals and Communitarians* (1992) and of a number of articles that reflect his interest in bringing together sociological and political-theoretical concerns. He is currently working on two collaborative and international-comparative projects: a study of social class, social mobility and meritocracy, and a book about popular beliefs about distributive justice.

JEREMY WALDRON is Professor of Law at the University of California at Berkeley and Chair of the Jurisprudence and Social Policy Program at Boalt Hall. He was educated in New Zealand and at Oxford, has taught at Oxford, Edinburgh, Cornell, and U.C. Berkeley, and has published widely in moral philosophy, political theory, and jurisprudence. His books include *Nonsense*

Upon Stilts (1987), *The Right to Private Property* (1988), and *Liberal Rights: Collected Papers, 1981–91* (1993).

MICHAEL WALZER is Professor of Social Science at the Institute for Advanced Study in Princeton and the co-editor of *Dissent* magazine. His previous books include *Just and Unjust Wars* (1977, 2nd edition 1992), *Spheres of Justice* (1983) and *The Company of Critics* (1989).

Introduction

DAVID MILLER

———◻▪◆▪◻———

In his book *Spheres of Justice* and associated writings,[1] Michael Walzer has given us an account of justice that is in several respects very different from the kind of account we are used to finding in works of political philosophy. Usually the theorist will search for some fundamental principle or axiom which he or she believes lies behind all the more concrete beliefs and judgements that we express when we say that this or that action or practice is a fair or just one. There are several principles that we might envisage occupying such a role. We might suggest, for instance, that the fundamental principle of justice is that of *equal treatment*: people are treated justly when they are all given the same consideration by whatever body or institution is allocating resources to them. Alternatively we might think that the fundamental principle was *desert*: people are treated fairly when each of them gets what he or she deserves, no more and no less. Yet again it might be said that what justice fundamentally requires is respect for each person's inalienable *rights*—to life, liberty, and property, say. Adopting such an approach, when we have to decide whether some practice like affirmative action in the assignment of jobs or taxing away inherited wealth is just or not, we consult the fundamental principle and follow out its implications for the particular case. We ask

[1] The most important of these writings for our purposes are the following: *Spheres of Justice* (New York: Basic Books, 1983); 'Philosophy and Democracy', *Political Theory*, 9 (1981), 379–99; 'Liberalism and the Art of Separation', *Political Theory*, 12 (1984), 315–30; 'Interpretation and Social Criticism', in S. M. McMurrin (ed.), *The Tanner Lectures on Human Values*, viii (Salt Lake City: Univ. of Utah Press, 1988); *The Company of Critics* (New York: Basic Books, 1989); 'Objectivity and Social Meaning', in M. Nussbaum and A. Sen (eds.), *The Quality of Life* (Oxford: Clarendon Press, 1992); 'Exclusion, Injustice, and the Democratic State', *Dissent*, 40 (1993), 55–64.

whether equal treatment requires that jobs should be awarded strictly on the basis of personal merit, or whether belonging to a disadvantaged group gives you a fair claim to preferential consideration; and so on. Our theory of justice is meant to look a bit like a scientific theory in which a small number of fundamental laws are established, and these are then applied to a range of concrete cases, bringing them into a common fold and showing how, despite their superficial differences, they share the same essential properties.

Walzer's account of justice is developed in conscious opposition to this approach. It is radically pluralistic in nature. There are no universal laws of justice.[2] Instead, we must see justice as the creation of a particular political community at a particular time, and the account we give must be given from within such a community. The account will also be pluralistic in a second sense: in liberal democracies especially, but in other societies too, there are many different kinds of social goods (and evils) whose distribution is a matter of justice, with each kind of good having its own particular criterion of distribution. The criteria used to determine who should get public honours, say, will not be the same as the criteria used to determine who should get medical care. And there is no underlying principle standing behind all these distributive criteria, no core idea which might *explain* why honours are to be distributed in one way and medical care in another.

Yet, despite the fact that Walzer deliberately rejects the search for any fundamental principle of justice, he none the less wants to make one general claim about societies which respect distributive pluralism of the kind just outlined: they may realize 'complex equality' among their members. Complex equality obtains when different people get ahead in each of the various spheres of distribution, but because they are unable to convert their advantages from one sphere into another, none is able to dominate the rest. As Walzer explains this idea:

In formal terms, complex equality means that no citizen's standing in one sphere or with regard to one social good can be undercut by his standing

---

[2] Walzer has qualified this view in one significant respect. In 'Interpretation and Social Criticism' he concedes that some requirements of justice run across all cultures and may on that account be regarded as 'a kind of minimal and universal moral code' (p. 22). These include prohibitions against murder, deception, and gross cruelty.

in some other sphere, with regard to some other good. Thus, citizen X may be chosen over citizen Y for political office, and then the two of them will be unequal in the sphere of politics. But they will not be unequal generally so long as X's office gives him no advantages over Y in any other sphere—superior medical care, access to better schools for his children, entrepreneurial opportunities, and so on. (*Spheres*, 19)

Complex equality in this sense can also be understood as an idea of equal citizenship, which I shall suggest plays a regulative role in Walzer's theory of justice. To say this, however, is not to say that it serves as a *fundamental* principle in the way in which equality, or desert, or inalienable rights have served in other theories. Complex equality cannot generate spheres of distribution; it is better understood as an ethically important *by-product* which, according to Walzer, appears in liberal societies when the autonomy of each distributive sphere is maintained.

One consequence of Walzer's general approach to justice is that his account must remain closer to the beliefs and understandings of ordinary people than is usually the case with abstract theories of justice. Identifying the kinds of goods available for distribution, and the criteria which are appropriate to each, means interpreting the culture of a particular society; in Walzer's metaphor, whereas the philosopher is conventionally supposed to 'walk out of the cave, leave the city, climb the mountain, fashion for oneself . . . an objective and universal standpoint', a better alternative is 'to stand in the cave, in the city, on the ground . . . to interpret to one's fellow citizens the world of meanings that we share' (*Spheres*, p. xiv). But this does not mean that the philosopher may not also be a critic of his society. What it does mean is that he or she must be a 'connected critic', a critic who attacks existing institutions and practices not by invoking some abstract principle but by highlighting the divergences between the ethical code espoused by his or her society and what actually takes place there. The critic, Walzer says, 'gives voice to the common complaints of the people or elucidates the values that underlie those complaints'.[3]

This account of justice is sure to provoke many questions and objections in the reader, among them the question whether a political philosophy which follows these prescriptions can engage in radical criticism of the status quo, or whether it is not bound to

---

[3] Walzer, *Company of Critics*, 16.

acquiesce in the prevailing ideology, to succumb to what Marx called 'the illusion of the epoch'. I shall raise some of these questions as I look in greater detail at the account of justice that I have so far sketched very rapidly.

Let us begin, then, by observing that, on Walzer's view, questions of justice always arise within a bounded political community. This is true, first of all, because unless we begin from a society with a determinate membership, there will be no social goods with shared meanings to distribute. Moreover, unless the society is politically organized, developing a theory of justice will be a pointless activity, because the state (in modern circumstances) is the institution whose job it is to maintain the boundaries between the spheres of distribution. In general, therefore, we cannot appeal to justice to fix the proper boundaries of the community; this is to put the cart before the horse. But there is an important qualification to be entered here. However the boundaries are fixed, Walzer argues, everyone inside them must be regarded as a fully fledged member of the community, entitled to take part in each of the spheres of justice. There cannot be more than one class of citizen: people in the position of *metics* in classical Athens or guest workers in contemporary Europe, deprived of political rights, are subject to a kind of tyranny which immediately and directly violates complex equality.

Each community creates its own social goods—their significance depends upon the way they are conceived by the members of that particular society. The roster of such goods will differ from place to place. In *Spheres* Walzer sees the following as the main categories of goods in contemporary liberal societies: security and welfare, money and commodities, office (i.e. positions of employment), hard work, free time, education, kinship and love, divine grace, recognition (i.e. marks of esteem, public honours, and so forth), political power. Most of these goods are likely to have analogues in other societies, but typically the analogues won't carry precisely the same meanings as the goods do with us. Much of Walzer's study is concerned with such contrasts, comparing, for example, the modern idea of the vacation with the Roman idea of the public holiday, or the old Chinese criteria for entry to the civil service with contemporary debates about appointment to public office. The point of these comparisons is to highlight what is specific about our own understanding of various goods—and by extension to reveal what we believe about their distribution.

This brings us to Walzer's third, and perhaps most controversial, claim: that the meaning of each social good determines its criterion of just distribution. Once we know what it is we have to allocate, he argues, we also know how we should allocate it—to whom and by what means. In the case of medical care, for instance, the distributive criterion is need; in the case of money and commodities, it is free exchange in the market; in the case of education, it is equality at the basic level, and capacity to benefit at a higher level. If there is disagreement about the distributive criterion, this must reflect disagreement about the nature of the good itself, so once we have settled the latter issue, the distributive question will resolve itself. Once we can establish what medical care, say, really means to us, we shall know by what methods and criteria it ought to be allocated among potential claimants.

How are we to understand this claim that distributive criteria are intrinsic to social goods? The strongest interpretation would be that there is a conceptual link between the meaning of the good and its principle of distribution, so that someone who proposed to distribute the good in another way would in the most literal sense be failing to understand what the good in question really was. Of the goods in Walzer's list, only love, divine grace, and recognition seem clearly to embody such a link. These are goods which it would be self-defeating to try to distribute other than by their proper principles. Love that is not freely given—'love' that is bought or coerced, say—is by that token not the genuine thing. Equally, if we have a system, formal or informal, of conferring honours on people, then it must be the case that the criterion of allocation is possession of the praiseworthy attributes which the honour is meant to celebrate. If you sell honours, or give them to everyone who reaches a certain rank in the party hierarchy, their value evaporates.[4] In these cases, then, the meaning of the good and its criterion of just distribution really are tightly interlocked. But that does not seem to be true for money, or medical aid, or education, or political power. Although it would be pointless to give medical aid to someone who was not ill, or education to

---

[4] The system can tolerate minor infractions so long as these are kept out of the public eye, but they remain parasitic on a practice in which the genuinely deserving are honoured.

someone incapable of benefiting from it, these constraints do not fully resolve the distributive question. You and I can agree about what education is—about what its value consists in—yet you may believe that access to education should be governed solely by pupils' ability, whereas I think it is all right for parents to buy better education for their children. Indeed, it is precisely the possibility of this sort of disagreement that fuels Walzer's anxiety about invasion across the spheres. Invasion occurs when people who have accumulated large quantities of good X use that advantage to acquire more than they are justly entitled to of good Y. If distributive criteria were always internal, invasion would be impossible, because the good that was acquired by illegitimate conversion would be a different good from the original one. If education has to be distributed on the basis of ability, then what is sold to parents for cash cannot be education. But that seems absurd.

In fact, Walzer never commits himself dogmatically to the strong version of the claim that the meaning of a good determines its proper distribution. He freely admits, for instance, that 'until recent times, the practice of medicine was mostly a matter of free enterprise'. But, he says, 'the distributive logic of the practice seems to be this: that care should be proportionate to illness and not to wealth'. What can 'distributive logic' mean here? It cannot be interpreted literally. The doctors who spent their time treating rich patients were not guilty of some kind of conceptual fallacy. In fact, what Walzer says about them is that they had a 'bad conscience'. But this suggests simply that there is a widely held distributive principle which holds that medicine ought to be allocated according to need. And although this principle may be suggested by the nature of medicine itself—the fact that medical need is a necessary condition for being able to benefit from this good—it is not entailed by it. It seems rather that we see medical aid as falling within a class of essential life-supporting goods about which people in contemporary democracies have a strong belief that they should be available to all who need them. The relationship between the meaning of the good and the distributive principle is not here a conceptual one; it is rather that, once we see what kind of good medicine is, this immediately *triggers* a particular distributive principle which we see as applying to all goods of that sort.

I am suggesting, then, that Walzer's claim that, when we understand what a social good is, we also understand how it should be distributed, should not be taken in its strongest and most literal sense. But this in no way diminishes the power or the distinctiveness of his theory of justice. We still face the injunction to begin our thinking not with general principles like equality or desert but with specific goods like money or education and to work upwards from there. The reading I have given does, however, force us to confront an issue that several of Walzer's critics have raised, namely how we are to go about establishing the proper distributive principle for a good like medicine, particularly where there appear to be conflicting views about this question in the society we are addressing.[5]

Walzer's method is an interpretive one. He claims to be providing us with the best interpretation of a set of social meanings, where 'social meanings' stretches to cover distributive criteria as well as the meaning of goods in its most literal sense. The raw material of such an interpretation are the institutions and practices of a society on the one hand, and people's beliefs about those institutions and practices on the other. So Walzer looks at how the education system in contemporary America is organized, but he also looks at what people think and say about it, at how teachers understand their role, at what parents demand for their children, and so forth. This duality of focus seems to me a source of strength. Practices are to some extent a precipitate of past and present belief. They are more stable than opinion, and it may be easier to discern the principles that lie behind them, particularly where, as in the case of education, the distributive criterion is complex rather than simple. To look only at practices, on the other hand, would be to sanctify the status quo and to deny justice its critical role, which is very far from Walzer's intention. Practices are always to some extent shaped by forms of power external to the distributive sphere in question, and this illegitimate shaping will be reflected in complaints and criticism from those involved in the practice. In the case of medicine, for instance, the practice takes the form (in the USA) of a semi-private, semi-public system where the quality of medical care available to each person depends upon their ability to

---

[5] Representative here are the views expressed in R. Dworkin, 'To Each His Own', *New York Review of Books*, 30/6 (Apr. 1983), 4–6, repr. as 'What Justice Isn't' in R. Dworkin, *A Matter of Principle* (Oxford: Clarendon Press, 1986). Dworkin argues that disputes about the right way to distribute particular social goods can only be resolved by an appeal to some more abstract principle of justice (such as the principle of equality that he favours).

pay for it. As we have seen, Walzer believes that the popular understanding of medicine requires that it be distributed on grounds of need alone, and this would require a radical reform of the practice, turning it into an American version of the welfare state.

We must, then, look beyond practices to people's opinions about those practices. But this does not entail conducting a simple opinion poll in which people are asked 'how do you think medicine (education, money, etc) should be allocated?' Challenged on the question of how we should distinguish between better and worse interpretations of our principles, Walzer has contrasted 'deep and inclusive accounts of our social life' with 'shallow and partisan accounts'.[6] How are we to understand this contrast? One requirement of a successful interpretation is simple consistency—the elimination of contradictory answers to the same question. Although this requirement may seem self-evident, it is not trivial, as any opinion researcher knows. Different ways of framing a question, different ways of placing a question in relation to other questions, will get you a significant number of contradictory responses. At this level, a good interpretation is simply one that discards people's aberrant opinions in favour of their regular ones, their off-the-cuff responses in favour of those they hold on to more obdurately, allowing the interpreter to build up a clear picture of public opinion on an issue like inherited wealth or the private purchase of medical care.

A stronger requirement than mere consistency is that beliefs should be *coherent*, where this means that the set of beliefs someone holds should have a certain structure to it; in particular, opinions about specific issues should be derived from principles of a more general sort. It is not straightforwardly inconsistent for someone to think that white racists should be permitted to express derogatory views about blacks, but that black racists should be prevented from saying similar things about whites. But since the first belief is likely to be supported by an appeal to the general principles of free thought and free speech, the two beliefs are incoherent unless the person holding them can give some plausible reason why blacks alone should be debarred from exercising the rights which, he admits, everyone should normally enjoy. Appealing to

---

[6] M. Walzer, 'Spheres of Justice: An Exchange', *New York Review of Books*, 30/12 (July 1983), 43.

coherence in support of an interpretation means, then, taking beliefs about one issue, extracting from them a more general principle which makes sense of those beliefs, and applying that principle by analogy to beliefs about some neighbouring issue. The results of such an appeal may be quite radical. A striking example may be found in *Spheres*. Walzer argues that the private ownership of factories and firms of other kinds constitutes a form of political power, which, therefore, should be subject to the same kinds of control as political power at the state level. It is a firmly held belief in democratic societies that public officials are accountable to those over whom they exercise their power; they may be removed from office if they abuse it. It follows that firms, too, should be subject to democratic control, primarily by those who work for them, though to some extent too by people outside the firms who may be seriously affected by their decisions. Walzer is arguing here that a coherent account of our beliefs about political power would include a commitment to industrial democracy. Obviously this is not a view that on the surface is widely held: people generally think of capitalist ownership as a legitimate extension of private property rights. But if Walzer is right, a coherent account would dispense with such a belief.

This should finally dispose of the charge that the Walzerian method of interpretation has conservative implications. Indeed, the arrangements that justice requires of us, he thinks, are those of

a decentralized democratic socialism; a strong welfare state run, at least in part, by local and amateur officials; a constrained market; an open and demystified civil service; independent public schools; the sharing of hard work and free time; the protection of religious and familial life; a system of public honoring and dishonoring free from considerations of rank or class; workers' control of companies and factories; a politics of parties, movements, meetings and public debate. (*Spheres*, 318)

These proposals are to different degrees radical when held up against contemporary public opinion (not least the general label that Walzer attaches to them: nine Americans out of ten reject the proposition that 'some form of socialism would certainly be better than the system we have now').[7] They are even more radical when

[7] H. McClosky and J. Zaller, *The American Ethos: Public Attitudes toward Capitalism and Democracy* (Cambridge, Mass.: Harvard Univ. Press, 1984), 135. Walzer's response to this, obviously, is that the most coherent reading of

compared to contemporary *practice*, which contravenes every one of them.

It might seem, though, that in the course of showing why Walzer's approach is not conservative, I have opened him up to the more damaging charge that the interpretation he gives of his society's culture is essentially an arbitrary one. Might there not be several equally plausible ways of rendering such a culture coherent, each with very different political implications? Couldn't one suppose, for instance, that Americans' most fundamental commitment, the focal point which best rendered their more specific opinions coherent, was a belief in fundamental rights to life, liberty, and property—and so arrive at the political ideals set out in Robert Nozick's *Anarchy, State and Utopia*? In this case Walzer's account of justice would take its place alongside several other accounts, and the choice between them would have to be made on grounds other than consistency and coherence as I have so far explained these ideas.

Walzer does not claim that there is any decisive test that could prove unequivocally that his interpretation of justice is the best available. In 'Interpretation and Social Criticism', he considers the problem of competing interpretations, and claims that the ultimate test of an interpretation must be its capacity to persuade participants in the culture at large that it gives the best 'reading' of their beliefs. 'The interpretation of a moral culture is aimed at all the men and women who participate in that culture—the members of what we might call a community of experience. It is a necessary, though not a sufficient, sign of a successful interpretation that such people be able to recognize themselves in it' (p. 28). There is, on this view, no final moment at which the success or failure of an interpretation is to be judged. The political philosopher throws his or her hat into the ring, readers assess the account that is given, and are persuaded or not, as the case may be, that it makes the best sense of their beliefs and attitudes. Walzer's view of interpretation is of a piece with his view of the role of a political philosopher in a democracy.

It is not possible to pursue the general issue of interpretive

Americans' political beliefs commits them to a set of arrangements that can legitimately be described as democratic socialism, whether or not they would accept the label—attitudes to the label are simply one raw ingredient to be considered alongside others when working out the best interpretation.

method further in this introductory essay. I want to look more closely at the structure of Walzer's own interpretation of contemporary beliefs about justice. We have seen that he holds these beliefs to be pluralistic in nature. There are many categories of goods, each constituting a separate sphere with its own internal principle of distribution. Yet the autonomy of the spheres is not inviolable. There is always a danger of invasion, when money, say, is used to buy its possessors political power, or a better education for their offspring. If these boundary-crossings were universally regarded as unjust there would be no theoretical challenge to Walzer's account, though the practical problem of preventing them would still of course remain. But Walzer acknowledges that the groups who benefit from the boundary-crossings offer ideological justifications for their doing so, and these ideologies have some resonance in public opinion. Thus many believe that if someone has fairly earned his money, he *should* be able to use it to buy better medical care for himself or better education for his children, subject perhaps to his not worsening the position of others in absolute terms. How does Walzer deal with the ensuing conflicts within his society's own culture?

He describes the state of affairs in which the holders of one good are systematically able to convert it into other goods as one of dominance. 'Dominance describes a way of using social goods that isn't limited by their intrinsic meanings or that shapes those meanings in its own image' (*Spheres*, 10–11). No single good has been dominant throughout history: money tends to be dominant in societies like ours, political power or priestly authority in other systems. But why should dominance matter in any case? It violates the norms of justice of those who are subjected to it, but perhaps they should simply abandon those norms, giving up the idea that medical care or education are distinct goods, and coming instead to regard them as commodities like any other, to be bought and sold in the market.

Walzer resists this conclusion because he thinks that dominance over goods translates into dominance over persons, or what he sometimes calls 'tyranny'. These ideas are used in a somewhat metaphorical way. The separate spheres of justice are conceived of as small republics in which different people rightly 'rule': in the sphere of politics the persuasive, in the sphere of love the beautiful and brave, and so forth. If money, say, can be converted into advantage in these spheres, then the holders of that good are like alien rulers tyrannizing over the local notables. But why should this matter? Here we come back to Walzer's overarching notion of complex equality, the idea that in a society in which different people succeed in different spheres, their relationships overall can manifest a certain kind of equality. This is not simple equality, the sort that might obtain if people had equal amounts of property, or income. It is equality that comes about through many separate inequalities, cancelling or offsetting one another in such a way that no one can be picked out as an all-round winner.

There are several ways in which we might try to understand more precisely this idea of complex equality; I examine several possibilities, and defend one particular interpretation, in Chapter 9 below. Here I wish to emphasize the pivotal role that the notion of equal citizenship plays in Walzer's account of justice. As we have already seen, equal citizenship of a formal kind is presupposed by that account: justice arises within a bounded community in which each person enjoys equal political and civil rights. But citizenship for Walzer is more than merely a formal status; to be a citizen one has to have a certain conception of oneself as able to take part in the direction of society, and that is not possible unless one enjoys in civil society a position that supports such a conception. (Being a servant, say, under the constant direction of a master's will, would violate this.) It is not possible, Walzer thinks, for every citizen to share in ruling in the traditional Aristotelean sense of having some share in political office. Nevertheless, 'what a larger conception of justice requires is not that citizens rule and are ruled in turn, but that they rule in one sphere and are ruled in another—where "rule" means not that they exercise power but that they enjoy a greater share than other people of whatever good is being distributed' (*Spheres*, 321). Someone who sees himself as an underdog across all the particular spheres of justice cannot have a sense of himself as an equal citizen, a full member of his political community.

This conception of citizenship provides a pivot from which we can tackle disputes about the distributive criteria appropriate to particular social goods. Broadly speaking, it guides us towards preserving as many distinct spheres of justice as possible, and enhancing those spheres which are in danger of becoming marginal to social life. The more spheres there are, the better the chance any

given person has of enjoying the experience of 'ruling'. Suppose we
go back to a controversial case I referred to earlier: ought medical
aid to be treated as a commodity or as a separate good with its
own distributive principle, namely that of need? We can now
address it in terms of how well different positions on this issue
cohere with the principle of equal citizenship. We ask which of the
two possible arrangements will do most to help foster complex
equality, and in this case the answer is clear. If we allow medical
aid to become a commodity like any other, we are enhancing a distributive sphere—the market economy—which in any case tends to
become dominant in societies like ours; and we are collapsing a
separate sphere which would otherwise serve to counterbalance it.
If we recognize medicine as a good provided outside the market on
grounds of need alone, this helps to reinforce equal citizenship
between people who in the market sphere may be highly unequal.
Again if the question arises whether places in higher education,
say, should be allocated on the basis of ability, or sold to the highest bidder, the question to ask is which practice best promotes
complex equality and thereby equal citizenship.

   To avoid misunderstanding here, I am not suggesting that we
might appeal directly to the principle of equal citizenship in order
to derive criteria for the proper distribution of goods like education. This would either be impossible or sinister—the latter if we
sought to subordinate every question of social distribution to political considerations in a narrow sense. I am suggesting instead that
we may appeal to the principle of citizenship in cases where goods
already have distributive criteria attached to them, but these criteria are in dispute: some people favour one mode of distribution,
others another—or perhaps all of us feel some pull in both directions and are unsure about the right answer. In these circumstances
it makes sense to take a broader view, to ask not only 'how do we
think medical aid should be allocated', but also 'how will implementing different answers to *that* question influence our standing
as equal citizens'.

   In assigning equal citizenship such a pivotal role within Walzer's
thought, I am not, then, suggesting that we should see it as a
supreme principle in the traditional sense—a basic axiom from
which other more specific principles of justice might be derived.
But the assignment does raise two critical questions which must
now be faced. The first is whether equal citizenship does not have

implications within the spheres of justice as well as between them.[8]
Might it not be helpful in terms of complex equality if money, say,
was more equally distributed—if there was some compression of
the income scale, for instance? If money threatens to become a
dominant good, why is it necessarily better to tackle the problem
by strengthening the boundaries between the sphere of the market
and the other spheres than by intervening in the market
itself? Walzer is clear that 'political power is always dominant—at
the boundaries, but not within them. The central problem of political life is to maintain that crucial distinction between "at" and
"in"' (*Spheres*, 15). What may be less clear is why he holds this
view.

The reason is that he is distrustful of political power, afraid that
to allow the state to operate inside the spheres of justice would be
to open the door to the simplest and worst form of tyranny: the
coercive assignment of social goods. Complex equality is the full
embodiment of the liberal 'art of separation' whose main achievement has been the limiting of state power.[9] Without dissenting
from this general perspective, it is permissible to wonder whether
power exercised with discretion within spheres is necessarily more
tyrannical than power exercised to prevent border-crossings. Is it
more coercive, for example, to tax incomes at a uniform progressive rate than to ban completely the purchase of private education?
Walzer concedes that, in any case, the state must intrude into the
market economy—to raise money to fund the welfare system, to
prevent coercive exchanges, and so forth. Why not at the same time
allow the intervention to be guided more directly by the demands
of complex equality? To fix wages politically would be to destroy
the integrity of the labour market; but to seek to control the spread
of incomes through the tax system would be compatible with
allowing goods, services, and labour to be exchanged in complete
freedom.[10]

[8] It is clear that for Walzer, citizenship has a direct role in shaping the spheres
of *power* and *education*. My question is whether this shaping influence should not
extend to other spheres too.

[9] This is stressed in Walzer's essay 'Liberalism and the Art of Separation'. But
see also his later discussion in 'Exclusion, Injustice, and the Democratic State',
where he envisages a more positive role for the state in combating injustice inside
the spheres as well as between them. This essay also underlines the pivotal role
played by citizenship in Walzer's theory of justice.

[10] We should bear in mind here that Walzer's proposal for worker-controlled
enterprises would have a very significant effect on the distribution of incomes. It is

The second question is whether an interpretive theory of justice can assign equal citizenship the pivotal role I have suggested it plays in Walzer's theory. Is citizenship indeed a central element in the culture of Western democracies? People are clearly committed to equal political rights and liberties, at least at the level of general principle.[11] No one nowadays wants to resurrect schemes for plural voting of the sort that our Victorian forefathers toyed with. Nor is the idea that citizenship has social implications, that we cannot tolerate 'second class citizens' in our midst, an unfamiliar one. But these principles appear to coexist somewhat uneasily with certain others. I am thinking particularly of ideas of desert and merit, which may threaten complex equality by suggesting that people's standing in various spheres of distribution should be correlated, not offsetting. Education, for instance, may be seen as an investment which properly brings with it better jobs, more money, greater political influence. Walzer seeks to confine the operation of desert criteria quite narrowly, suggesting that they can properly be applied only to the distribution of honours and other forms of recognition. Whatever the philosophical merits of this argument,[12] as a piece of interpretation it underestimates the role played by desert in popular thinking—for instance in determining both the allocation of jobs and offices, and in fixing the financial rewards attached to them.[13] Although common opinion in these areas may not be coherent in its raw state, so to speak, it would be possible to develop an interpretive theory of justice which rendered it coherent and which took desert as its fundamental principle.

I have suggested that Walzer uses equal citizenship as a guiding principle in cases where first-order criteria for distributing goods are in dispute. It seems that this strategy cannot be defended as self-evidently consistent with prevailing beliefs. Rather it reveals Walzer in his role of social critic, seeking to persuade us that the

possible that, in these circumstances, complex equality would not demand any further equalization of income by the state.

[11] Rather less so when they are asked to make specific judgements, say about allowing groups they strongly dislike to exercise their political rights. I am indebted here to George Klosko's paper 'Rawls' "Political" Philosophy and American Democracy', *American Political Science Review*, 87 (1993), 348–59.

[12] I have criticized Walzer's position in the case of jobs in 'Deserving Jobs', *Philosophical Quarterly*, 42 (1992), 161–81.

[13] See my discussion in 'Distributive Justice: What the People Think', *Ethics*, 102 (1991–2), 555–93.

best interpretation of our culture is one that gives citizenship this pivotal role. Are we persuaded? If so, how ought we to change our specific practices of distribution and how should we redraw the boundaries between them? These are the questions that Walzer challenges us to answer.

1

Equality in Post-Modern Times

MICHAEL RUSTIN

EQUALITY, DIFFERENCE, AND SOCIALISM

In the decade since the first publication of *Spheres of Justice*,[1] the concept of 'difference' has acquired a much greater importance and resonance in social theory than it had earlier possessed. The critique of 'foundationalism', the rejection of 'grand narratives' (notably the narrative of historical materialism), the equation of the unified world-views of the left with 'totalitarianism', have all contributed to making 'equality' a singularly unfashionable value. Walzer's attempt to reformulate the concept of equality—defined by him in its earlier one-dimensional form as 'simple equality'—in his difference-respecting terms of 'complex equality' can now be seen as an indispensable contribution to this 'post-modern' field of debate, though this was not its original point of departure.[2] One of the primary intentions of *Spheres* was to renew and revitalize the socialist understanding of egalitarian ideas, through attention to the desirable variety and plurality of things, and by inclusion of these within an enlarged concept of equality. Walzer's purpose was not to set up 'difference' as an alternative, essentially anti- or post-socialist value as many of the avatars of post-modernism have done. The implications of his arguments for this significant division in contemporary social thought are, nevertheless, ambiguous.

Spheres is a book remarkable for its commitment to understand, describe, and value the variety of ways in which human lives are actually lived, and the meanings and norms which shape them. It

[1] (New York: Basic Books, 1983).

[2] Walzer's principal points of departure in the literature of political theory were liberal foundationalists like Nozick and Rawls, not radical conventionalists and relativists like Rorty. French writers crucial to the anti-foundationalist and thus post-socialist movement of thought, such as Lyotard, Derrida, or Foucault, scarcely figured in *Spheres*.

takes as its premiss the idea that if a socialist view of the world is to be in the least bit plausible, it must be grounded in good aspects of the lives that people have now. Walzer's method is to argue not from abstract principles, like most of his fellow contributors to the debate about social justice, but from meanings grounded in everyday social experience. 'Another way of doing philosophy', he writes, 'is to interpret to one's fellow-citizens the world of meanings that we share' (*Spheres*, p. xiv). Socialism is sometimes thought to be a doctrine fed by jealousy of the good fortune of others, or, even worse, by envy, or hatred of the good in itself (this was Nietzsche's (in part) insightful view of the matter). Walzer's writing (and his quotations from some of the classics of socialist literature: Wilde, Tawney, Shaw) show that this need not be so. The foundation of Walzer's view of a just society is the recognition of what men and women already are and achieve in their own spheres of life—in families, conceived as contexts of unconditional love and responsibility, in workers' co-operatives such as the San Francisco Scavenging Company giving dignity to the most stigmatized form of manual labour, in (some) schools espousing learning as an intrinsic good. Neither abstract principles nor utopian speculation appeal much to him as guides to political action. It is a lasting achievement to have shown that writing identifying itself with socialist values could be the very reverse of envious in its valuation of different spheres of achievement and in its commitment to defend and extend these.

Post-modernist social thought speaks in its various forms (the theory of 'post-Fordism', 'disorganized capitalism', consumer society, the information society, post-industrial society) of the elaborated division of labour and diversity of goods and services generated by advanced capitalism. Though Walzer does not actually say so, the ideas of 'simple equality' of most recent currency, calling for decent basic living standards and social services for all, even Raymond Williams's concept of a 'common culture', were rooted in the political experiences of the early post-war period. That is to say, in the nearly achieved possibility, in the advanced countries of the West, of full employment, social security, and rising living standards and expectations. The dominant élites of these societies, including their most left-leaning segments,[3] were at this

---

[3] In Britain, the leadership of the Labour Party in this period drew heavily on radicals from the upper middle class, formed like Clement Attlee in a tradition of

time struggling to get used to the idea of democratization, and still formulated social objectives ambivalently in terms of the needs of the 'masses' (mass production, mass housing, mass communication, etc.).[4] So 'equality' in social democratic discourse still generally meant 'simple equality', this value being grounded in the solidaristic universes of working-class factory and community life and in the political outlooks generated by identification with these. In Communist Eastern Europe, ruled by a more severe ideology of proletarian needs and desires, the operative concept of equality for the masses was even more simplistic and uniform. This ideology is represented in concrete in many huge housing projects throughout Eastern Europe.

The idea of 'simple equality'—equated with 'sameness' and uniformity, imposed or chosen—has become untenable or at least insufficient because the social experience of the majority in 'developed' societies has changed so radically. For reasons of prosperity, enhanced individual mobility, and a greater diversity of lifestyles, the resonance of the ideal of equality as a shared condition of life is not what it was. Of course there has been a relentless and effective ideological assault on this conception of life too, in the era of Reaganism and Thatcherism, but this individualist ideology would not have had its success unless it had corresponded to some emergent features of actual social experience.

Walzer was therefore prescient in recognizing that a philosophical defence of equality during the 1980s would have to be done in quite new terms. It would need to embrace and celebrate, not ignore or disparage, the diversity of experiences and choices which people made (and increasingly wished to make) in their lives. But if this more pluralist and differentiated view of the world were to remain part of the socialist tradition, it would be vital that it be formulated in social rather than individual terms. The grounding of the retained socialist core of Walzer's position became the idea of the social itself (as it was for an earlier democratic socialist, Emile Durkheim), and not, as in the Marxist tradition, the idea of

élite public service. See G. Stedman Jones, 'Why is the Labour Party in a Mess', in his *Languages of Class* (Cambridge: Cambridge Univ. Press, 1983).

[4] Raymond Williams memorably said there were no masses, only ways of thinking of people as masses. In his explication of this concept in his *Keywords* (London: Fontana, 1976) his main contrast is between 'the masses as the subject and . . . as the object of social action'.

the primacy of the material or economic over all other dimensions of life and society.

WALZER'S HISTORICAL METHOD

To ground this idea of the inherently social constitution of values, Walzer turned away, as he says, from the intellectual disciplines of psychology and economics, founded as they are on concepts of rational self-interest and on axiomatic deduction from these premisses. Concepts of individual interests and rights, whether from utilitarian or Kantian origins, are the building blocks of liberal theories of social justice, and even of some socialist redistributive versions of these.[5] Walzer chose to look instead to the more holistic and 'culturalist' methods central to anthropology, and to historical writing conceived as the investigation and interpretation of whole ways of life. It is plausible to suggest that anthropology does have at its core the assumption that societies are inherently 'cultures' (ensembles or assemblages of meanings and values), and that if one understands the cultures, one understands the societies. (And more critically, if one doesn't, then one hasn't.[6])

But whilst it may be reasonable to understand anthropology in terms which give priority to cultural interpretation, the adoption by Walzer of a historical method based largely on this same perspective creates some difficulties for his argument, as well as bringing some strengths to it. Walzer presents a number of vivid historical sketches to demonstrate the ways in which different societies have framed distinctive spheres of justice. He explores, for example, the status of *metics* (resident aliens) in classical Athens,

[5] See e.g. J. Le Grand and R. Robinson, *The Strategy of Equality* (London: Allen & Unwin, 1982); J. Le Grand and S. Estrin (eds.), *Market Socialism* (Oxford: Oxford Univ. Press, 1988); and at least half of the argument of S. Mulhall and A. Swift, *Liberals and Communitarians* (Oxford: Blackwell, 1992).

[6] Walzer has in these matters been deeply influenced by the writings of his anthropological colleague at the Institute of Advanced Study, Clifford Geertz. *Spheres* has as its basic method the 'interpretation of cultures', in the form of elucidating the meaning of a whole variety of embedded social practices both of his own and of other societies. A less conspicuous but nevertheless also telling presence in this book may also be the work of Walzer's other long-time Institute colleague, Albert Hirschman, who has helped Walzer to see what liberal models of behaviour can and cannot explain, to locate the edges and fault-lines, so to speak, of this intellectual continent.

identifying some contradiction between the idea of political citizenship and the criteria of membership by birth and blood that determined to whom in practice the rights of a citizen were accorded. His argument is that these caste-like norms to some extent justified the Athenians' treatment of first-generation *metics*, even though by Athenian criteria of citizenship they could be regarded as objects of tyrannical rule. Walzer's method of 'internalist' critique enables him to argue that in modern Western societies, unlike in classical Athens, the disqualification of guest workers or their children from citizenship rights cannot be justified, since the qualifying norm of hereditary membership in a political caste has (allegedly) disappeared.[7]

The second most important historical example which Walzer cites (grounding his argument in Judaeo-Christian as well as classical traditions) is that of medieval Jewry, with its distinctive commitment to sustaining membership in a community of believers. This strong concept of cultural membership explains for Walzer the commitment of this community to education and to the provision of social welfare, as means of maintaining the membership of individuals and families who might otherwise have been lost to it. Walzer illustrates here how the allocation of economic goods in these two exemplary societies—universal payments for the services of political citizens on the one hand, the obligation to support charity on the other—is determined by the central meanings and values of the communities concerned. They each depend on a culturally specific idea of membership.

The tradition of political theory, in which Walzer chiefly locates himself, has always made use of historical example to illustrate and justify concepts of good or just societies. The more interested the philosopher in the variety of goods there are, the greater the relevance of historical exemplification. More definite kinds of story, as

---

[7] The problem with this argument is that some citizens of Western societies continue to claim that hereditary citizenship remains a just category, defining who should have access to national territory on either a permanent or temporary basis. 'Patriality' (or ancestry) has since 1971 been enshrined in British immigration law. A shared normative consensus may be subsequently challenged, and defeated arguments re-emerge to win substantial support. In Britain the argument from hereditary birthright is currently made more effectively against would-be immigrants entering a territory than against the citizenship rights of immigrants or their children already present in it. But there seem to be no limits on the arguments that can be made. In some European nations the case for the repatriation of former immigrants and their children has won significant political support.

Ernest Gellner has pointed out, are told by philosophers who are interested above all in historical transitions, either where these are perceived to be for the better, in a narrative of 'modernization' of some kind (social-contract theorists, Marxists), or for the worse, from the perspective of a lost or threatened coherence (St Augustine, Plato, Alasdair MacIntyre, or, despite his ostensible critique of all such narratives, Nietzsche).[8] In such cases more deductive arguments are constructed from first principles, and the point of the history is to show what happened when these principles were embodied in action, or alternatively, neglected.

These contrasting approaches to historical method crucially divide the opposed camps of 'post-modernist' (i.e. relativist, contingent, difference-based) and 'modernist' (foundationalist, emancipatory) approaches to social theory. The rejection of 'grand narrative', of generalizing explanations of how modern society and its values came to be, was a decisive step in the attack on totalizing moral and theoretical perspectives.[9] Mostly, this has been an attack on Marxism, but by extension it has also been an attack on the socialist tradition.

In this context, Walzer's choice of historical method cannot lack serious consequences, whatever his intention may be.[10] Democratic socialism, no less than its Marxist opposite number, has depended on coherent narratives of historical development, usually derived from and extending liberal theories of emancipation, whether of Hegelian, Kantian, or utilitarian origin. It is not easy to see how any remotely socialist concept of 'complex equality' could be

---

[8] See E. Gellner, *Though and Change* (London: Weidenfeld & Nicolson, 1964) and *Plough, Sword and Book* (London: Collins Harvill, 1988) for an earlier and later version of this idea. Perry Anderson's essay 'Max Weber and Ernest Gellner: Science, Politics, Enchantment', in his *A Zone of Engagement* (London: Verso, 1992) has a valuable discussion of these issues in Gellner's work.

[9] See esp. J.-F. Lyotard, *The Post-Modern Condition* (Manchester: Manchester Univ. Press, 1984).

[10] Walzer, in post-modern mode, reverses the priority usually given by emancipatory theorists to temporal and spatial categories. In enlightenment-based historical narratives (Hegel, Marx, Gellner), a strong temporal sequence regulates the argument, and empirical instances occurring in some place or other are categorized in relation to the primary developmental and thus temporal schema. No such privilege is assigned in *Spheres* to a developmental progression. Valuing 'difference' leads to a privilege being given to the 'places', the contingent and spatially located moments in which particular complexes of moral interest have occurred. These are widely separated in space and time—Jewish life in medieval Cairo, Kula exchange in Polynesia (presumably over a very long period, though studied only in this century)—and are not set in a meaningful historical frame.

sustained as the desirable moral goal of industrial societies without some convincing historical account of how this causally emerges, is sociologically fitting and consistent with social stability, and is consonant with the emerging norms of contemporary society. Walzer provides little of this kind of argument either in *Spheres* or in his subsequent writings. Where he seeks to justify social democratic concepts of social justice (and a good part of *Spheres* is in fact devoted to such justifications), he uses a different method of argument from existing social understandings. His attempts to argue that social democracy is the direction in which everyday American understandings point are not especially convincing, as others have already noted.

BOUNDARIES, BLOCKED EXCHANGES, AND COMPLEX EQUALITY

Instead, Walzer has concentrated on a different task, one with which his historical and anthropological methods are more consistent. This is the task of demonstrating that there *are*, in fact, many 'spheres of justice', grounded in distinctive social communities and institutional practices, both at the level of 'whole societies' (such as ancient Athens and the medieval Jewish communities) and in institutional segments of contemporary society (the Japanese school system or American family life).[11] Walzer is able to demonstrate, often very beautifully, that there is a greater diversity of relevant values even in our everyday experience of society, and that our view of the world is grossly impoverished when we allow this to be forgotten.

Walzer's implicit aim is instead to recover and recuperate such

---

[11] A recent critique of absolutist methodologies in the social sciences has rejected the idea of a 'whole society' as a referent for explanations. These have been held to privilege a particular model of transition (functionalist or Marxist), and to neglect the infinity of points of view from which any set of social relations (the proper object of social inquiry) can be viewed. Walzer perceives 'coherence' in a variety of social formations and 'spheres of meaning' within them, without (ostensibly at least) assigning any of these relative priority over one another. His method is vulnerable to still more radical deconstruction by those who might look for the repressed or unheard voices within any such reading. Michael Mann, *The Sources of Social Power*, i. *A History of Power from the Beginning to A.D. 1760* (Cambridge: Cambridge Univ. Press, 1986) provides a neo-Weberian critique of methodological holism.

values, where they might have significance for us. The 'thick descriptions' to which we should pay attention include accounts of ways of life situated at a temporal as well as a spatial distance. Walzer's approach is antipathetic not only to invasive spheres of justice in the present, but also to one-dimensional narratives of progress which flatten our sense of the richness of past social forms. 'Progress', in this perspective, might be measured not by our distance from the 'pre-modern' past, but by the extent to which its diversity becomes a cultural resource for us. This view is not without its appeal.[12]

Differentiation of 'spheres of justice' is, Walzer points out, institutionalized in democratic capitalist societies by what he calls, following Arthur Okun, a variety of 'blocked exchanges'. There are the 'blocked exchanges' of the market; those things—votes, persons, children, judicial verdicts—which are not to be bought and sold. There are similarly 'blocked exchanges' or blocked relationships within the sphere of kinship: illicit and improper extensions of favour to kin outside of their proper sphere, or of illicit sexual relationships within kinship groups. And there are equally 'blocked uses of power' within the relationships of politics, limiting what can properly be decided or allocated as a matter of political preference or value, and what cannot. Walzer provides an impressive list of such restraints (*Spheres*, 282–4), which map the constitutional liberties of subjects achieved in liberal societies, but which he rightly points out are a source of equality between citizens as well as guarantees of their freedom. Walzer is able to use the idiom of 'blocked exchanges' in these different institutional sectors to map the actual differentiations of complex societies, and the carefully evolved insulation of its different spheres of activity from one another. This is a source of individual liberty, as it was a main achievement of the classical sociologists to recognize, since it means that control exercised over individuals in one sphere will normally not be extended to another. It is also, and this is Walzer's original point, a beneficial source of *social* diversity, since the values prevailing in one social sphere do not necessarily dominate another. (This was also Durkheim's reason for seeing the division

---

[12] How we should relate to the traditions of the past has been the central issue of the debate between 'modernists' and 'post-modernists' in architecture, a debate which has helped to define the meaning of post-modern culture.

of labour, when given its due forms of moral integration through occupational guilds, as ethically desirable.)

One way of viewing Walzer's exploration of this complexity of moral boundaries through his most powerful concept of 'blocked exchange' is simply as a phenomenology of the existing institutional differentiation of liberal capitalist societies. The differentiations thus charted by Walzer correspond to the insulation between economic and political institutions which modern Weberians have characterized as a key feature of democratic capitalism.[13] Walzer's most powerful concept of 'blocked exchanges' thus provides descriptions of the rules which in practice maintain boundaries between institutions. It is this insulation between sectors which has enabled class conflict to be conducted in at least some capitalist societies without jeopardy to political liberty or stability, and which has also allowed 'mixed economies' to operate, as systems of market entitlements mitigated by criteria of social need.

Sometimes Walzer seems largely to endorse these mixed arrangements, albeit somewhat critically, arguing that the sphere of commodity production and distribution in America might be more satisfactory if only there was also (for example) a National Health Service to ensure that at least health care was exempted from this system of exchange and was subject to its own intrinsic norms of allocation by medical need.[14]

One might reasonably expect that someone arguing as a

---

[13] On the institutional segregation of economic and political spheres in democratic capitalism, see e.g. A. Giddens, *The Class Structure of the Advanced Societies* (London: Hutchinson, 1981).

[14] The sphere of medicine provides a good test of the validity of Walzer's main argument in which values are grounded in defined social practices. Though decisions about the distribution of resources leave much scope for conflict and disagreement (e.g. between the claims of curative and preventive medicine, or regarding the priority to be given to scientific progress over immediate patient need), such arguments are often pursued within the framework of a fundamental commitment to health. A 'sphere of justice' thus delimits a discursive space in which such arguments can be made, and need not imply a set of specific outcomes. But how can problems at the interface between one such sphere (e.g. health) and another (e.g. the idea of just reward for individual merits or efforts) be resolved? Walzer's argument suggests that health has its own intrinsic norms of allocation, which should override more general entitlements derived from the market. But what *should* the extent be of such overriding? Perhaps this can only, in any society, be an issue for discursive negotiation. Secondly, and perhaps more seriously, isn't the argument for the priority of health in substance an argument for the priority of basic human needs in general? The force of any case for the priority of health would then depend on more general and universal considerations than Walzer's argument suggests.

democratic socialist would be not too far distant from a conventional liberal pluralism, and would favour a 'mixed economy' of institutions. Some combination of democratic decision-making with market-based allocations is accepted by most socialists to be unavoidable, if not exactly desirable, following dire experience of the imposed monopolies of political decision-making under state socialism. Walzer is also trying to base part of his argument in the common-sense thinking of his own society, and therefore needs to ground his critical differences with the mainstream of that society on beliefs and values that citizens actually hold. *Spheres* combines a number of different purposes, however, and these do not all seem consistent with one another.

These purposes can be identified as threefold. First, and most successfully, Walzer seeks to demonstrate that equality is or should be a complex concept, that different norms of distribution should prevail in distinct spheres of activity. Secondly, and more problematically, Walzer attempts to establish a more general idea of justice or a just society, which would be one whose specific spheres of justice are duly and mutually respected. This is the state of affairs he characterizes as 'complex equality'. This concept will have a variable substantive existence, according to Walzer, depending on the different 'spheres of justice' which can properly claim autonomous respect within the understandings of a particular society. But although the empirical reality of 'complex equality' will differ between societies, its meaning and the procedures by which it is to be achieved are held to be consistent. Thirdly, in the large central section of his book, Walzer seeks to set out the implications of his concept of complex equality for contemporary American society, suggesting the kinds of arrangements that actually do embody respect for distinct spheres of justice at present, and that might to a greater degree do so in the future. Walzer argues here as a social democrat, attempting to ground his own conceptions of social justice in the shared understandings of contemporary America.

The first of these purposes is the most important to the project of *Spheres*, and the one that is most fully achieved by it. Walzer might even have had more success in achieving a much-needed enrichment and redefinition of the concept of equality if he had confined himself to this task, to demonstrating that various criteria of justice do obtain in different spheres of life, and that no single criterion of equality can properly override these. His arguments against the 'invasion' of discrete spheres of justice by criteria derived from a single dominant sphere (whether this be political ideology, monetary value, or religious doctrine) would be valid even if no definite procedure for resolution of these conflicting spheres of value was proposed or imagined. Indeed, the idea that different criteria of value and thus distribution properly hold for different spheres of activity, and that good societies recognize many kinds of value, is the main achievement of Walzer's book, rendering untenable earlier conceptions of equality that in the light of his argument can now be seen as simplistic or reductionist.

This moral discovery (or rediscovery) is properly supported by the evidence, both historical and contemporary, which Walzer brings to bear, since he is able to show the power and attractiveness of different conceptions of justice in their historical settings, and to indicate the moral traditions to which these have given rise. Our own conceptions of justice are in fact composed of many strands, each with its own long history (the range stretches from the Hippocratic oath to the rights of suspects to receive a fair trial), and Walzer suggests a method—others might see this as an archaeological or genealogical method—for tracing these origins and sources of credibility.

To have left the argument at that point—at a demonstration of the unavoidable plurality of values—would, however, have been to settle for less than Walzer wanted to achieve. He is committed to a version of pluralism that is in some sense egalitarian. This is evident not only in his attempt to justify more egalitarian distributions in the context of the USA but in the central place he gives to the idea of complex equality in his view of social justice.

Walzer sets out a state of 'complex equality' as a possible outcome of a state of plurality of values, and of the inevitable conflicts between 'spheres of justice'. Measured against the contrasted ideas of simple inequality or simple equality, the concept of 'complex equality' has obvious attractions, since it alone seems to acknowledge the desirable variety of goods that exist. But there is a fourth conceptual possibility which disappears from sight in Walzer's classification, but which describes by far the most common and probable state of affairs. This is the state of *complex inequality*:[15] the

---

[15] I outlined but did not develop the idea that one might more accurately substitute four conceptual possibilities (simple equality, simple inequality, complex

condition in which many goods and values are recognized, with *some* insulation between 'spheres', but in which nevertheless certain forms of allocation or 'spheres of justice' remain dominant over others.

This dominance can be understood in two related ways. Sociologically, different institutional sectors will usually have different causal weight in determining the shape of any society and the distribution of life-chances within it. Societies based on principles of caste, or on the rights of property, or on kinship ties, or on religious belief, are likely to be largely ordered by what happens within these decision-making spheres. Some autonomy will remain for other spheres (not even totalitarian societies were able completely to subordinate every sphere to their central will, if only for reasons of efficiency and cost), but not such as to cause doubt that a dominant sphere exists. Walzer's argument by contrast has the shape of a normative or idealized kind of pluralism, and sets up an implicitly functionalist (or equilibrium) model in which every part of the social order is, or should be, assigned equal causal weight.[16] It is not easy to set out counter-factual measures of relative dominance of the elements of a social order, but it nevertheless seems obvious that such relative dominance (of, in Walzer's terms, some spheres over others) is the usual case.

Such dominance is explained in Walzer's argument through his concepts of boundaries and 'blocked exchanges'. It arises from the frequency or normality of 'leakages' across boundaries, which lead

equality, and complex inequality) in place of Walzer's contrasting two, in *For a Pluralist Socialism* (London: Verso, 1985).

[16] Walzer's arguments reproduce a number of the problems identified in functionalist sociology generally. That is, they make unwarranted assumptions about attainable consensus and fail to take note of the inequalities of power which determine the actual weight of specific institutions and actors. Of course, Walzer's argument is chiefly normative, not explanatory in its purpose. To elaborate rules of procedures by which social justice could be secured, is not to say that they already prevail. Indeed, Walzer's arguments (like those in his *Just and Unjust Wars* against the unjust use of violence) can be read as a critique of all forms of power that are not normatively justified. In *Spheres*, Walzer characterizes relationships of power quite properly, in his vocabulary of justice, as 'invasive spheres', in order to bring them within the domain of normative discourse. Yet his implicit recourse to functionalist (or consensualist) assumptions predisposes him to underestimate the actual sources of division and conflict in contemporary society. It is questionable how far values are in fact held in common in societies where power is unequally exercised. The extent to which normative argument may be a central resource for resolving distributional conflicts may be historically variable. Such issues are explored on a grand historical scale by Mann, *Sources of Social Power*, i, ii.

to the 'invasion' of subordinate spheres by greater ones. Societies dominated by religious consensus impose religious values on what in secularized societies are seen as 'other spheres'—indeed religious societies may decline to recognize such boundaries as legitimate at all. (Walzer's defence of 'membership' as a precondition for any coherent society allows him to gloss the normative origins of many kinds of invasion.) Capitalist societies have of their essence created highly liquid and convertible forms of power, which invade and undermine all previous boundaries, whether of birth, religious belief, or ethnicity.[17] Whilst political democracies, through their universalistic rules of due process and by conferring equal rights of participation on their citizens, may appear to be egalitarian, their norms were nevertheless once experienced as invasive of traditionalist and more élitist forms of power distribution. One can rationally defend liberal and democratic procedures, but to do so one seems to need recourse to a priori universalistic principles, not merely reference to normative boundaries as these have historically existed.

STRATEGIES OF JUSTIFICATION

What kinds of argument might support the idea that 'complex equality' is at any rate the most desirable outcome of this inherent pluralism of values and spheres? Walzer himself seems to rely on an a priori concept of cultural coherence, on the idea that 'ways of life' are generally consistent or have a predisposition to arrive at consistency. This coherence is to be elicited by hermeneutic methods, the interpretation of meanings of a given society.[18] Walzer seems to think that everyday meanings will reveal consistency and order, rather than inconsistency, disorder, and irresolvable conflicts. His latent functionalism and consensualism is surprisingly

---

[17] See Marx and Engels's classic description of this in the *Communist Manifesto*, and its elaboration by Marshal Berman, *All That is Solid Melts into Air* (New York: Simon & Schuster, 1982). 'All fixed, fast-frozen relations, with their train of ancient and venerable prejudices and opinions, are swept away, all new-formed ones become antiquated before they can ossify. All that is solid melts into air, all that is holy is profaned, and men at last are forced to face . . . the real conditions of their lives and their relations with their fellow-men.'

[18] On the relation of this approach to *Spheres* see Georgia Warnke, *Justice and Interpretation* (Cambridge: Polity Press, 1992), esp. ch. 2.

consistent in this respect with the philosophical methods of both Wittgenstein and Plato, though he has different and more liberal expectations than they of what is to be found beneath the surfaces of everyday language.

What Walzer expects is that the logic of every sphere of justice that is recognized within a society will in principle enable members to define what the appropriate boundaries between the spheres should be. The appearance and recognition of a concept (e.g. of family, or of health, or of scholarship) are held to bring with them some intrinsic idea of what is due to the sphere which the concept denotes. (This is the 'essentialist' aspect of Walzer's approach.) But this seems to assume far too much. All that such concepts usually identify is that *some* limit or boundary is appropriate, not what this limit should be, or what the jurisdiction of one sphere should be relative to others.

Consider, for example, the concept of family and the rights and duties attaching to family members. Acknowledgement of some such duties (recognized in nearly all societies) by no means clarifies what the scope of these should properly be, for example in the allocation of property by bequest to new generations, or in responsibilities for educating children or caring for the sick or old. Even the doctrine that political rights should be independent of kinship roles (which Walzer presents as an elementary example of proper respect for boundaries) required the revolutionary defeat of *ancien régimes* to come into effect (a victory still not complete in some supposedly 'modern' states such as Great Britain, in which a hereditary monarchy and aristocracy continue to enjoy significant powers and privileges). Walzer's argument elides the emergence of fields of legitimate debate in societies, once distinct spheres of action emerge, with the idea that there can be expected to be any natural or logical resolution to such debates. He proposes a 'strong programme' of social justice, asserting that 'complex equality' is its logical outcome. In fact his arguments better support 'a weak programme' (still an important one) which merely identifies scope for argument about appropriate boundaries between spheres, or a discursive space in which this can occur.

One of the options opened up by Walzer's argument—it is one of its implicitly 'post-modern' features—is that differences between spheres of justice are simply undecidable by any rational means. A benign American version of this is Richard Rorty's vision of

politics as a 'conversation of mankind', in which no rational reso-
lutions can be expected since no underlying criteria can be located
or agreed upon. Rorty makes an exception for the framework of
democratic discourse itself, as a 'collective cogito' without which
there can be no social identity, though it is far from clear why those
committed to undemocratic values should be expected to respect
this self-enforced limitation on their actions. The less benign
European version of this position belongs to the tradition of
Nietzsche and Foucault, where it is more plainly stated that the
rules of engagement, including discursive engagement, are usually
set by the dominant groups in any society, and that their domination is the result of their power, not of the validity or rational consistency of their arguments. Clearly, Walzer does not wish his
plurality of values to amount to the definition of a state of moral
war. But it is not at all clear that the actual arguments he presents,
from 'internal consensus', preclude this outcome.

It is for example difficult to find grounds within Walzer's
relativist position for intervention to end or mitigate gross social
injustices (for example, the oppression of women) where these
injustices have not already become the subject of contention within
a society. But it is surely unreasonable to assign such overwhelming weight in deciding questions of justice and injustice to internal
states of (real or apparent) consensus when these may depend so
largely on force or ignorance. To do so may seem to require practical indifference to barbarity until and unless effective 'internal'
resistance to it has emerged among members. The more powerful
and effective oppressors may be in squashing opposition to them
in thought or action, the less grounds there will be for intervening
against them.

One strategy for getting around this apparent problem of tacit
consent, is to presuppose that 'internal resistance' exists a priori,
once certain degrees of mistreatment have occurred. One might
plausibly assume that some basic needs and aspirations are shared
by any community, such that no community could consent to certain levels of abuse of them. The problem with this attempt to
escape the implications of moral relativism is that it tacitly evokes
universalistic norms to override particularistic conditions to which
there is apparent consent, or at least where visible dissent is absent.
This option may be good for the defence of what we think of as
human rights, but it is in fact inconsistent with moral relativism.

The attraction of the universalist and historicist approaches to social justice which are the two principal alternatives to Walzer's is that they do surmount some of these problems of relativism or undecidability.

A consequence of arguments founded on the value attributed to the fulfilment of human desires as such, or on the exercise of free choice by rational agents, is that they appear to give the idea of 'justice' a definite and decidable form, in a way which can be transferred impartially from one social context to another. Either the factual summation of human desires and kinds of human happiness, or the assignment of absolute status to each individual's rights, once defined, offers a definite resolution to the problem of distinguishing between just and unjust allocations. Rawls's limitation of justified inequalities to circumstances where they can be seen to benefit the worst off has the advantage of incorporating a calculus of relative power and well-being into a primarily libertarian position, as a limiting condition on the exercise of free choices by the fortunate. (Whilst this is formulated in terms of relative entitlements to primary goods, in order to respect the primacy of self-determination by all individuals, its effect is to constrain the rights of some individuals in order to preserve the well-being of others.) These frameworks can also be deployed to give meaning to ideas of material and historical progress towards the attainment of social justice, since measures both of freedom and happiness can be envisaged which would enable one rationally to prefer more materially or politically developed societies to more repressive or poverty-stricken ones. (This is in effect the approach taken by Ernest Gellner to the transition to the modern.) Concepts of basic human needs,[19] or in the terms of the early Marx of essential human powers, as material and cultural preconditions of almost any significant sphere of activity, are other kinds of foundation for distributive justice. All these arguments assume that individuals should in some respects be counted as equal. It might be argued that 'complex equality' will only *be* a state of equality, if this condition is met.

Alternative to liberal discourses of justice are teleological accounts of a sociological or Marxist kind, which have set out to explain how the social values characteristic of 'modernity'—justice between individuals, freedom, equality—have been historically

[19] See Len Doyal and Ian Gough, *A Theory of Human Need* (London: Macmillan, 1991).

generated and made possible. Freedom which in one epoch was conceivable only as freedom for property owners, at a later stage becomes generalizable to all who labour. The limited rights of political 'subjects' under constitutional law become extended to the democratic rights of all citizens. Within the sociological tradition, freedom is seen as a product of urbanized and marketized social structures. Within Marxism, ethical possibilities are seen as the outcomes of stages of development of the modes and relations of production. The sphere of morality therefore extends beyond the consideration of the consequences of actions to individuals, to their probable effects on these larger processes of development. Historicist ethics, elaborated by Merleau-Ponty for example, has been subject to violent political abuse, but some element of ethical argument from probable historical consequences seems nevertheless indispensable.[20] Consequentialist arguments of this form are routinely deployed in defence of military actions by states, harmful as these invariably are for many individuals, where it is held that some broader societal good is thereby advanced. The crucial issue in legitimizing such arguments is whether societies are viewed holistically, such that systemic outcomes can properly be taken into moral account. Attacks on historicist ethics, as by Popper, have often depended on an extreme methodological individualism and derived their plausibility from this.

Walzer is unsympathetic both to abstract universalist and to historicist approaches to social justice. Pluralism, in the sociological version of historicism, is the consequence of the division of labour, of social processes which make differentiation possible. Walzer tries to disconnect justice from any particular state of differentiation. Just societies are simply those organized in accordance with the shared understandings of their members, whatever they may be. But he nevertheless acknowledges that differentiation changes the possibilities. Whilst social justice does not depend on it, complex equality as Walzer's particular and preferred version of justice does.

The theory of justice is alert to differences, sensitive to boundaries. It doesn't follow from the theory, however, that societies are more just if

---

[20] See M. Merleau-Ponty, *Humanism and Terror*, tr. J. O'Neill (Boston, Mass.: Beacon Press, 1969) and, for his more considered second thoughts, *The Adventures of the Dialectic*, tr. J. Bien (Evanston, Ill.: Norwestern Univ. Press, 1973). See also Steven Lukes, *Marxism and Morality* (Oxford: Oxford Univ. Press, 1985).

they are more differentiated. Justice simply has more scope in such societies, because there are more distinct goods, more distributive principles,
more agents, more procedures. And the more scope justice has, the more
certain it is that complex equality will be the form that justice takes
(*Spheres*, 315).

Walzer seems to be acknowledging that, although social differentiation is not a sufficient condition of complex equality, it is nevertheless its necessary condition. Without differentiation, there will
be few boundaries to respect. The argument that justice in its
specific forms might have anterior sociological (or material) conditions, offers an external dimension to Walzer's otherwise 'internalist' arguments. It seems that the move from 'justice', as consistency
with shared meanings, to 'complex equality', as respect for many
different spheres, does after all depend on assumptions about an
emergent social division of labour.

WALZER'S CRITIQUE OF CONTEMPORARY AMERICA

Walzer's rather reluctant concession to sociological realities leads
one, finally, to assess his arguments for complex equality in modern American society. Walzer here relies on two kinds of argument,
neither of them universalistic or historicist. The first is the argument from shared social understandings. Walzer tries to show both
that many existing boundaries and 'blocked exchanges' are rooted
in shared understandings (they could hardly exist without these)
and that it is possible to argue from such understandings for
changes to these boundaries. For example, Walzer argues for a
stronger insulation of health care from the market, and for the
democratic entitlements of employees to regulate their places of
work.

   These arguments are not convincing as logical implications of
the understandings which most Americans presently share.
Whereas it does follow from the existence of a sphere of health,
and a sphere of market exchange, that there is a boundary to be
negotiated between them ('the weak programme' for justice
referred to above), there seems no consensual reason for drawing
this boundary at the point of providing for a universal rather than
residual health-care system. Citizens seem to be committed *both* to
a view of health as an intrinsic good, *and* to a conception of prop-

erty rights which makes health care a legitimate object of purchase. They may similarly be committed *both* to a conception of human need which requires intervention to assist the very poor, whether in the United States or elsewhere, *and* to a view of property rights which makes excessive taxation, such as would be entailed by radical aid programmes, an unjust imposition. The proper boundaries between these 'spheres of justice' are not obvious, natural, or logical. Shared understandings now lead to them being in practice drawn at a more conservative point that Walzer (or I) would like.

In the case of Walzer's arguments for industrial democracy, or for the extension of political control in the workplace, the difficulty is even greater. Here, despite recent legislation in the USA supporting Employment Share Ownership Plans (ESOPS), the overwhelming consensus favours the rights of property and capital over the political rights of labour. A significant change in the balance of these rights would require not a mere boundary adjustment, but a tumultuous change in the value system and division of power in American society. Walzer's model of parallel 'spheres' between which some notional parity is assumed is here seriously misleading. Descriptions of the market economy in terms mainly of the (often harmless or beneficial) supply and exchange of commodities subtly misrepresents the nature of a capitalist economy in shaping most of what happens within it—in generating or destroying employment, in shaping the landscape, in securing superior or inferior life-chances through education, in influencing the political and cultural systems.[21] The 'convertibility' of money across boundaries, and the general rights and powers attaching to private property, are decisive. The 'blocked exchanges' described by Walzer mark out important boundaries and limits to the powers and rights of capital, but they do not establish parity between competing spheres. The relation between the different spheres of capitalist societies is, in effect, a deeply hierarchical one.

Walzer nevertheless does describe the 'invasion' of spheres by the market as the central problem of capitalist societies. Even though his description of American society analytically understates the power of capital, his programmatic argument is radical. He

---

[21] See Sharon Zukin's recent discussion in *Landscapes of Power: From Detroit to Disneyworld* (Berkeley, Calif.: Univ. of Calif. Press, 1991) of the pervasive power of capital in shaping the physical environment of American cities, and the opportunities for employment and consumption which they accord to citizens.

seeks to justify a significant democratization and equalization of life-chances in American society, within his framework of respect for differences. But it does not seem that this can be convincingly achieved simply by 'internalist' argument from shared American values. Americans mostly know they live in a society dominated by the rights of property owners, and they are in the majority contented to do so. (Or at least, whilst they may be discontented, they do not think they are discontented about *that*.) Indeed, the meanings that Walzer draws upon to criticize these allocations in part come from outside the American mainstream, from traditions of European socialism and of communitarianism more generally.

There is a trivial sense in which social criticism must depend on the understandings shared by members of a society. This is because, unless there is some commensurability between critique and existing meanings, no dialogue will be possible at all. At a deeper level, the idea that justice is circumscribed by shared understandings is an empty one.[22] If this were wholly so, change would be ruled out a priori, since new ideas must by definition of their newness be different from and thus in some respect break with old ones. Walzer seems to make a category mistake in confusing the preconditions of intelligibility, or shared membership, and the kinds of arguments which are properly invoked by social critics.

Such arguments necessarily make reference to principles and facts which point outside our existing assumptions, and provide reasons 'external' to them for holding to them or not. It is only within very closed societies that arguments are only admissible in debate if they are already elements of accepted doctrine. It is only in such societies that arguments must be settled by reference to consistency with already-accepted positions. (This is the social state of mind usually called 'fundamentalism'.) The more modern and pluralistic the society, the less this recourse to an existing consen-

[22] Charles Taylor has criticized the incoherence of utilitarian views of the good which allow no possibility for moral discrimination between desires and wishes, *Philosophy and the Human Sciences*, ii (Cambridge: Cambridge Univ. Press, 1985) and *The Ethics of Authenticity* (Cambridge, Mass.: Harvard Univ. Press, 1991). He argues that human freedom depends on being able to elaborate choices between ends. Fulfilment of human desires, including those that are socially constructed, is not self-evidently a good. The point of moral debate in societies is to decide between one socially generated value and another, and we cannot assume that what has been socially generated (in effect, everything) is by definition of value. It may have meaning, but that is something else.

sus is possible or normal. The undecidability of disputes within such plural societies is what makes appeal to facts or principles not sanctioned mainly by tradition so central to their discourses. It is only at the end of such debates that it may become clear whether an idea was indeed a radical departure from precedent, or whether it merely developed some meaning latent in existing beliefs. The more 'complex' a society (in Walzer's terms of competing spheres of justice), the less likely it is that its arguments will be confined by its existing traditions. The universalistic forms of argument, which Walzer criticizes as one-dimensional and reductive, have in fact been the natural products of complex social organization. Walzer's cultural particularism and stress on internal 'coherence' runs dangerously close to cultural closure. They appear to reject one inherent feature of 'modernity'—namely its rationalistic discursive procedures—even whilst arguing for its distinctive values of plurality and complexity.[23]

DEMOCRATIC CITIZENSHIP AND COMPLEX QUALITY

The final issue I want to address is whether Walzer's concept of 'complex equality' could in fact be set on a firmer basis than he now provides for it. I have argued that 'a strong programme' for complex equality cannot depend merely on the existence of shared meanings, for both logical and factual reasons. Arguments within American society, on for example the scope of health care and industrial democracy, depend on contrasting and conflicting belief systems, not merely on negotiating minor boundary adjustments between existing spheres. If a change were to occur in several of the areas of reform which Walzer recommends, it would signify a deep shift in the balance of prevailing values and powers, and would have to be justified in such terms.

[23] This may be because Walzer usually tries to imagine these arguments taking place at some point within moral communities, rather than in the spaces between them. (*Gemeinschaft* preferred to *Gesellschaft*.) One might also argue that some of the apparent rationalism of universalistic discourse in fact enforces the one-dimensionality of a dominant order (e.g. capitalism), and therefore represents a 'false universalism'. There is in any case much to be gained from the recovery of the local densities of moral argument, and showing this has been one of the main achievements of Walzer's book.

In such arguments, both universalist approaches (concerning the general happiness, or political rights of citizens) and historicist or sociological arguments (drawing attention to needs of the society at its particular stage of material or cultural or technological development) would need to have a place. These are indeed the terms in which arguments for social justice are now routinely presented. Paradoxically, Walzer's 'internalist' criteria, in 'modern' societies like ours, legitimize the invocation of the universalist or 'externalist' criteria which he is seeking on the whole to exclude, since these are the abstract terms in which 'modern' moral and political debates are typically conducted.[24] Such forms of argument are a distinctive product of societies which have become rationalized and differentiated. To rule such logics out *tout court* is to give implicit preference to 'pre-rationalized' forms of discourse in which local norms (or 'local knowledge' in Geertz's term) count for everything.

It seems that different kinds of argument than the particularist kind advanced by Walzer are in any case needed if a 'strong programme' for complex equality is to have plausibility. Not merely boundary demarcations between spheres, but the underlying logics of meaning and value which sustain different spheres of action need to be the subjects of debate and contestation, as in practice they already are. Major changes in conceptions of social justice (for example, those charted by Albert Hirschman in his account of the emergence of interest-based models of society in opposition to aristocratic norms) lead to deep-seated changes in such frameworks of justification.[25] The idea of complex equality, as an attempt to reformulate a uniformitarian concept of equality to take account of a more differentiated form of society, may itself signify such a change in ethos. In the nature of the case, arguments of this kind seem necessarily to evoke both universalistic criteria (as the basis of critique of existing arrangements) and historicist narratives (legitimating values by reference to changing social facts), as

[24] This argument has its equivalent in modern moral philosophy. Critics of ethical 'naturalism' have pointed out that it is characteristic of modern ethical debates (the meaning of 'modern' being explicated from usages in current ordinary language) that general principles are invoked to question particularistic cultural assumptions. Critics of this position, such as Alasdair MacIntyre, argue that this merely demonstrates the empty texture of modern moral thinking.

[25] A. Hirschman, *The Passions and the Interests* (Princeton, NJ: Princeton Univ. Press, 1977).

well as making particularistic reference to locally shared meanings.[26]

Only one major element of Walzer's argument in *Spheres* supports a universalistic form of social critique. This is the idea that shared political citizenship might be a defining egalitarian attribute of 'complex equality'. Walzer falls short of saying that only where procedures of political democracy exist can any consensus of values on which relative justice depends be ascertained. He seems to wish to maintain a more inclusive conception of consensus, in order not to rule out of court immediately distributional arrangements (caste societies are a case in point) which are sanctioned by different customs and conventions. But it might be agreed with Walzer, nevertheless, that there are some attributes of political citizenship which do make it the key dimension of the 'equality' of 'complex equality'.

The hallmark of the separation of 'spheres of justice' is that entitlements and claims derived from one sphere do not automatically carry over as claims and entitlements into others. Another way of putting this is to say that individual bearers of status, rewards, or recognition should not be able to remove these, as 'portable benefits', from the sphere in which they are earned, or at least should not be able to deploy these as power-resources in others. This condition is best respected where the ultimate 'ownership' of the good or reward in question is retained by the 'moral community' in which it is earned, and does not become the alienable property of the individual.

The recognition afforded to talented artists or performers, or to scientists, has this quality in high measure, since it depends on a continuing regard accorded by audiences or peer groups. It does not travel well, neither spatially (outside these spheres of communities of value) nor temporally (value has to be continually rediscovered and renewed in the minds of audiences).

One reason for the respect accorded to spheres of activity such as science, or to arts such as the theatre or jazz, and even to the communities constructed around sports, is that the communities in

---

[26] Gellner's earlier critique of the 'ordinary language philosophy' of Wittgenstein and his followers from a rationalistic liberal point of view has some critical application to Walzer's hermeneutic approach. See E. Gellner, *Words and Things* (London: Gollancz, 1959) and *Spectacles and Predicaments* (Cambridge: Cambridge Univ. Press, 1979).

question and their own memories and traditions remain highly and continuously in evidence. The *processes* by which achievements are made possible and recognized, and the relationships between new achievements and their predecessors, are very public ones. The cultures of jazz, baseball, or theatre are imbued with shared memories of filiations and apprenticeships, memorable performances, great careers, which provide a strong model for creative activity and for its recognition throughout entire societies. Routinely, on BBC television, commentators refer to cricket matches played forty or even eighty years ago, and compare the performance figures of players of many successive generations. This seems to constitute a much 'thicker' texture of recognition than the competitive denomination of money earnings, which increasingly prevails in certain sports, and which seems to signify the invasion of a moral sphere by a more general materialism. Relative limitation of material reward within a sphere of activity can be a positive benefit in this respect. By requiring that performers remain connected to their primary peer group and audience, as their main source of reward and recognition,[27] such limits encourage a reciprocal relationship and return of value to the community from which their activity has derived.[28]

The dependence of recognition and reward on the continuing respect of the community that provides it is also an attribute of political democracy, at least in principle, since office follows competitive election, is subject to periodic renewal, and involves some explicit consideration of candidates' intentions and qualities. Formalized appointment procedures (which derive from the public domain, even though they have been widely transferred to the private) also have some of these attributes.

[27] Carole Satyamurti, author of *Broken Moon* (Oxford: Oxford Univ. Press, 1987), has made me aware of the dense networks of poetry schools and public readings on which poetry as a calling in Britain depends, and which provides a milieu in which new poets are helped to learn to write. Material rewards are, of course, small, but the intrinsic satisfactions provided by these communities seem to ensure that there is no shortage of new members.

[28] At least in the days when track and field athletes were not able to command large attendance or sponsorship fees, successful athletes were often constrained to remain in contact with their local roots, taking up positions as coaches and managers when their performing careers declined. This is still, of course, the majority pattern, but the idea that the really successful will want to use their success to rise out of these worlds must impoverish these primary communities and perhaps to some degree spoil the motives of those who enter them in the first place.

The importance of such allocations of reward and status by political procedure is twofold. The first is its revocability, and the relationship which it enforces between office-holders and the 'publics' who award office. The second is the formal role of the structures of political sovereignty in determining the boundaries and limits of all other forms of power. If structures of political decision-making are democratic, and based on equal citizenship, there is some likelihood that other forms of power will be kept within bounds. Political structures are themselves subject to internal corruption, and to invasion from other spheres. The totalitarian abuse of political authority has been the worst form of power the world has seen, with power grossly to invade every domain, including the sanctity of kinship ties, cultures, life itself.[29]

But such abuses have scarcely been those of states which were (or continued to be, after an initial conquest of power) *democratic*. Where democratic procedures have survived, limits upon and redresses for abuses of power have usually remained. Democratic political authority does not, it is obvious, guarantee that 'complex equality' will result. Democratic majorities can be sustained for many forms of inequality, along many dimensions, though less easily when such inequalities are prohibited from invading (through the deployment of wealth or violence) the political process itself. In so far as 'complex equality' is defined by Walzer procedurally, as the outcome of negotiation between competing value systems, then guarantees of the procedures of negotiation (roughly speaking, democracy) are its necessary though not its sufficient conditions. There seem therefore to be strong reasons for giving priority, as Walzer does, to the sphere of democratic political sovereignty. Measures, via social revolutions, to rectify social injustice which have bypassed the institution of political democracy have usually led to other severe injustices, sometimes greater than those they initially sought to rectify. The achievement of a measure of justice in the sphere of legal and political rights may thus be a precondition

---

[29] The distinction made by Michael Mann, *Sources of Social Power*, i, and *The Sources of Social Power*, ii. *The Rise of Classes and Nation-States, 1760–1914* (Cambridge: Cambridge Univ. Press, 1993), between the scope and intensity of different forms of power helps to explain the extreme qualities of modern totalitarian power. Anthony Giddens, *A Contemporary Critique of Historical Materialism* (London: Macmillan, 1981) and *The Nation State and Violence* (Cambridge: Polity Press, 1985) draws similar distinctions.

of progress towards the achievement of social and economic justice. It has in historical practice usually preceded it.[30]

Ulrich Beck in his recent book *Risk Society*[31] has argued persuasively for a view of the process of 'modernization' as the hitherto incomplete historical realization of an ideal of self-reflective rationality, that is, of the possibility that individuals can take full responsibility for decisions concerning their own lives, powers, and environment. He argues that this process is radically incomplete, and remains qualified by many survivals of 'transitional' retentions of unequal authority. For example, within the family, by male heads of household; in the field of science, by a scientific community claiming absolute authority in the public sphere whilst it claims to observe norms of infinite corrigibility in its own sphere of action; and in the corporate economic sphere (about which however Beck remains somewhat vague).[32] Beck's programmatic argument, which is close in spirit to Habermas's view of modernity, though more grounded and empirical in its method, is for the further development of this process of a still incomplete modernity, so that a fuller and more general rational responsibility can be attained by humankind for its affairs. This perspective locates democratic political sovereignty as the key (and historically the formative) instance of rational autonomy. It offers some possibility of grounding Walzer's idea of 'complex equality' in a historical evolution, and provides empirical hope for its eventual fulfilment. The idea of an emergent rationality, taking the form of responsible, democratic citizenship, and rooted in conceptions both of human nature and of material possibility, is one possible discursive basis of a 'strong programme' for social justice conceived as complex equality. It is hard to see how such an argument can be sustained without the support of general principles of this kind.

Walzer's primary theoretical and methodological presupposition is the idea that goods are generated by a process of cultural and social definition, and are rooted in membership of a moral

---

[30] This was T. H. Marshall's view of the historical development of the idea of citizenship in *Citizenship and Social Class and Other Essays* (Cambridge: Cambridge Univ. Press, 1950).

[31] *Risk Society: Towards a New Modernity*, tr. M. Ritter (London: Sage, 1983).

[32] In an otherwise appreciative discussion of Beck's book in M. J. Rustin, 'Incomplete Modernity: Ulrich Beck's "Risk Society"', *Radical Philosophy*, 67 (Summer 1994), 3–12, I give attention to what I see as some evasiveness in regard to the obstacles posed to his enlightenment project by the operations of capitalism.

community. Walzer presents this as the foundation of his argument, and the grounds of his disagreement about methods with individualist theorists of social justice. This cultural particularism sustains Walzer's commitment to difference, but does not prevent him from making his qualified case for a version of equality compatible with a full recognition of difference.

In fact, Walzer's assumptions that concepts of justice are generated only within moral communities are more deeply contentious than he acknowledges. One reason why his arguments for complex equality have less purchase than he would like in American society is that there is not even agreement about his basic assumption that goods are socially generated. This is not merely an issue in the procedural terms in which Walzer presents it (of how philosophers should define and defend justice). It also defines how the issue of justice is framed and perceived in everyday social practice. (This integral link between philosophical assumptions and taken-for-granted beliefs is however what one would expect from Walzer's interpretative view of political philosophy.) The idea that distributions should be regulated on normative grounds, by reference to different communities of value, is denied by individualists, who assert that entitlements and claims exist *prior* to their sanction by a political community ('This property, these possessions, these freedoms are *mine* and no one else has any claim on them'). Community, in this frame of reference, comes *post facto*, as a way of clubbing together to protect individual rights, not as the source and justification of those rights. The story of the American settlement of the West is a mythical legitimation of this idea: first individual claims were asserted by force, then a law-enforcing structure was constructed to defend them. First the pioneer, then the sheriff, not, as in Europe, first the king's law, then the citizen. It is characteristic of a certain kind of individualism that it denies its actual social origins, and defines the individual as the source of all value.[33] In this way private property, the rule of the strongest, and

[33] These fundamental differences of outlook are brought out beautifully by G. A. Cohen in his critique of Nozick. He points out that Nozick's Lockean idea that individuals are entitled to what they appropriate and create with their labour assumes that 'nature' belongs to no one before individuals engage in their appropriations, rather than being the property of the community. This precisely defines the difference of view between America's settlers and its pre-existing Indian population. G. A. Cohen, 'Self-Ownership, World-Ownership, and Equality', in F. S. Lukash (ed.), *Justice and Equality Here and Now* (Ithaca, NY: Cornell Univ. Press, 1986)

individualism, have been able to pre-empt social critique by denying the legitimacy of any of the supra-individual values which are
necessary to formulate such critiques.

Utilitarian and universalistic rights-based theories are attempts
to repair the damage to social coherence which arises from such an
individualist starting-point. They attempt to 'construct' an imaginary 'society' from the building blocks of individual desires or
choices alone, to solve the intractable problems of aggrandizement
which otherwise follow from these conflictful assumptions. Walzer
describes contemporary America as if it were a set of competing
moral communities, between which moral boundaries are open to
negotiation and adjustment. The problems of achieving agreement
on social justice are made more severe than he suggests by the fact
that, for many citizens, the debate is not between competing moral
communities at all, but between individuals and the claims of any
moral community upon them. Sociologists like Durkheim and
Talcott Parsons, and cultural interpreters like Walzer, may argue
that individualism is the derivative of a certain kind of historically
emergent community, but not all members of such communities
think so. What Walzer presents as a neutral frame of debate
between different claims to reward is in fact itself a widely contested one. This is one reason why the 'internal' meanings of
Walzer's own society are much less hospitable to the idea of complex equality than he suggests.

Contested or not, Walzer's assumption that the essence of value
is social is the essential precondition of any viable egalitarian philosophy. Not only regard for 'differences', as the culturally specific
values of particular societies, but the idea of complex equality as
the definition and allocation of goods by the decision of moral
communities, depends on this 'social' starting-point. *Spheres*, as I
have suggested, does not altogether succeed in defending 'complex
equality' as the form of justice natural to a differentiated society.
But it does establish several of the essential preconditions for doing
so.

and 'Self-Ownership, World-Ownership and Equality, Part II', in E. F. Paul *et al.*
(eds.), *Marxism and Liberalism* (Oxford: Blackwell, 1986).

2

Complex Justice, Cultural Difference, and Political Community

JOSEPH H. CARENS

———◁◆▷———

'Justice is a human construction . . . The questions posed by the theory of distributive justice admit of a range of answers, and there is room within the range for cultural diversity and political choice.'[1] How much room? How wide is the range? Which constructions of justice should we respect and which should we criticize? These are the questions I will explore in this chapter.

The basic claim I want to make here is that the picture Walzer draws in *Spheres* of the moral autonomy of political communities is not true to the moral standard that he invokes, namely our shared understanding of justice. There are two related aspects to the critique. The first concerns the kinds of judgements we make regarding justice, the second who constitutes the 'we' making the judgements. With respect to the first, I will argue that our understanding of justice requires us sometimes to respect and sometimes to criticize the institutions and policies of political communities to which we do not belong. With respect to the second, I will argue that the 'we' who make these judgements sometimes correspond to the members of a political community and sometimes constitute a moral community, wider or narrower than any political community to which we belong. In developing this critique, I will try to argue that the more complex picture of justice that I want to paint corresponds in fact to the understanding of justice that Walzer displays in *Spheres*, even though it conflicts with some of his central formulations.

I want to thank Ed Andrew, Rainer Bauböck, Ronnie Beiner, Heiner Bielefeldt, Dilek Çinar, Peter Lindsay, and David Miller for comments on an earlier version of this chapter.

[1] Michael Walzer, *Spheres of Justice* (New York: Basic Books, 1983), 5–6.

STYLES OF POLITICAL PHILOSOPHY

I begin with a few remarks about Walzer's philosophical style because I think that it is intimately linked to and is a manifestation of his commitment to a deep moral pluralism. Too often we think of intellectual exchange on the model of a fight: you try to knock down my argument and I'll try to knock down yours. Sometimes it is a friendly fight, sometimes not, but it is rarely a shared exploration. Our goal becomes constructing an airtight case, warding off or even submerging doubts, problems, and countervailing considerations (except perhaps as objections to be rebutted). I have certainly written in that style, and I am not alone.

By contrast Walzer's approach is much more conversational. One has the sense that he is listening as well as speaking. He draws our attention rather than commanding it. He evokes more than he insists. At times he expresses ambivalence and uncertainty. He opens up issues for consideration and invites reflection and response. Walzer takes positions—many of them controversial—and he offers reasons and arguments in support of his views. But his arguments are not, and I think not intended to be, knock-down arguments On the whole, that is to the good. We are rarely persuaded or enlightened by knock-down arguments even when we cannot refute them. I do not mean to deny that we can occasionally learn something from pushing an argument as far as it will go or seeing someone else do so. There is something to be gained from a pluralism of styles as well as from a pluralist style. But it seems to me that Walzer's approach is relatively rare among philosophers and political theorists, and that we would learn more if more people followed his lead.

One way to appreciate Walzer's approach to political philosophy is to contrast it with that of Rawls in *A Theory of Justice*, a contrast to which Walzer alludes in the preface to *Spheres*. I mean this not as a criticism of Rawls but as a way of drawing attention to the virtues of both. In my view, every political theory worth taking seriously will have interconnected strengths and weaknesses. In bringing light to bear on some questions, concerns, arguments, and ideas, a theory inevitably casts others into the shadows. It is a mark of a good theory to be both illuminating and comprehensive but no theory can make everything clear.

Rawls, at least the Rawls of *A Theory of Justice*, offers a model of political theory as an engineer's blueprint. He shows how something can be built from scratch, though, of course, it requires appropriate building materials. Every principle and argument is carefully related to every other one like the beams of a building, with the weight that each will bear carefully specified, and the entire structure resting upon a foundation whose characteristics are essential to the success of the project. By contrast, Walzer offers a model of political theory as an impressionist painting of our moral landscape. He says, in effect, 'See. Isn't it like this?' I am not suggesting that he just points to what people already think is right and wrong. To see a landscape through a painting is not the same as to view it with the naked eye. The artist offers a reconstructive interpretation, drawing attention to colours, shadings, interconnections. Once we've seen the artist's painting, the landscape actually looks different to us, though in important ways what the artist sees was always already there.

I do not mean to offer an unqualified endorsement of Walzer's approach. At times reading Walzer's work I would like to see a little more of the Rawlsian structure, some further specifications of what weight particular arguments and principles will bear and of their relation to one another. (Perhaps what we need is some combination of the two approaches—say, political theory as architecture.) But, on the whole, I think that Walzer's artistic and pluralist style of philosophy is underrepresented.

LOCAL UNDERSTANDINGS
AND THE MORAL COMMUNITY

Now consider the way Walzer's approach shapes an inquiry into justice. The most important lesson I have learnt from *Spheres* and related works by Michael Walzer is how much we gain as political theorists if we begin our theoretical reflections with ordinary moral discourse about public affairs—with the concrete judgements we make, the characteristic language we use, the particular principles we invoke, the specific problems we recognize, and the actual arguments we advance when we talk about questions of justice in ordinary life. In a sense, Walzer is a left-wing Burkian. He would rather rest his moral claims and criticisms on the history, traditions, and practices of a particular community than on abstract general principles, on the rights of Englishmen rather than the rights of man (though Walzer, I suspect, would construe the rights of Englishmen much more expansively than Burke with respect to class and gender).

Walzer is not opposed in principle to general theoretical formulations but he is very sensitive to the blinkers they can impose and to the ways they can embody, in disguised form, moral insights that grow out of, and are only applicable to, particular contexts. *Spheres* is filled with examples of social practices that are either neglected by, or in apparent conflict with, conventional theories of justice but that, upon reflection, raise issues of justice and seem morally justifiable. Indeed, the book emphasizes the variety and variability of the social goods with which a theory of justice must be concerned. Once we see the richness and complexity of social goods, once we appreciate the different ways in which different communities understand goods, value goods, and think various goods ought to be distributed, we will no longer imagine that it is possible to construct an adequate theory of justice without beginning from and returning to the actual practices of particular societies.

One thing we will discover from such an approach is that we inhabit a rich and complex moral world, a world in which history, culture, and community matter. Theory can clarify and criticize some aspects of this moral world, and no aspect is off limits in principle. But theory cannot replace our moral world or entirely reconstruct it. Indeed, critical reflection should lead us to appreciate not only the morally problematic character of some local practices and understandings but also the limitations of general principles. The adequacy of a political theory depends in part on its ability to bring into its compass the complex variety of moral considerations that we actually think are morally relevant, even after reflection and self-criticism.

This kind of approach is particularly helpful in thinking about how we should respond to different ways of understanding justice. To say why we should respect some version of local justice in one case and criticize it in another requires a contextual inquiry that begins with actual moral problems and moral judgements and moves back and forth between these particulars and general principles, paying attention in a critical and reflective way to the actual features of our moral world. I think this approach provides an extremely valuable corrective to the dangers of abstract theorizing. Walzer is surely right to insist upon how much we can learn simply by paying attention to the way people in different societies think about the problems of justice. Unfortunately, Walzer's picture of the moral autonomy of political communities would lead away from the kind of contextual inquiry that he invites.

Walzer claims that justice *is* what the people in a particular community *think* it is. More precisely, he argues that when goods are distributed in accordance with the meaning that people in a community attach to those goods then the goods are distributed justly. The most striking illustration of this argument is his discussion of a caste system in which, by hypothesis, all participants agree to the principles governing it. According to Walzer, criticism of such a cohesive internal society by outsiders would be inappropriate if not incoherent.

Every substantive account of distributive justice is a local account . . . One characteristic above all is central to my argument. We are (all of us) culture-producing creatures; we make and inhabit meaningful worlds. Since there is no way to rank and order these worlds with regard to their understanding of social goods, we do justice to actual men and women by respecting their particular creations . . . Justice is rooted in the distinct understandings of places, honours, jobs, things of all sorts, that constitute a shared way of life. To override those understandings is (always) to act unjustly. (*Spheres*, 314)

Elsewhere in the book, Walzer says that the locus of these shared cultural understandings is the political community: 'The political community is the appropriate setting for this enterprise . . . [It] is probably the closest we can come to a world of common meanings' (*Spheres*, 28). He describes the way of doing philosophy that he pursues as 'interpret[ing] to one's fellow citizens the world of meanings that we share' (*Spheres*, p. xiv).

This broad picture of how we should think about justice fits poorly with important aspects of Walzer's own discussion in *Spheres*. Let me mention two examples. First, Walzer says that it is wrong for new states formed after the demise of colonialism to expel current inhabitants who do not share the race or ethnicity of the newly established dominant majority. The sort of case he has in mind presumably is the expulsion of Asians from Kenya and Uganda in the 1970s. But he makes no appeal to African or even

Asian understandings of community and of responsibilities towards those seen in some way as outsiders. Instead, he cites Hobbes (*Spheres*, 42–3). Second, Walzer criticizes the treatment of 'guest workers' in Western Europe, arguing that people who live and work in a country should also be given access to citizenship. The German exclusion of Turks from citizenship is perhaps the clearest example of the sort of practice Walzer is criticizing, but he says nothing about German or Turkish history, culture, traditions, or conceptions of membership and community. Instead, he offers an argument based on general, even abstract, liberal democratic principles (*Spheres*, 56–60).

Let me pursue this second example in more detail. The German policy that makes naturalization so difficult for guest workers is rooted in an understanding of citizenship that has very deep roots in German history and culture. Even many of the Turks share that understanding. As William Rogers Brubaker puts it:

The ethnocultural inflection of German self-understanding and German citizenship law makes it difficult to reconcile—in the political imagination of Germans and immigrants alike—the preservation of Turkish cultural identity and autonomy, for example, with the preservation of German citizenship. State-membership is too closely tied to nation-membership. To take on German citizenship, in the self-understanding of Germans and Turks alike, requires that one become German in some thicker, richer sense than merely acquiring a new passport.[2]

This view of German citizenship is probably as close as we get empirically to a distinctive and shared understanding of the meaning of a good within a political community. Walzer's theory of justice effectively requires the German political community to abandon or at least radically transform this shared understanding. Is this not the very sort of overriding of local understandings that Walzer declared would be unjust?[3]

---

[2] *Citizenship and Nationhood in France and Germany* (Cambridge, Mass.: Harvard Univ. Press, 1992), 178.

[3] Could one argue that the term 'overriding' refers not to judgement and criticism, as I suppose, but to intervention whether military or economic? I do not think that would be a reasonable reading of *Spheres*. Non-intervention was a central theme of Walzer's earlier work *Just and Unjust Wars* (New York: Basic Books, 1977), but in *Spheres* the central focus is on the appropriateness of different standards of justice and on the relation between those making moral evaluations and the communities they wish to evaluate. Walzer's position seems to be: anyone may try to persuade anyone else; you do not have to be a member of a community to

One possible way to try to preserve the Walzerian emphasis on local understandings is to say that his argument is based on liberal democratic principles that Germany too claims to embrace. In that sense, it remains an immanent critique, though it requires the commitment to liberal democracy to trump conflicting commitments to German history and culture.[4] To construct the argument in this way, however, is to assume that Germans and Americans share an understanding of what democracy means and what it requires. If, as Walzer says, 'in matters of morality, argument simply is the appeal to common meanings' (*Spheres*, 29), this argument presupposes that our world of common meanings at least partly transcends the boundaries of the particular political community to which we belong. It assumes a shared moral community—to some degree—even among people who are not members of the same political community.

That sort of assumption corresponds much better both to our ordinary moral practices and to Walzer's own theory of justice than do some of his formulations about the moral autonomy of political communities. In fact, *Spheres* does not strike me as exclusively, or even predominantly, an account of the *American* understanding of justice. It is much less explicitly tied to American history and culture than, for example, Judith Shklar's recent book on citizenship.[5] Many of the arguments and examples refer to the experience of a variety of Western states, and not with the goal of illustrating how different societies may understand goods differently (which is often the point of Walzer's use of historical examples) but in order to articulate 'our' understanding of goods like

---

engage in conversation about justice (see e.g. *Spheres*, 314). If you want to persuade others, Walzer assumes, you will have to draw heavily upon some of their existing moral understandings, even if your goal is to transform those understandings in some respects. In any event, what counts morally is what the members of the community think. Their judgements are the ones that determine the content of justice. To grant moral weight to the views of an external critic constitutes the kind of overriding to which Walzer objects.

[4] I am assuming here that Walzer's argument is correct, i.e. that the German exclusionary policy on naturalization is incompatible with liberal democratic principles. I have argued for this view in 'Membership and Morality: Admission to Citizenship in Liberal Democratic States', in William Rogers Brubaker (ed.), *Immigration and the Politics of Citizenship in Europe and North America* (Lanham, Md.: The German Marshall Fund of the US and Univ. Press of America, Inc., 1989), 31–49.

[5] *American Citizenship: The Quest for Inclusion* (Cambridge, Mass.: Harvard Univ. Press, 1991).

money, political power, and position. That is the way the book has been read and discussed in Europe and elsewhere. David Miller's introduction to this volume, for example, assumes that Walzer is talking about 'the main categories of goods in contemporary liberal societies' and about the ways that 'we in contemporary democracies' think about these goods.

All this suggests that it is a serious mistake to equate the moral community with the political community. The 'we' who share a set of moral understandings should not be identified exclusively with the 'we' who share a political community. It is not merely that there is a minimal morality shared by all contemporary societies, as Walzer sometimes suggests. Rather there is a thick, highly developed, richly textured morality shared by many people who do not live in the same political community. We often engage in debates about what is just and unjust, in ways that presuppose this wider moral community. But I do not mean to suggest that recognition of this wider moral community resolves all of the puzzles about the connections between justice, culture, and political community. On the contrary, it opens the door to more complexity.

First, even if we assume a shared commitment to liberal democratic principles, we have to acknowledge (a) some range of morally permissible implementations on any given account of the principles and (b) some range of reasonable disagreement about how to interpret the principles themselves. Within these extents, it is morally appropriate to treat the institutions and policies of a particular democratic community as legitimate, even when they differ from the institutions and policies of your own community or from the ones that you think would be best. No one supposes that every liberal democracy is morally obliged to adopt exactly the same institutions and policies. These legitimate differences in institutions and policies will presumably reflect in part historical and cultural differences between democratic states. So, we cannot entirely dismiss Walzer's emphasis on the political community as the locus of shared moral understandings that deserve respect.

THE CANADIAN CHARTER AND THE OVERRIDE CLAUSE

How wide is this range of legitimate differences? How closely are our interpretations of liberal democratic principles and our understandings of appropriate institutional implementations tied to particular cultures? Consider briefly an example from Canada. One essential component of most contemporary conceptions of democratic justice is the protection of basic human rights such as freedom of religion, freedom of thought and expression, equal treatment under the law, and so on. In 1982 Canada adopted as part of its constitution a bill of rights, called the Charter of Rights and Freedoms, designed to protect such basic rights. The Canadian Charter is like the American Bill of Rights in many ways, but it has some interesting differences. For example, it says at the very beginning that the rights and freedoms it guarantees are 'subject . . . to such reasonable limits prescribed by law as can be demonstrably justified in a free and democratic society', thus rejecting any absolutist conception of rights and drawing attention to the need for public deliberation about the relationship between individuals as rights-bearers and the political community to which they belong.[6] It also has clauses explicitly endorsing affirmative action in various contexts, acknowledging distinct aboriginal rights, prohibiting gender discrimination, affirming multiculturalism, and so on.

The particular feature of the Charter that I want to highlight concerns the limits on judicial review. As in the USA, Canada's Supreme Court can declare laws that violate the Charter to be invalid, but there is this important difference. A simple majority, either of Parliament *or of a provincial legislature*, can pass a law that is immune to such judicial scrutiny, with respect to certain sections of the Charter, simply by announcing that as its intent. This is the so-called notwithstanding clause.[7] The law has to be renewed every five years or it automatically lapses.

---

[6] Constitution Act, 1982. [Schedule B to Canada Act 1982 (U.K.)] Part I: Canadian Charter of Rights and Freedoms, s. 1, repr. in Rainer Knopff and F. L. Morton (eds.), *Charter Politics* (Scarborough, Ontario: Nelson Canada, 1992), 385. Of course, many interpreters of the US Constitution would argue that it does not provide for absolute rights either, but the language of the Bill of Rights creates scope for absolutist readings that would be much harder to defend in the Canadian context.

[7] Ibid., s. 33: 'Parliament or the legislature of a province may expressly declare in an Act of Parliament or of the legislature, as the case may be, that the Act or a provision thereof shall operate notwithstanding a provision included in section 2 or sections 7 to 15 of this Charter.' These sections deal with such rights as freedom of religion, freedom of expression, freedom of assembly, freedom of association, the right to habeas corpus, and other basic legal rights.

Americans may be tempted to think that this provision just shows that the Canadian constitution is built on a misunderstanding of the nature of fundamental rights, which are supposed to be trumps (to use Dworkin's famous phrase), not something that can be overridden by a democratic majority. Many Canadians would agree with this.[8] But the override clause, as it is also called, has many defenders as well, and I am now inclined to be one of them.

The short version of my defence goes like this.[9] We should assess political institutions, including institutions for protecting human rights, not only by their announced aspirations but also, and more fundamentally, by how well they work in practice. The US Supreme Court, for example, whose task (one might say) is to interpret and apply the Constitution in an uncompromising fashion, without regard for democratic majorities, immune from easy democratic override, is the very Court that has brought us such decisions as *Dred Scott* v. *Sanford* and *Plessy* v. *Ferguson*.[10] To put it very cautiously, the Court has not been an unqualified success in protecting basic human rights, especially of minorities.

The way an institution works depends in part on the history and culture of the society in which it is embedded. Any institution has to be evaluated in context. The Canadian Charter is too new for any reliable evaluation, but one can make an argument that, given the Canadian context, the override clause is a reasonable experiment whose goal is to promote public deliberation about individual rights and to assign political responsibility for transgressions. In a society like Canada where people are deeply attached to fun-

[8] See e.g. John Whyte, 'On Not Standing for Notwithstanding', *Alberta Law Review*, 28 (1990), 347.

[9] The account that follows is heavily influenced by Peter Russell, 'Standing up for Notwithstanding', *Alberta Law Review*, 29 (1991), 293–309.

[10] In *Dred Scott* (1857) the Court struck down as unconstitutional a federal law prohibiting slavery in certain territories of the USA and held that 'negroes' were not citizens of the USA and could not become so, even if free, saying that the Constitution reflected the long-standing view that negroes were 'beings of an inferior order . . . and so far inferior that they had no rights which the white man was bound to respect'. In *Plessy* v. *Ferguson* (1896) the Court held that compulsory segregation of the races did not violate the Fourteenth Amendment, an amendment explicitly passed to overturn *Dred Scott* and to guarantee equal protection of the laws to all. According to the Court, it was fallacious to assume that 'The enforced separation of the two races stamps the colored man with a badge of inferiority. If this is so, it is not by reason of anything found in the act, but solely because the colored race chooses to put that construction upon it.' (Quotations from Court opinions excerpted in Stanley Kutler (ed.), *The Supreme Court and the Constitution*, 3rd edn. (New York: Norton, 1984), 153 and 216.)

damental rights, invocation of the override clause will be likely to generate public criticism and debate. Canadian parliamentarian traditions ensure that, in most cases, a debate will occur and political responsibility for the action will be clear. If an override can be publicly defended as a correction of judicial injustice or perhaps judicial imperialism, then it will provide a better outcome than the judicial decision. If it cannot be reasonably defended in this way, it may well be a significant factor in the next election. This might ultimately secure rights more effectively, because more democratically, than an American style system of judicial review would have in the Canadian context.[11]

So goes one argument for the notwithstanding clause, and, if you accept it, you can already see that cultural differences *between* democratic societies can have an impact on what democratic justice requires and permits. It may be tempting to reply that Canada and the USA agree on basic principles, and that the institutional differences are just differences of application. There is a lot to that reply, but it misses something as well. All principles require mediation, instantiation, embeddedness in some concrete social context. Different forms of mediation have different advantages and disadvantages, different features and quirks, and they may fit together more or less well with other forms of mediation. But sometimes the particularity of the mediation overwhelms the abstract principle it allegedly instantiates. To put it another way, people are supposed to experience the realization of principles of justice through various concrete institutions, but they may actually experience a lot of the institutions and very little of the principles. Moreover, how the institutions work may depend greatly on the background culture of the society in which they are established.

Some people will not be persuaded by my defence of the override clause. As I said, many people in Canada think the override is a bad idea. But even if one thinks the American approach to protecting rights would be superior, would it be appropriate for non-Canadians to call the override clause unjust, or is this the sort of judgement that ought to be left to Canadians? If you consider the override clause unjust, what would you say about the system in

---

[11] I am not arguing that an override clause would be a desirable innovation in the American context. On the contrary, given the different history, traditions, and culture of American politics, I would suppose that such an innovation would be extremely unwise.

place before the Charter (with its override clause) was adopted, the system of parliamentary sovereignty that continues in Britain today? Is that sort of system unjust?

The point of this example is to unsettle a bit the sense that we know what liberal democratic justice entails, with respect to institutions and policies, and to draw attention to the ways in which even similar countries can have understandings that are very different. I am not suggesting that there are no limits to these differences. On the contrary, in discussing German citizenship policies, I have already drawn attention to one sort of limit. But we should try to map out the range of the morally permissible (and also the range of reasonable disagreements), and in constructing this map, we should begin by identifying some of the actual differences of institutions and policies in existing states and by considering their connections to cultural differences. When we speak of 'contemporary liberal societies' or 'contemporary democracies', as David Miller does above, do we include Japan and India in the mental list conjured up by this phrase? Do the cultural differences between countries like Japan and India on the one hand and Western countries on the other have any bearing on how we think about democratic justice? I would be surprised if they do not.

Consider again the issue of German citizenship policy. When defenders of that policy argue that a critique like Walzer's is a form of North American cultural and moral imperialism, an attempt to project an understanding of membership appropriate to the immigrant societies of North America on to European societies with very different histories and traditions, this is an argument that deserves to be considered seriously.[12] In this case I would ultimately reject that argument, but I do find it somewhat troubling that the model that Walzer and I hold up as a standard fits so comfortably with the practices of the societies of which we are members.

We make moral arguments against a background of cultural assumptions that are never fully explicit and often not even conscious. I may have enough of a feel for the way that German culture is similar to and different from the North American cultures

---

[12] See e.g. Kay Hailbronner, 'Citizenship and Nationhood in Germany', in Rogers Brubaker (ed.), *Immigration and Politics*, 67–79. Hailbronner's essay is, in part, a response to my article (see n. 4 above), but since I defend Walzer's position, Hailbronner's objections to me would presumably apply to Walzer as well.

that I know best that I can make reasonable critical judgements about German citizenship policy, despite the fact that I do not know German culture well. Would I be willing to make the same critical judgements with respect to Japan's citizenship policy? Japan, like Germany, has a restrictive naturalization policy and an understanding of citizenship closely tied to an ethnocultural conception of the nation. In the end, I would criticize Japan's policies too, but I would do so with somewhat more trepidation. The cultural differences between Japan and North America are much greater than the cultural differences between Germany and North America, and so the risk of missing something that would make a difference to the moral argument seems greater.

I draw attention to my doubts and trepidations not as a way of providing information about my psychic life but because I regard these feelings as morally relevant. In moral deliberation, what matters is not only the ultimate conclusion we reach but also the considerations we regard as relevant (even when they are outweighed) and the degree of confidence we feel in our judgements. These things matter because they affect our view of the range of reasonable disagreement, which in turn affects our view of the kinds of differences that deserve respect.[13]

UNIVERSAL AND PARTICULAR PRINCIPLES OF JUSTICE

So far, I have been exploring some of the implications of cultural differences for the ways in which we think about justice in liberal democracies. Would it be appropriate for us to extend the critique of exclusionary citizenship policies to a state like Kuwait or Saudi Arabia that does not claim to be a liberal democracy? I am not sure how Walzer would answer this. On the one hand, this sort of critique can no longer easily be construed as an appeal to shared moral understandings.[14] For that reason, one might expect Walzer

[13] See Amy Gutmann and Dennis Thompson, 'Moral Conflict and Political Consensus', *Ethics*, 101 (1990), 64–88; John Rawls, *Political Liberalism* (New York: Columbia Univ. Press, 1993); and Amy Gutmann, 'The Challenge of Multiculturalism in Political Ethics', *Philosophy and Public Affairs*, 22 (1993), 171–206.

[14] To construe the critique as an appeal to local shared understandings would presumably require one to argue that most people in Saudi Arabia or Kuwait accept

to oppose it. On the other hand, Walzer's criticism of the expulsion of current inhabitants from new states formed after the demise of colonialism, which I mentioned earlier, seems to point to the existence of moral standards not derived from local shared understandings. In the same context, he says that he will later consider and reject the possibility that such inhabitants should be permitted to stay but excluded from citizenship, thus connecting his critique of exclusionary citizenship policies to this wider minimal morality (*Spheres*, 43).

For the moment, I don't want to try to settle the question of how Walzer would answer this question or how it ought to be answered. Instead, I want to explore what these ambiguities in his analysis reveal. I think that they point to a richer, more complex theory of justice than his rhetoric sometimes suggests. One way to read (or reconstruct) *Spheres* would be to say that it reveals that Walzer's theory of justice contains four distinct parts. To employ an alternative spherical model, we might think of these four parts as concentric circles, the later contained within the earlier.

The first part concerns minimal standards of justice applicable to all contemporary states, regardless of their own particular histories, cultures, or political arrangements. The theory is universal in the sense that it applies to all, at least all in the present.[15] It is

democratic principles that their governments reject. This throws up the further problem of whose understandings count. Do the views of those living there but currently excluded from citizenship matter? How do we judge whose interpretation of the shared moral understandings of Saudi Arabia or Kuwait is the best? Nevertheless, it would be difficult to make a convincing case that a critique of Saudi Arabian or Kuwaiti policy from a liberal democratic perspective is driven by an appeal to shared understandings.

[15] Walzer's frequent use of historical examples evokes, without directly addressing, the question of the relationship between contemporary moral standards and the past. One of Walzer's goals seems to be to make us aware of differences in social understandings of goods without arousing the urge to judge these differences because moral criticism would be anachronistic. Yet a different and more critical theme also plays a role in his discussions. For example, he spends some time exploring, without finally resolving, the question of whether the Athenian treatment of *metics* was unjust, given the conception of citizenship that prevailed in Athens. He focuses on *metics* rather than slaves because, he says, 'the injustice of slavery is not disputed these days, at least not openly' (*Spheres*, 53). Given Walzer's general approach, that seems already a puzzling form of deference to today's standards of justice. If he had asked the same question about slaves that he asked about *metics*—whether Athenians ought to have viewed slavery as unjust given their shared social understandings—the answer would be far from clear. In my view, there is a real danger of anachronism in making critical judgements about the past. It violates the maxim 'ought implies can' to criticize people for failing to meet moral

particular in the sense that this understanding of justice is acknowledged to be the product of a particular time and place, a particular culture and history. It is *our* understanding of justice. The 'we'
here is indeterminate and open but includes more than the members of any particular political community and presumably less
than all humanity. Thus there are some policies, practices, and
institutions that we will criticize in the name of justice, even though
we recognize that the people whose policies, practices, and institutions are being criticized may not share our understanding of justice. Walzer has self-consciously discussed this part of the theory
of justice in *Just and Unjust Wars*, but how much of *Spheres* and
related subsequent work ought to be read as falling within this circle, whether he recognizes that or not?

The second and third parts of the theory concern standards of
justice applicable to contemporary liberal democratic states, but in
somewhat different ways. The second part identifies standards that
apply regardless of the particular history or culture of a given state.
These standards are derived from liberal democratic principles.
Many arguments of this kind can be found in *Spheres*, not only in
the critique of the treatment of guest workers cited above but in
many parts of the discussion of money, power, office, and so on.

The third part identifies standards that are more contingently
linked to commonalities of culture and history among liberal
democratic states. Walzer's discussion of medical care provides a
good example. While he focuses on the American case, he never
suggests that he is presenting a distinctive American understanding. (It is the opponents of communal provision who insist that
there is a distinctive American understanding of medical care.) The
understanding of medical care that Walzer presents—that it is a
basic need that ought to be provided by the community to all—is
a cultural understanding shared (at the least) by all affluent liberal

standards that are entirely unknown and unarticulated in their own time. Yet criticism may be appropriate if moral standards are within people's cognitive reach
even if not actually in their grasp. For example, in the *Philosophy of Right*, Hegel,
who had some appreciation for the importance of historical development, was
sharply critical of the Roman legal system for treating children as the property of
their father, because the Roman legal system was built upon a conception of the
distinction between persons and things that should have enabled them to understand why treating children as property was wrong. By contrast, Hegel has nothing
comparably judgemental to say about Babylonian practices even more at odds with
modern ethical norms, presumably because Babylonian civilization did not have the
conceptual resources for a critical perspective on these practices.

democratic societies. In such societies, justice requires communal provision of medical care to all citizens, where that is economically feasible. Yet Walzer is surely right to insist that this view of what justice requires is a historical and cultural development, closely linked to a particular understanding of medical care. It is not intrinsically linked to the principles of liberal democracy or to any universal conception of justice.

The fourth part of the theory—the innermost concentric circle—contains standards of justice that are intimately linked to the history and culture of a particular political community. Walzer's discussion of integration and school bussing offers one prime example. It is impossible to separate our sense of what justice requires with respect to this issue from the history of American racism, and the particular forms it has taken. Indeed, Will Kymlicka has argued, persuasively in my view, that liberal theorists like Rawls and Dworkin have failed to appreciate the ways in which the famous claim 'separate is inherently unequal' was tied to the particular case of African-Americans and thus have not seen that justice may not only permit but require separate arrangements for cultural minorities in other circumstances.[16]

Walzer's rhetoric suggests that the fourth part of the theory constitutes the core of his theory of justice, but his actual discussion in *Spheres* ranges over all four parts. One crucial question, then, is how wide or thin the various circles are. In other words, how much of our understanding of justice is universalistic and how much is particularistic? I don't mean to suggest that these matters are precisely quantifiable but rather that it is important to try to specify what kind of room we think it appropriate to provide for various forms of particularity in our understanding of justice. One way to provide this specification is to look at crucial topics where our understanding of justice is not shared by others, to see whether we regard these different understandings as ones we should respect or not.

---

[16] Will Kymlicka, *Liberalism, Community, and Culture* (Oxford: Oxford Univ. Press, 1989). Kymlicka does not connect his project to Walzer's and indeed devotes a whole chapter to a critique of *Spheres*, but I think Kymlicka's argument fits very well with Walzer's emphasis on what we can learn about justice from looking at the problems and practices of different societies.

GENDER AND DEMOCRACY

Consider then some questions about gender and democracy. How should we think about the way women are treated in other countries? Of course, we need to *understand* how they are treated before passing judgement. We cannot simply assume that what would be a form of oppression in our society is necessarily one in theirs as well. But should we limit *our* judgements to *their* understanding of what justice requires in relations between men and women, with respect to economic opportunity, education, health care, access to office, and so on? If we recognize that both justice and gender are cultural constructions, what should we think about the ways in which cultures that are not our own have constructed them?

I wonder how Walzer would respond to these questions. His discussion of the caste system suggests that the only meaningful criticism is internal criticism, but, as I have tried to show, other parts of his discussion are less particularistic. Walzer is surely right to draw our attention to the fact that cultures vary and to insist that justice, like all morality, is a cultural creation, at least in many important respects. It is all too easy to project our own particularistic understanding as a universal norm and to misunderstand institutions and practices different from our own. As liberals, we have good historical and theoretical reasons to be wary of such projections and misunderstandings. Would anyone today want to endorse (or reproduce) the smug superiority displayed by so many nineteenth-century liberals towards indigenous cultures in Asia, Africa, and America? On the other hand, appeal to difference is every tyranny's first line of defence against external criticism: 'You don't understand our circumstances, our way of life, or our people.'

Take the issue of female circumcision, a practice carried on in a number of countries, mainly in Africa but also in the Middle East and South-east Asia, by people from various cultural and religious traditions, some of whom are Muslims (though it is not a practice followed by most Muslims). Those who object to Western criticism of female circumcision usually argue that the criticism is a contemporary manifestation of Western cultural imperialism and hence is illegitimate. It seems essential, however, to distinguish between two kinds of objections to Western or external criticism of female circumcision. One challenges the intrinsic merits of external criticism, insisting that the moral status of the practice can only be evaluated in terms of the values and understandings of the culture in which it is practised. The other challenges the effectiveness of such criticism or seeks to interrogate its meaning and purpose in a particular context.

I have some sympathy for the second sort of objection. In its simplest form, this amounts to the argument that external criticism is counter-productive, causing people to be defensive and to continue the practice longer than they would if left to their own internal debates and deliberations. Note that this argument presupposes the illegitimacy of the practice and merely claims that one set of tactics is better than another in arriving at the agreed-upon goal of eliminating it. This kind of argument is valid in some cases and not in others, and I don't know how well it works in this case.

A more complex, and, to my mind, more compelling form of the objection draws attention to the symbolic role played by female circumcision in many contemporary discussions of immigration.[17] Such discussions often focus on the 'problems' raised by the 'alien' values of Islamic immigrants especially with respect to the issue of gender equality. In this context, the issue of female circumcision is frequently used to illustrate and define the nature of the presumed conflict of values. The effect is implicitly to create an identification of the West with civilization and Islam with barbarism, and to define immigrants from Islamic countries as threats because they are bearers of this barbaric culture. These identifications are possible because nothing is said about the considerable internal opposition to the practice of female circumcision within Islamic countries on cultural and religious grounds, about the ways in which immigrants may not fully embrace the dominant cultural traditions of the countries they have chosen to leave, or, for that matter, about the failures and inadequacies of Western liberal democratic states with respect to gender equality.[18]

This objection rightly alerts us to the fact that moral discussions of particular issues may have symbolic and political functions that deserve critical scrutiny. Thinking about the issue of female circumcision reminded me that when I was educated in primary and

---

[17] I owe the argument in this paragraph to Dilek Çinar.
[18] One criticism of female circumcision frequently advanced within Islamic countries is that it is a pre-Islamic tradition and thus without any foundation in Islam.

secondary school, the only thing I ever learnt about India concerned suttee, the Hindu practice in which widows were burnt alive
on their husbands' funeral pyres and which was outlawed by
British colonial authorities. It is no defence of suttee to suggest that
there are other, perhaps more important things one could learn
about Indian civilization and that the focus on this practice was
not an accident.

Yet one can grant the force of the objection to the symbolic mis-
use of female circumcision without accepting the view that the only
legitimate moral critique of female circumcision is one based on the
local understandings of the community in which it is practiced.
Female circumcision is clearly a practice loaded with cultural significance, intimately connected to the meaning of sexuality and
gender in particular communities. Nevertheless, I consider the
practice to be unjust, because it causes permanent physical harm
to young girls. In the face of this fact, its local meaning and the
degree to which that meaning is accepted by people subject to the
practice seem to me irrelevant.

Because it involves painful, permanent, and debilitating physical
mutilation of children, female circumcision is a hard case to defend
on grounds of local understanding. What about gender-related
practices in which such physical harm is not involved? Here the
answer is less obvious. One way to test how much of one's theory
of justice falls within the outermost circle and how much within the
innermost would be to ask the following question. Are there any
gender-related norms or practices that you would regard as just (at
least in the sense of being morally permissible) on the grounds that
they are accepted by the people of a particular society as integral
to their culture and way of life, even though you would regard such
practices as unjust in your own society on the grounds that they
are incompatible with a commitment to equal citizenship?

In formulating the question in this way, I do not mean to imply
that contemporary liberal democratic states have achieved gender
equality. On the contrary, I take it to be obvious that the opposite
is the case with respect to physical security, economic opportunity,
political power, and virtually every other important life-chance.
But I do assume that gender equality (the meaning of which is, of
course, contested) provides a critical standard of justice for evaluating public institutions and practices in Canada, the USA, and
every other liberal democratic state. The question is whether it

provides the same kind of critical standard for evaluating public institutions and policies in other societies.

I hope that Walzer will address this question in his response to the essays in this volume, and that readers will think about it for themselves. I confess myself to be uncertain about how to respond. On the one hand, I feel the power of Walzer's argument about the importance of cultural particularity. On the other hand, I cannot think of any actual example of a gender-differentiated practice that I would be willing to defend as just in another society but not in my own. I could probably construct an imaginary example, but it seems to me to be crucial to appeal only to actual, not hypothetical cases, and to ones drawn from contemporary societies so as to avoid the problems of anachronism that emerge with historical cases. I am not ruling out the use of hypotheticals in moral inquiry. Rather the point is that if you cannot think of (m)any actual examples of gender-differentiated practices that are just in other societies but would be unjust in your own, then your understanding of justice has a powerful universalistic cast in practice, whatever its formal room for particularity.

These questions emerge not only as theoretical puzzles about how to think about justice but also as concrete problems requiring action. For example, several Third World countries led by China have pressed for revision of various international human rights codes, especially with respect to gender, on the grounds that they reflect a specifically Western liberal view of the proper role of women in society. How should we respond to these demands? Moreover, despite the problematic aspects of the use of the issue of female circumcision in debates about immigration, immigrants to Europe and North America do arrive with a variety of cultural commitments different from those of most of the existing population, some of them related to gender, and some of those emerging as public political issues. In what ways should those already present respect and in what ways should they challenge these pre-existing cultural commitments? If we think of an inquiry into justice as a matter of evaluating conflicting interpretations of shared understandings, what do we say when disagreements about what justice requires come from deep differences in cultural traditions?[19]

---

[19] Of course, these deep cultural differences may come not from immigrants but from long-established groups in the population. As Will Kymlicka has argued, Walzer's prescriptions seem to privilege the dominant group in such circumstances,

The kinds of questions I have asked about gender can be extended to the idea of democracy. Again, I pose these in the first instance as questions for Michael Walzer to address, but also as questions for the reader to use in clarifying the character of his or her own understanding of justice. In general form, the question about democracy is this: to what extent is the normative force of the democratic ideal contingent upon the shared understanding of particular communities other than our own?

This question has two dimensions. First, is not the idea that we should respect the shared understandings of other communities itself a democratic argument, a kind of modified consent theory with shared understandings substituting for other forms of consent as the basis of legitimacy? But we get *that* argument from *our own* traditions and understandings, not from the particularistic cultures of other societies. Some of them may share this commitment to democracy and some may not. So then the fundamental question is not really what do *they* think is right, but rather what do *we* think is right or what *should* we think is right? *Our* conception of justice includes respect for cultural difference as one of its components, but one that is balanced against concern for human rights and gender equality among other things.

Second, is there any actual state today in which the absence of democratic institutions—to put it more starkly, let me say liberal democratic institutions—should not be regarded as deeply problematic from a moral perspective? In less convoluted form, is there any actual state that is undemocratic but not unjust because of the absence of democracy? If the answer is 'no'—for whatever reason—that would suggest that the idea that justice is determined by the shared understandings of particular communities is far less radically relativistic and justice far less culturally specific than many readers of *Spheres* would have supposed. Indeed, the distinction between the first and second concentric circles collapses. If the answer is 'yes', then the challenge is 'name it' and say why it is not unjust.

As in the discussion of gender, I want to make a plea here for actual examples. The undemocratic but just state has to be a real

in ways that hardly do justice to the notion of shared understandings (see *Liberalism*, ch. 11). On the other hand, I think that Kymlicka's conception of a cultural community is excessively rigid and underestimates the extent to which people from different cultures may create a common political culture.

state, not an imaginary one, and a contemporary state, not a historical one. It is one of the great virtues of Walzer's approach to theory that he starts with real moral arguments and real political cases. He rightly criticizes some philosophers for relying too heavily upon implausible hypotheticals to support their intuitions. So it is striking that, while the general principle of *Spheres*—particularly the arguments about shared understandings—*seem* to open the prospect of a just state with social arrangements radically at odds with contemporary liberalism, the only actual example of such a radical yet just departure that he gives is an idealized picture of an Indian village based on the caste system. It is not a state. India is a state, but such a description could not plausibly apply to the entire state of India. It is not even an actual village, with all the complexities and messiness that actual village cultures contain. If there are no real cases to support these principles, perhaps the principles themselves are less sturdy than they appear.

Let me conclude with a caution. I don't want to overstate the universalism of the last few pages. I think there are indeed many important areas of local justice, many situations in which we should simply respect the shared understandings of other communities even when they differ from our own. But there are many other situations where we do not and should not respect these shared understandings. How we sort these cases out, and on what basis and whether our sorting makes sense, are all important questions. Answering them requires just the sort of comparative and interpretative inquiry that Walzer invites. But that is not what Walzer himself says. In granting such strong priority to the shared understandings of particular communities, he stops a bit short of the more fully satisfying sort of political theory that his own work has enabled us to see.

3

Spherical Justice and Global Injustice

BRIAN BARRY

———————

Thanks to David Miller's excellent Introduction, there is no need for me to engage in an exposition of the leading ideas in *Spheres of Justice*.[1] The existence of this book is itself an indication of the lasting importance of the contribution made by *Spheres* to debates among political philosophers about justice. Let me therefore get down to business.

SOCIAL MEANINGS AND CRITERIA OF JUSTICE

The most distinctive and challenging claim to be found in *Spheres* is that the demands of justice in a given society can be ascertained by interpreting to members of that society their shared under-standings of the meanings of the goods they distribute among themselves. Once the meaning of a good has been established, the appropriate criteria of distribution follow directly. Now, I think that it is possible to find a pure case of this, where the good to be distributed is literally constituted out of the social understanding of the criteria for its distribution. Consider a prize of no intrinsic value, to be awarded for best satisfying certain criteria. (At the extreme there may be no physical object at all, not even a rosette or a piece of paper, and no official awarding ceremony, but simply the recognition of the spectators and the other competitors that so-and-so has won.) Here it does seem plausible to say that it is just (not merely is believed by the participants to be just but really is just) for the person who best satisfies the criteria to get the prize. The value of the prize simply lies in its meaning: that it is supposed

This chapter adapts some material which first appeared in 'Intimations of Justice', *Columbia Law Review*, 84 (1984), 806–15.

[1] (New York: Basic Books, 1983).

to go to the person who best satisfies the criteria. To say that the prize should be given for something else instead has an air of absurdity about it, since *that* prize would not exist any longer if the criteria for its award were different.

Georg Simmel's discussion of honorary prizes in *The Philosophy of Money* illustrates what has just been said, but the continuation of his discussion points to the limitations of the pure case.

The honour that does not subordinate its representative to others but brings him into prominence also requires a certain narrowness and solidarity of the group; the name of the victor at the Olympics resounded through the whole of that part of Greece that was closely knit together by this interest. The money prize has an egotistic quality which suggests itself to members of a large group. The unegotistic character which corresponds to the solidarity of the small group is most beautifully symbolized by the custom that the golden wreath presented by the Athenian Council of the Five Hundred for good administration was set aside in the temple. Within smaller and closed interest groups, as for instance for sport affairs or for industrial experts, the honorary prize is fully justified even today. But in so far as the restriction and homogeneity of the group is replaced by openness and heterogeneity, the honorary prize, which reflects the co-operation of the whole group, has to be replaced by the money prize, which reflects the ultimate recognition of the performance. The enlargement of the social group requires the transition to expressing merit in money terms because it means the inescapable atomization of such a group. Since it is impossible to provoke the same sentiment in the same manner in a large group as in a small one, distinction within a large group requires a means by which the recipient is no longer dependent upon the agreement and co-operation of the whole group.[2]

Whereas the value of a rosette or a certificate is constituted by the criteria on the basis of which it is awarded, the value of a monetary prize is constituted both by that and by the money. There would be no advantage in my appropriating your 'Best of Breed' rosette unless I could persuade people that my dog had won it. But it would be well worth my while to purloin your Nobel Prize cheque, even if I left you the plaque that came with it. Given the interest of the police in the matter, the attraction of the money to me indeed depends on the possibility of divorcing the value of the monetary aspect of the prize from its provenance. As Simmel

[2] Georg Simmel, *The Philosophy of Money*, tr. Tom Bottomore and David Frisby (London: Routledge & Kegan Paul, 1978), 348.

emphasized in *The Philosophy of Money*, the essential feature of money is its anonymity: its ability to retain the same value as it passes from hand to hand.

The point of all this for Walzer's thesis is as follows: the meaning of a prize is no longer solely constituted by the criteria for its award in an era when the most prestigious prizes tend to consist of 'large cheques in small envelopes'. *Qua* public honour, the meaning of the prize is constituted by its criteria, but *qua* cold cash, the meaning of the prize is simply the meaning of money, which is simply the social recognition of it as a valid claim on goods and services. Money is, indeed, constituted by a social convention, but it is not a social convention that automatically carries with it any particular understanding of the criteria on the basis of which it should be distributed.

The notion that the meaning of money does not entail any distributional criteria might perhaps be challenged. In an earlier essay, 'In Defence of Equality', which anticipated *Spheres*, Walzer said that he was 'tempted by "equality of results" in the sphere of money'.[3] And he tried out an argument with egalitarian implications, namely that, if people had equal incomes, a luxury item such as a sailboat would 'be bought by the person who is willing to forgo other goods and services, that is, by the person who really wants it'.[4] Although he did not make an explicit connection with the intrinsic meaning of money (that idea was not yet present), this might be done by saying that the meaning of money is that it is a way of satisfying wants, and the best way of ensuring that it satisfies the most intense wants is to distribute it equally. If this worked, it would be a neat way of getting from the meaning of money to a utilitarian criterion for its distribution and then (via diminishing marginal utility) to an egalitarian one. But it is fairly clear that the argument does not hold up without the insertion of a substantial premiss to the effect that commodities ought to go to those who will enjoy them the most. Otherwise somebody could accept the conventional meaning of money, as a claim on goods and services, while maintaining that nothing follows from this about the criteria for its distribution. In the chapter of *Spheres* devoted to 'Money and Commodities', we hear no more of the idea, so Walzer has presumably concluded that it will not hold water. We are therefore

---

[3] Michael Walzer, *Radical Principles* (New York: Basic Books, 1980), 250.
[4] Ibid. 251.

back at the conclusion that the meaning of money carries no implications for its just distribution.

This opens up a way of testing the claim that Walzer wishes to hold, and thinks he is holding, the strong conventionalist view that the criteria for distribution and the meaning of a good are indissolubly linked. If the meaning of money does not entail any particular criteria of distribution, Walzer will conclude that justice is consistent with any distribution of money, and this we do in fact find. The only reason, from the point of view of justice, for concern about the distribution of money is that money constantly threatens to escape from its own proper sphere and influence other distributions, such as that of political power, which should have their own independent criteria of distribution. But no distribution of money is unjust in itself, according to Walzer.

Once we have blocked every wrongful exchange and controlled the sheer weight of money itself, we have no reason to worry about the answers the market provides. . . . Given the right blocks, there is no such thing as a maldistribution of consumer goods. It just doesn't matter, from the standpoint of complex equality, that you have a yacht and I don't, or that the sound system of her hi-fi set is greatly superior to his, or that we buy our rugs from Sears Roebuck and they get theirs from the Orient. People will focus on such matters, or not: that is a question of culture, not of distributive justice. So long as yachts and hi-fi sets and rugs have only use value and individualized symbolic value, their unequal distribution doesn't matter. (*Spheres*, 107–8)

There is, it seems to me, something quite bizarre in claiming that the distribution of money is not a matter of distributive justice and that an unequal distribution does not matter. It is perfectly clear that it matters to most people, and rightly so. Walzer's examples of things that do not matter are such things as yachts, Oriental rugs, and top-quality hi-fi equipment. As the possessor of two out of the three, I would not wish to write off the significance of even these. But confining the discussion to luxuries is tendentious. For there is nothing in a market distribution that guarantees everybody even bare necessities. Blocking all the exchanges that Walzer thinks should be blocked would still be quite consistent with leaving a segment of the population lacking the resources to purchase food, shelter, or clothing. (The only 'commodification' that he explicitly resists, as we shall see, is of medical care.)

It is an obvious embarrassment for Walzer's analysis that people do actually argue about the distribution of money (both wealth and income) and that they argue in terms of social justice. Walzer and Hayek make strange bedfellows in denying that this kind of talk makes any sense. They are both wrong. Leaving entirely on one side the issue of money escaping from its 'sphere', and simply treating its 'meaning' as that of enabling its possessor to buy consumer goods, there is a legitimate question about the moral defensibility of the enormous inequality in purchasing power thrown up by market allocations. It is, moreover, economically illiterate to treat 'the market' as if it were itself an unproblematic and uniquely specified institution. How any given market system works depends on the details of the legislative framework in which it is embedded, including consumer protection law, environmental law, workers' health and safety law, and trade union law, to mention only some leading examples. And these are characteristically argued about, be it noted, in terms of fairness between the parties.

Walzer believes that, because the 'meaning' of money does not determine a distribution, the distribution of money is not a matter of justice. In the case of other goods, he does appear to wish to claim that the 'meaning' of the good determines its right distribution. I believe that this claim fails and that in each case he has in the end to build the criteria of distribution into the meaning in order to make the theory work. But the circularity is less blatant than that way of describing it makes it sound because the notion that the meaning of the good affects the criteria is also doing some independent work. Making a distinction that Walzer needs to make and does not, we may say that to talk about what justice requires we have to know the social meanings of the goods to be distributed, but that knowing the social meanings of the goods does not uniquely determine what is a just distribution of them. Walzer is adept at showing how the social meaning of such things as work, leisure, health, education, and religious salvation varies from one society to another. And he is unquestionably correct in thinking that it would be absurd to talk about justice in a society without having this kind of information about the significance to the people concerned of different goods that they distribute among themselves. But the trouble is that this is not enough for his purposes. What Walzer needs to be able to show is that, once he has established the meaning, the just distribution will fall out of it. But this cannot be done. Let me give some illustrations.

In his chapter on 'Security and Welfare', Walzer argues forcefully and effectively that what counts as a 'need' is, to a great extent, a matter of social determination. For ancient Greeks and Romans an accessible public bath was a high priority need, but this would not figure on a contemporary list of basic needs. For us, medical care is a need, but this has by no means always been so. One reason for this, which Walzer does not mention, is that it is only since the 1940s that it has been clearly advantageous on balance to undergo state-of-the-art medical treatment. That the emphasis in the hundred years before that was on public-health measures—sanitation and immunization—was a reasonable response to what actually worked.

So far so good. Walzer now argues that, because of the status of health care in contemporary societies (including the USA), it should be taken out of the market and be communally provided on a basis of medical need alone. I think so too, as it happens, but I cannot see that he can get there by saying that 'needed goods are not commodities' (*Spheres*, 90). After all, food, clothing, and shelter (including heat and utilities) are even more basic needs; yet Walzer has no argument to the effect that these things should not be sold for what the market will bear. Perhaps (though, as I have noted, he does not say so), he thinks that here needs should be taken care of by providing people who could not otherwise afford a decent minimum with a standard sum of money, and leaving them to spend it as they wish. But then medical insurance could be assimilated to the same analysis and regarded as another needed commodity. Good arguments can be made against this model, pointing to ways in which medical care is special—in particular the difficulty, in any fee-for-service scheme, of controlling the providers. But this is a long way from deducing the supersession of the market from the social recognition of health care as a need.

The point can, however, be pressed further. Leaving aside the form that provision should take—whether the need should be supplied as a public service or by allocating funds or vouchers—I do not see how the social recognition of something as a need entails anything immediately about what justice requires. Surely every society has recognized that people need food in order to stay alive—it is the most basic of all needs—yet many societies have not drawn the conclusion that starvation must be prevented by public provision. It seems to me that Walzer will have to reply here that a society that does not recognize a peremptory claim to be saved from starvation does not understand food as a need. But then, of course, the way in which we find out what is regarded as a need is to see what is agreed on as a good that must be supplied to everyone who lacks it. The logical order, which appeared to be 'it is a need, so it should be supplied', actually becomes 'it should be supplied, so it is a need'.

I believe that the same line of criticism may be made of the chapters on, for example, office and education. I shall briefly discuss one of the best chapters in the book, that on 'Free Time'. Here, Walzer offers an enlightening discussion of the way in which free time has different meanings in different societies, contrasting the public holiday, devoted to religious or civic celebration, with the contemporary individualistic vacation. He is surely correct in suggesting that 'free time' would be too abstract a category to use in talking about just distribution and that we must know *what* it is that is being distributed. 'Free time has no single just or necessary structure' (*Spheres*, 196). But I do not see how Walzer gets from there to the assertion that 'the right that requires protection . . . is not to be excluded from the forms of rest central to one's own time and place' (ibid.). Surely somebody could agree that in the USA most people have vacations without being constrained to agree that everyone has, or should have, a right to one. Walzer's egalitarian assertion that what is central should be available to all takes him right outside his own self-imposed constraints.

As we have seen, the only way in which Walzer can get a definite distribution out of the meaning of most goods is to include the criteria of distribution in the meaning. So the assertion that goods have the meaning for Americans that they would need to have in order to yield his conclusions amounts to saying that Americans already in some sense accept the relevant distributive criteria. However much Walzer tries to gain room for manœuvre by looking for implications of existing practices that the members of the society may not currently recognize, it seems to me that he has left himself with a desperate case to argue. I should at this point mention an argument made by David Miller against the suggestion that Walzer's methodological commitments are inherently conservative. Miller's reply is that Walzer himself derives radical conclusions from them. But this is beside the point. The question is not what Walzer thinks but whether he is entitled to think it.

My own view is that Walzer's radical conclusions can be resisted quite easily by those who accept his methods. To succeed in saying that the logic of American institutions points towards a national health service and workers' self-management, he has to show that there is no rationale for the existing institutions that is internally coherent. This seems to me a patently absurd claim. Like it or not, it is perfectly coherent to hold that state intervention in health care should come in only where the market fails: to provide cover for the old and poor, who cannot afford insurance; and to finance fundamental medical research, which is a public good. Similarly, there is a coherent rationale for the private ownership and control of firms, based on widely diffused ideas about the rights of private ownership. Given that scarcely any Americans believe that support for political democracy entails workers' control of firms, it would be a quite extraordinary feat for Walzer to be able to show convincingly that they are so wildly wrong about the implications of their actual beliefs. This is not to say that a good case for workers' self-management cannot be made. But it is futile to make it in the way proposed by Walzer.

JUSTICE AND CONSENT

What *is* the theory of justice in *Spheres*? It is natural to suppose that it lies in two ideas. One is that of 'complex equality': the idea that justice depends upon the maintenance of the separate 'spheres', each with its own criteria of distribution. The other is the one on which I have been focusing here: that the appropriate criteria of distribution are given by the meaning attributed to each good by the members of the society. However, these ideas are in tension—the second has a potential for subverting the first. To see this, we have to observe that justice requires 'the art of separation' only in societies where this is the common view of what justice requires. If the members of some caste, race, or ethnic group manage to persuade enough other people in their society that their birth entitles them to wealth, power, education, spiritual superiority, and pleasant occupations, then that is what justice calls for in their society. Only a general theory of the kind that Walzer anathemizes can say what Walzer would obviously like to say but cannot: that justice has certain formal characteristics and that the universal validity of this proposition cannot be challenged by showing that a lot of people in some benighted society think otherwise.

It is important to see that Walzer is not embracing the position usually called moral relativism, though more accurately described as moral scepticism. Nor is he taking the position, advanced for example by Bernard Williams, that we simply cannot sensibly criticize societies whose ways of life are not live possibilities for us here and now.[5] For, although he does say that his object is to 'interpret to [his] fellow citizens the world of meanings that we share' (*Spheres*, p. xiv), he is prepared to do the same for, say, fifth-century BC Athenians, and on the basis of that interpretation to draw conclusions about what was just among them—to make moral rather than historical assertions about it. His position would best be described not as relativism at all but as conventionalism: the view that justice (what really is just, not merely what is locally called just) is determined for each society by the shared beliefs of the members of that society about the meanings of the goods that are to be distributed among them. Since these meanings are socially defined, what is just is a matter of convention.

The obvious objection to this is that 'justice' is a word in *our* vocabulary, and it is not correct, according to the way in which most speakers of English use the word, to say that the caste system is just in India—and it would not be correct to say so even if there was a consensus among Indians that it was just. Similarly, most of us are prepared to say, on the strength of what *we* believe, that it is unjust for women to be prohibited from pursuing higher education or paid employment, even if this is acceptable in their society according to the locally prevailing ideas about justice. If Walzer wants to dissent, he has to make a universalistic moral argument for the proposition that (roughly speaking) justice is what the members of each society think it is. But to do so, be it noted, he cannot appeal to what most Americans believe, since I should imagine that most Americans believe in human rights.

---

[5] Bernard Williams, 'The Truth in Relativism', *Proceedings of the Aristotelian Society*, 75 (1974–5), 215–28. Repr. in Michael Krausz and Jack W. Meiland (eds.), *Relativism Cognitive and Moral* (Notre Dame, Ind.: Univ. of Notre Dame Press, 1982), 175–85, and in Bernard Williams, *Moral Luck* (Cambridge: Cambridge Univ. Press, 1981), 132–43.

(They must, of course, if they believe in their founding document, the Declaration of Independence.)

As far as I can see, Walzer has two arguments in favour of his hyper-conventionalist position. One argument, which runs through a number of his writings, is in my view simply confused. It is an elaborate way of changing the subject by assuming that we can determine what is just and unjust by deciding what outsiders may legitimately do in the way of coercive intervention. Thus, in *Just and Unjust Wars*[6] and even more clearly in a later reply to critics,[7] Walzer defended a strong doctrine of non-interventionism. There is, of course, much of a prudential kind to be said against intervention in the affairs of other countries: it is seldom altruistically motivated; even if it is, it may well be counterproductive. Walzer wanted to go beyond that and argue that no country has a right to intervene in order to promote its own values. This is more questionable, but let us grant it for the sake of argument. We could still quite consistently with that hold that we are entitled to form views about the justice of what goes on in other countries, using our own criteria of justice rather than those of the people in the country. Thus, the desired conclusion would not follow even if we granted the premiss.

In Walzer's article 'Philosophy and Democracy',[8] he argued for the proposition that 'the people' should be able to do more or less whatever pleases them without judicial restraint. This is also, fairly evidently, a controversial view. But, again, let us grant it. Nothing follows from this about justice. We recognize with little difficulty that individual people may behave unjustly, and in other ways wrongly, without exceeding their rights. The opportunities for a collectivity to do what it has a right to do but still behave unjustly are far greater. At the time of writing that article (which preceded *Spheres* by a couple of years), Walzer seemed prepared to admit that philosophers could legitimately develop their own theories of justice, even though they should not try to get them implemented outside the ordinary political process. But his subsequent hostility to the independent role of political philosophers even in formulating theories of justice may, I surmise, rest on his bringing his views

---

[6] Michael Walzer, *Just and Unjust Wars* (New York: Basic Books, 1977).

[7] 'The Moral Standing of States: A Response to Four Critics', *Philosophy and Public Affairs*, 9 (1980), 209–29.

[8] *Political Theory*, 9 (1981), 379–99.

about internal intervention into line with those on external intervention. That is, he may now think that, if 'the people' have a right to legislate according to their shared understandings, this somehow undermines any criticism of those shared understandings on the basis of a philosophical theory of justice.

What may, perhaps, be intended as an alternative justification of conventionalism can be found in a much-cited passage in *Spheres*. This comes in answer to the question: 'By virtue of what characteristics are we one another's equals?' Walzer's answer runs as follows: 'We are (all of us) culture-producing creatures; we make and inhabit meaningful worlds. Since there is no way to rank and order these worlds with regard to their understanding of social goods, we do justice to actual men and women by respecting their particular creations. . . . To override those understandings is (always) to act unjustly (*Spheres*, 314). 'Overriding' and 'acting' suggest that Walzer is still thinking of political intervention. I think, however, that Walzer may believe he has an independent argument here for the conventionalism of justice. This is that consent creates justice. It should be recalled that, in a much earlier book, *Obligations*,[9] Walzer claimed that we should look for a theory of political obligation based not (as in most social-contract theories) on hypothetical consent but on actual consent, as manifested in various ways. If justice is taken to be constructed out of actual consent, we can see how Walzer gets to his conclusion that outside judgements are invalid.

But how valid is actual consent? We are all, Walzer tells us, culture-producing creatures. But if this is (as he suggests) the fundamental respect in which human beings are equal, the obvious retort is that some are more equal than others. Walzer resolutely refuses to investigate the micro-processes that go into the formation and sustenance of beliefs. A noticeable absentee in the list of spheres of justice is that of communications. How would communications be organized if the power of money were eliminated from newspaper publication, television-programming, and so on? And, given that it is so omnipresent, what would consent be worth even if there *were* consensus?

These are awkward questions for Walzer. Once admit that consent is invalidated by unequal access to the means of persuasion,

<hr />

[9] New York: Simon & Schuster, 1970.

or by lack of education, lack of opportunity (or indeed the suppression of opportunity) for speculation about alternatives, and ignorance about one's own and other societies, and the theory fails to have application. We might add that, even if none of those conditions existed, consent would still be suspect in a society of actual inequality. For if those who do relatively poorly do not see any early prospect of improvement, they can make themselves feel better about things by persuading themselves that their position is deserved.

So far I have not even bothered to mention the most obvious objection to Walzer's conventionalism, which is that it presupposes the existence of a consensus on criteria of distribution. If there is no consensus (and there is not in the USA, for example), the appeal to common understandings is merely a tendentious way for the theorist to advance his own ideas. (The suspicion that this is so is strengthened by noticing the wide array of positions that different theorists claim to find implicit in common beliefs—and the uncanny way in which these correspond to the positions they hold themselves.) However, the crucial point that emerges from the discussion here is that, even if we found a society in which there were something approaching a consensus, the most plausible initial hypothesis to explain the phenomenon would be that it had come about as the result of power over communications, education, and religious doctrine exerted by the beneficiaries from the *status quo*.

We are led by the logic of the argument to the idea that justice is connected not to actual consent but to hypothetical consent. Whether a society is marked by consensus or dissensus, it makes sense to ask what *would* be agreed on if the sources of distortion were removed. Now, I have no doubt that what would be agreed on by well-informed people negotiating under conditions of equality would include the idea that the criteria of distribution for different goods would be different. That idea is in itself utterly banal. It is what everybody who is not a philosopher thinks and what almost all philosophers think. The question is how the criteria are to be justified. The alternative to Walzer's appeal to 'social meanings' is, I suggest, to construct a theory of justice and then show how the criteria flow from it.

I cannot do that here but I can offer as an example of the genre Rawls's *A Theory of Justice*—a book that (judging by his comments on it at *Spheres*, 5 and elsewhere) Walzer has never comprehended.[10] Rawls agrees with Walzer that basic civil and political rights should be equally distributed, that jobs should be distributed according to the principle of equal opportunity, and that education should be distributed according to capacity to benefit from it. He also agrees that it is essential to prevent inequality of wealth from undermining political equality, and his discussion of the institutions needed to achieve this compares favourably with Walzer's.[11] Unlike Walzer, he also has a criterion for the distribution of income, the difference principle. But where he scores over Walzer most decisively is by having a theory of justice within which these criteria can be articulated and defended.

ONLY CONNECT?

I want to conclude by adverting to my title, 'Spherical Justice and Global Injustice'. It is an immediate implication of Walzer's particularism—and one he happily embraces—that there can be no such thing as international distributive justice. For there is manifestly no international community in Walzer's sense of a set of people with shared understandings of the meaning of social goods. I wish to suggest that we should regard as self-refuting any theory of justice entailing that there is nothing unjust about a world in which poor countries are making net transfers to rich ones and in which the USA uses up 40 per cent of total resources while a quarter of the world's population goes without the most basic necessities. If Walzer wants to know who says that this violates the demands of justice, my reply is: *I* say so, and I believe that I can give reasons of an appropriately general kind for saying so.[12]

Walzer might respond that setting out my views about what justice demands, even if they are backed up by what seem to me good reason, has a very small chance of bringing about the kind of

[10] I have spelt out my objections to Walzer's treatment of Rawls elsewhere and shall not repeat them here. See my 'Social Criticism and Political Philosophy', *Philosophy and Public Affairs*, 19 (1990), 360–73; repr. (with some new material) in my *Liberty and Justice* (Oxford: Clarendon Press, 1991), 9–22. This discusses two later books by Walzer, but the seeds of his persistent misinterpretation of Rawls lie in *Spheres*.

[11] John Rawls, *A Theory of Justice* (Oxford: Clarendon Press, 1971), esp. 226–7.

[12] The theory that I would wish to defend is developed in *Theories of Justice* (Hemel Hempstead: Harvester-Wheatsheaf/Berkeley, Calif.: Univ. of Calif. Press, 1989), and *Justice as Impartiality* (Oxford: Clarendon Press, 1995).

global transformation that I believe is required. I of course concede this: how could I deny it? I think the most likely future for most of the world is a continuation of current trends towards overpopulation, degradation of the environment, and the breakdown of civil order. Since justice has never been prominent in the relations between states in the past, or in the internal arrangements of the great majority of states for that matter, why should we expect it suddenly to begin to do so now?

I could make the *ad hominem* observation that Walzer has had no more success in shifting the USA towards the kind of social democracy with workers' control that he alleges is implicit in the beliefs of his fellow citizens. A more serious response is that the search for influence is at best distracting and at worst corrupting. Political philosophers should say what they think is right, whether what they have to say is popular or unpopular. Perhaps they will with luck eventually extend the boundaries of what is politically thinkable. But even this is not likely to be achieved if we start by flattering our audience and telling them that if enough of them believe the same thing it makes no sense to say they are all wrong.

4

The Empirical Study of Justice

JON ELSTER

Studies of justice fall into three main categories: descriptive, explanatory, and normative. The descriptive study of justice aims to identify the perceptions of justice held—or acted upon—by social actors. The explanatory approach tries to identify independent variables that can account for the findings of such descriptive studies. The normative study of justice aims at identifying valid and defensible conceptions of justice. Michael Walzer's *Spheres of Justice*[1] certainly includes the first and the last of these perspectives. Throughout the book, Walzer seeks to identify and describe the 'common understandings' of the citizen with respect to the allocation of goods in a number of different realms or 'spheres'. Moreover, on various occasions he offers normative criticism or recommendations with respect to specific allocative practices. As far as I can see, he does not offer a causal explanation of the common understandings (i.e. perceptions of justice). The gap in his account is demonstrated in Fig. 1.

In Fig. 1, thin arrows stand for relations of justification (or criticism) and the thick arrow for a causal relationship. In his discussion of the American welfare system, Walzer writes that 'the established pattern of provision doesn't measure up to the internal requirements of the sphere of security and welfare, and the common understandings of the citizens point toward a more elaborate pattern' (*Spheres*, 85). This illustrates how common understandings and sphere-specific logic can be brought to bear on the assessment of specific practices. When discussing the policy of veteran's preference in civil-service employment, he first writes that the

I am grateful to David Miller for his patient and constructive help with this article. It is organized as a running dialogue with Michael Walzer, although conducted within a more general framework.

[1] (New York: Basic Books, 1983).

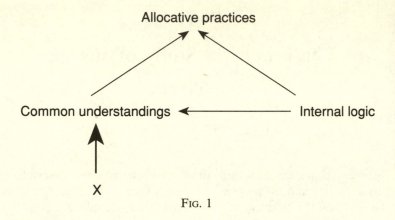

Fɪɢ. 1

principle 'seems to have been widely accepted' but also that 'surely offices are the wrong currency with which to pay such debts' (*Spheres*, 154 n.) If I understand him correctly, he is asserting here that the common understanding of the citizens violates the internal logic of the sphere of office.[2] Although Walzer does not offer a causal explanation of the common understanding, I assume he would agree that the search for an unknown X would be a legitimate enterprise in such cases. By contrast, he might not accept it as relevant or interesting in cases where the internal logic and the common understanding coincide.

In the main part of this chapter I look more closely at the three approaches to distributive justice (descriptive, explanatory, normative) and the relations among them. In doing so, I shall also be in a position to compare Walzer's analysis and my own on a number of specific issues. The most difficult is the relevance of empirical findings for normative analysis. For Walzer, 'Every substantive account of distributive justice is a local account'. To criticize the caste system, for instance, one would need (*a*) to locate (possibly repressed) feelings of anger and indignation among low-caste members, and (*b*) to explain those emotions in terms of village perceptions of justice (*Spheres*, 314). If low-caste villagers harbour no feelings of resentment, even at the repressed, unconscious level, the

---

[2] He might also claim that the example illustrates how one part of our common understandings (how to reward veterans) contradicts another part (how to allocate offices). But in that case it is hard to see why it is the former rather than the latter that has to be adjusted.

discriminatory practices to which they are subjected are unobjectionable. To me, this is close to a *reductio ad absurdum* of Walzer's view. But even if I do not accept this particular claim about the relevance of empirical facts for normative conceptions of justice, other claims might be more plausible. When I set out a few years ago to study 'local justice'—how institutions allocate scarce goods and necessary burdens—I did so partly in the hope that the empirical findings might eventually throw some light on the basic normative issues. For reasons explained below, that hope was largely frustrated. The question remains open.

DESCRIPTIVE STUDIES

Generally speaking, descriptive studies can be directed either at behaviour or at attitudes, and take place either in real-life contexts or in artificial settings such as surveys or experiments (see Table 1). I shall briefly discuss and illustrate the various categories.

TABLE 1. *Descriptive studies of justice*

	Attitudes	Behaviour
Real-life settings	(A) Content analysis	(D) Local justice; fairness in wage determination, taxation, etc.
Artificial settings	(B) Surveys; experiments	(C) Experiments

The study of attitudes towards justice in real-life settings (A) is not, to my knowledge, highly developed. I do not here have in mind the attitudes that may be revealed in allocative situations, but attitudes as manifested in verbal behaviour *not elicited for this purpose*. I have tried to study the *Records of the Federal Convention* and the speeches at the Assemblée Constituante in Paris 1789–91 in this perspective.[3] It is possible to identify, for instance, how

---

[3] For some samples of this ongoing work, see my 'Constitutional Bootstrapping in Philadelphia and Paris', *Cardozo Law Review*, 14 (1993), 549–75; 'Majority Rule and Individual Rights', in S. Shute and S. Hurley (eds.), *On Human Rights* (New York: Basic Books, 1993), 175–216, 249–56; 'Strategic Uses of Argument', in K. Arrow *et al.* (eds.), *Barriers to the Negotiated Resolution of Conflict* (New York: W. W. Norton, forthcoming).

different speakers weigh consequentialist and non-consequentialist values; conditional and unconditional rights; individual rights and collective rights; and so on.

The study of normative attitudes in an artificial context (B) can be illustrated by a well-known article by Daniel Kahneman, Jack Knetsch, and Richard Thaler.[4] Using a telephone survey they were able to identify the conceptions of market fairness held by their respondents. They found, among other things, that ideas of fair allocation are governed by a reference-point effect similar to that previously identified in choice situations. Another instance of this approach is an equally well-known article by Menachem Yaari and Maya Bar-Hillel,[5] who showed that their subjects tended to approve the utilitarian criterion for some goods and the maximin criterion for others. The work by Norman Frolich and Joe Oppenheimer comparing Rawls's 'difference principle' with other distributive schemes also falls into this category.[6]

The experimental-behavioural study of justice (C) can be illustrated by the 'ultimatum bargaining' experiments conducted by Werner Güth and others.[7] Two subjects are asked to divide (say) $10 according to the following procedure. One subject proposes a division of the sum between himself and the other. If the other accepts the proposal, it is implemented. If the other turns the offer down, neither gets anything. The salient findings in these experiments were that (*a*) the person who makes the offer usually leaves a substantial share for the other, and (*b*) if the other is not given a substantial share, he is likely to reject the proposal.

The real-life behavioural study of distributive justice (D) can be directed to the processes of wage formation and income transfers.[8] It can also be directed to the allocation by institutions of goods other than money. This kind of analysis, pioneered by Guido Calebresi's and Philip Bobbit's *Tragic Choices*,[9] is at the core of

---

[4] 'Fairness as a Constraint on Profit-Seeking', *American Economic Review*, 76 (1986), 728–41.

[5] 'On Dividing Justly', *Social Choice and Welfare*, 1 (1984), 1–14.

[6] *Choosing Justice* (Berkeley, Calif.: Univ. of Calif. Press, 1992).

[7] W. Güth, R. Schmittberger, and B. Schwarze, 'An Experimental Analysis of Ultimatum Bargaining', *Journal of Economic Behavior and Organization*, 3 (1982), 367–88.

[8] See e.g. ch. 6 of my *The Cement of Society* (Cambridge: Cambridge Univ. Press, 1989) for a discussion of conceptions of justice as a determinant of wages.

[9] (New York: W. W. Norton, 1978).

Spheres and, more recently, of my *Local Justice*.[10] Examples that figure prominently in these books include the allocation of dialysis and kidneys for transplantation to patients with end-stage renal disease, induction into the army, the hiring and firing of workers, admission to selective institutions of higher education, the allocation of rights to procreate, and immigration policies. These decentralized systems of allocations, unlike wages and taxes, are not part of a global system of distribution, redistribution, and compensation. Rather, they are overwhelmingly local in the sense that they are made independently of allocative decisions in other spheres or arenas. (An exception is the practice, noted by Walzer, of preferential treatment of veterans for federal jobs or college admission.) They are subject to a bewildering variety of distributive criteria and mechanisms, including lotteries, queuing, need, effort, merit, efficiency, or some combination of these.

These approaches can obviously be combined in various ways. For many years, the dominant paradigm in the experimental study of justice was equity theory, organized around the hypothesis that rewards should be proportional to contribution.[11] To test this hypothesis, behavioural as well as attitudinal techniques have been used. In studies of lay-offs, comparisons have been made between actual practice and the results of opinion surveys regarding the fairness of various lay-off procedures. To determine which soldiers should be demobilized first from the American army after the Second World War, the military authorities first conducted a survey to determine which principles were perceived as being more just, and then used the findings to construct the actual procedure.[12]

EXPLANATORY STUDIES

In causally oriented approaches to justice, the explanadum may be either the attitudes and behaviour of an individual, or the allocative behaviour of an institution. The second case typically includes the first. If we take seriously the principle of

[10] (New York: The Russell Sage Foundation, 1992).
[11] For a survey, see D. M. Messick and K. S. Cook (eds.), *Equity Theory* (New York: Praeger, 1983).
[12] S. Stouffer *et al.*, *The American Soldier* (Princeton, NJ: Princeton Univ. Press, 1949), ii, ch. 11.

methodological individualism, as I do, it is nonsense to claim that an institution 'does' this or that. What we observe is that individuals in the institution and in its environment, each of whom may have a specific conception of justice, interact to bring about a particular allocative scheme. In this case there is a need for a two-step explanation, in which the first stage focuses on preference formation and the second on preference aggregation. Consider first the explanation of individual attitudes and individual behaviour. I shall distinguish among six approaches that have been put forward.

A first line of argument is that individuals have different conceptions of justice depending on the *context* in which they are to be applied. Thus Morton Deutsch claims that distributive relations among friends are governed by the principle of equality, relations in the family by the principle of need, and professional relations by the principle of equity (to each according to his contribution).[13]

A second argument explains the preferred conception of justice in terms of the *good* to be allocated (or the reasons for valuing it). Thus Yaari and Bar-Hillel found that the preferred allocation of a set of grapefruits and avocados depended on whether their value was seen mainly to lie in their taste or in their vitamin content. In the former case, a utilitarian allocation was preferred, whereas in the latter an egalitarian solution was found to dominate. A more ambitious version of this approach is advanced in *Spheres*. Walzer claims that different spheres, defined by the goods to be allocated, are regulated by different conceptions of justice. However, the connection between the sphere and the principle is conceptual rather than causal. It follows from the nature of medical care, for instance, that its allocation 'should be proportional to illness and not to wealth' (*Spheres*, 86). Similarly, 'Special education is necessarily a monopoly of the talented' (*Spheres*, 211). In my opinion, Walzer has neither identified our 'common understandings' nor an alleged 'inner logic'. Rather, many of the principles he discusses are those typically held by professional dispensers of these scarce goods, but not necessarily held by the population at large. (See the next paragraph.)

A third line of argument is to relate the preferred conceptions of justice to *properties of the individual* rather than to the context or

---

[13] 'Equity, Equality and Need', *Journal of Social Issues*, 31 (1975), 137–49.

to the good. Thus it has been claimed that age, gender, and nationality are determinants of subjective justice. Following Jean Piaget, Lawrence Kohlberg claimed to be able to identify well-defined stages in moral thinking in the development of the child.[14] Another well-known example is Carol Gilligan's claim that men and women have different conceptions of justice, with men being more oriented towards abstract considerations of consistency and universalizability and women more towards care and the alleviation of suffering.[15] A different line of argument is that alluded to in the previous paragraph, viz. that intuitions about justice may depend on one's professional status. Doctors want to give priority to critically ill patients, whereas hospital administrators want to allocate scarce medical resources to patients whose probability of survival would be most increased.[16]

A fourth approach is to explain the answers to queries about justice by an appeal to the *phrasing of the question*. From studies of psychological 'framing', it is well-known that the same person, in the same context, can react differently to a half-full glass and a half-empty one.[17] For instance, people who will not use a credit card if there is a credit-card surcharge, will be less reluctant to do so if there is instead a cash discount—even though the two are substantially equivalent. The study by Kahneman, Knetsch, and Thaler cited in n. 4 applied this reasoning to issues of fairness. They found, for instance, that the respondents perceived a wage cut as being more fair if it takes the form of a reduction of an annual bonus than if it is an outright reduction of the basic wage. Yaari and Bar-Hillel also found that different conceptions of justice could be elicited by describing the same allocative issue in superficially different terms.[18] These findings question the robustness and relevance of 'common understandings'. I believe, for instance, that it is part of our common understanding that direct wage subsidies to workers in ailing industries is wrong, but that cheap energy for the purpose of maintaining employment is not, and yet the two phenomena are essentially equivalent.

[14] L. Kohlberg, *The Philosophy of Moral Development* (San Francisco: Harper & Row, 1981).

[15] *In a Different Voice* (Cambridge, Mass.: Harvard Univ. Press, 1982).

[16] Elster, *Local Justice*, 91 ff.

[17] The seminal work is A. Tversky and D. Kahneman, 'The Framing of Decisions and the Psychology of Choice', *Science*, 211 (1981), 453–8.

[18] 'On Dividing Justly', 8.

A fifth and radically different approach is to explain the preferred conceptions of justice in terms of *self-interest*.[19] In the crudest version of this line of argument it is claimed that individuals subscribe to the norms of distributive justice that coincide maximally with their self-interest.[20] Thus when industry-level trade unions within a central labour union negotiate over the wage demands to present to the central association of employers, workers in low-wage industries appeal to a norm of equality whereas those in high-wage industries appeal to a norm of equity (wages should be proportional to contribution).[21] A more sophisticated version takes account of the fact that it may not be in the self-interest of actors to show too clearly that they are moved exclusively by their self-interest.[22] They will subscribe to norms of distributive justice that correspond optimally rather than maximally to their self-interest. Thus a member of a given minority group may argue on behalf of all minority groups, or on behalf of disadvantaged groups more generally.[23] The reluctance to be seen as moved by self-interest may even induce actors to subscribe to the norms that are least favourable to themselves.[24]

A sixth and final approach in the spirit of the preceding one, although with a different focus, suggests that 'moral sentiments' are to be explained in terms of their contribution to genetic *fitness*. After the pioneering studies of Robert Trivers,[25] this line of argument has recently been restated by Robert Frank, in *Passion within Reason*. Discussing the ultimatum bargaining experiments cited above, he argues that if recipients of offers in these games tend to reject very unequal proposals as unfair, it is because such behaviour is to their evolutionary advantage. 'Perhaps people who are concerned about fairness for its own sake are observably different from others. If so, the concern for fairness, and the willingness to act irrationally that follows from it, can yield material benefits even in one-shot bargaining encounters.'[26]

[19] I have in mind here conceptions that are genuinely held by the individuals in question, not simply conceptions which they merely profess publicly without believing in them. Self-interest often operates 'behind the back' of the individual.

[20] D. Messick and K. Sentis, 'Fairness, Preference and Fairness Biases', in Messick and Cook (eds.), *Equity Theory* (see n. 11), 61–94.

[21] See my *Cement of Society*, ch. 6.   [22] See my 'Strategic Uses of Argument'.

[23] For some examples, see ch. 4 of my *Local Justice*.

[24] References in *Cement of Society*, 126 n. 95.

[25] See notably 'The Evolution of Reciprocal Altruism', *Quarterly Review of Biology*, 46 (1971), 35–57.

[26] (New York: W. W. Norton, 1988), 169–70.

I now consider the two-stage problems involved in explaining the allocative behaviour of institutions.[27] First, we need to explain the normative preferences of the main actors that are involved. First-order actors (political authorities) care mainly about the efficient use of scarce resources.[28] In addition, their concern about re-election may generate a derived concern for the kind of fairness issues that preoccupy public opinion (see below). Second-order actors (the staff of the allocating institution) are concerned both with local efficiency and with various non-instrumental norms. To explain the idea of local efficiency, consider the allocation of scarce medical goods such as kidneys for transplantation. The concern for global efficiency that characterizes first-order actors would suggest that priority be given to patients who can resume their work so as not to be a burden on society. Local efficiency, by contrast, would dictate a preference for the patients who are least likely to reject the graft. As indicated above, however, this concern may conflict with such non-instrumental concerns as the 'norm of compassion', according to which the kidney should go to the most critically ill patients. Third-order actors (potential recipients of the scarce good) tend to form allocative conceptions under the influence of their self-interest, as explained above. Thus in the selection of workers for lay-offs, the more senior workers tend to argue for lay-offs in the order of inverse seniority as the most fair procedure. Finally, public opinion is concerned with a subclass of fairness issues. Scandals can arise when manifestly needy individuals fail to get a scarce good, or when people get the good by manipulating the criteria (e.g. avoid military service by entering college).

The second stage in this process is the aggregation of these normative preferences into a final scheme. Two central mechanisms are bargaining and coalition formation. A pure form of bargaining is observed when workers and employers negotiate over lay-off procedures, with the former advocating seniority and the latter ability as the main criterion for retention. Typically, the outcome is a compromise in which seniority is used to break ties among workers of equal ability or to select among workers who pass a minimal ability requirement. Sometimes, the bargaining results in the adoption of a point system, in which the point-generating

---

[27] The following draws heavily on ch. 5 of my *Local Justice*.
[28] The distinction between first-order and second-order actors is due to G. Calabresi and P. Bobbit, *Tragic Choices* (New York: W. W. Norton, 1978).

criteria reflect the demands of the different parties and the weights reflect their bargaining power. Thus in the American scheme for kidney allocation, points are given both for the number of antigens that are shared between the donor and the recipients and for time on the waiting list for transplantation. The former is a criterion of local efficiency, whereas the latter embodies a concern for fairness which ensures that patients with unusual antigen patterns, such as blacks and other minority group members, have some chance of getting a transplant. There is some indication that the weights accorded to these criteria reflect the bargaining strength of the different groups of doctors that are involved. I suspect that bargaining also was behind the unique system of admission to medical school in the Netherlands, where applicants are selected on the basis of a weighted lottery, with the high-school grades being used as weights. The fact that applicants with better grades have higher chances of being admitted satisfies the advocates of meritocracy, whereas the fact that everybody (above a certain minimal level) has some chance of admission satisfies the believers in equality.

Coalitions can arise because of the general fact that procedures are overdetermined by principles. Different actors, who subscribe to different principles of justice, may nevertheless agree on the procedure to adopt in specific cases. Need–efficiency coalitions can arise when the worst off individuals are also those who can benefit most from the scarce good. Because of the decreasing marginal utility of consumption goods, this coalition will form, for instance, in the allocation of food in disaster situations. (However, as indicated above, need and efficiency may point in different directions with regard to the allocation of scarce medical resources.) Efficiency–desert coalitions can arise because of the good incentive properties of many desert systems. When workers argue that the more senior workers deserve to retain their jobs, employers sometimes concur on the grounds that seniority tends to stabilize the workforce by creating a disincentive to leave the firm. Use of time on the waiting list as a criterion for allocating kidneys may be supported by a coalition of (a) advocates of affirmative action in favour of blacks, (b) those who want to compensate patients with bad medical luck, and (c) those who believe in the inherent fairness of queuing.

NORMATIVE STUDIES

The idea that normative, philosophical conceptions of justice need empirical foundations is controversial. One approach to the issue is to distinguish between 'hard' and 'soft' theories of justice. Hard theories start from first principles and accept all their implications, however counterintuitive. Suppose one could show that total welfare in society would be maximized by killing randomly selected individuals and using their organs for transplantations that could save the lives of many more others.[29] A hard-nosed utilitarian would then have to recommend this practice. More soft-minded theorists would see this implication as a *reductio ad absurdum* against utilitarianism. For them, theories are constrained by intuitions about what it would be fair or just to do in particular cases. Utilitarians have an answer, of course, to the charge that their theories have unacceptable consequences. Typically, they deny that situations in which total utility would be maximized by torturing infants or killing people randomly would ever arise.[30] Although such replies may be plausible in any given case, the strongly felt need to come up with a reply itself indicates that the utilitarians may have a guilty, non-utilitarian conscience they are trying to pacify. Elizabeth Anderson has argued convincingly that the resort of utilitarians to *occult numbers*—confident appeals to remote effects of various sorts, without actually carrying out the calculations—betrays that they are really moved by non-consequentialist concerns.[31]

Similarly, Walzer's appeal to the 'repressed' indignation of low-caste Indians looks like an occult quantity, introduced to insulate the theory against counterintuitive implications. His discussion of the caste system betrays a (fully comprehensible) uneasiness with the idea that the extreme subjection and abject misery of low-caste villagers might be part of a society that is just as any other. 'Assume now', he writes,

that the Indian villagers really do accept the doctrines that support the caste system. A visitor to the village might still try to convince them—it is

---

[29] J. Harris, 'The Survival Lottery', *Philosophy*, 50 (1975), 81–7.
[30] This for instance is the response by Peter Singer ('Utility and the Survival Lottery', *Philosophy*, 52 (1977), 218–22) to the article cited in n. 29.
[31] *Value in Ethics and Economics* (Cambridge, Mass.: Harvard Univ. Press, 1993), 69.

an entirely respectable activity—that those doctrines are false. He might argue, for example, that men and women are created equal not across many incarnations but within the compass of this one. If he succeeded, a variety of new distributive principles would come into view. (*Spheres*, 314)

The words used here—'false', 'argue', 'convince'—introduce an appearance of cross-cultural commensurability and argument for which Walzer has hardly any space within his framework.

Taking intuitions seriously, rather than trying to accommodate them by occult methods, commits us to the methodology of 'reflective equilibrium' proposed by John Rawls in *A Theory of Justice*.[32] Just as theoretical grammar is constrained and limited by the intuitions that people have about which sentences are grammatical, theories of justice have to take as their data our strongly held intuitions about what justice requires us to do in concrete situations. However, as Rawls explains, the intuitions are not data in the sense of the natural sciences. The theory that we elaborate to account for our intuitions may also lead us to give up some of them as unfounded, when we perceive that they were based on superficial similarities between different situations.[33]

According to Rawls, these intuitions are established by simple introspection rather than by any kind of empirically oriented moral sociology.[34] It would be a fundamental mistake to think that information about the proportion of people in society who believe, say, in the moral wrongness of abortion is relevant in the construction of a theory of morality or justice. For if such statistical data were relevant, the idea that they might come to be modified in light of the theory would lose its meaning—unless one were to carry out new surveys every time somebody came up with an objection that might affect the attitudes in the population. And even if new surveys were carried out, the finding that a given prejudice survived rational criticism would not invalidate that criticism.

In a Rawlsian perspective it would be more appropriate, I believe, to talk about the contingent aspects of justice than about its empirical foundations. The contingency—the possibility of mul-

---

[32] (Cambridge, Mass.: Harvard Univ. Press, 1971), 48–51.

[33] This impact of theory on data should not be confused with the more generally valid proposition that data, even in the natural sciences, are 'theory-laden'. That proposition does not imply, as in the case being discussed, that the data are modified by the very theory that we construct to account for them.

[34] *Theory of Justice*, 50.

tiple reflective equilibria—arises for two reasons. First, the initial set of intuitions depends on historical and cultural circumstances. There is no reason to believe (nor, perhaps, to exclude the possibility) that all such sets will converge to the same reflective equilibrium. Second, the modifications made to a given set of intuitions could depend on the theory we choose to account for them. A utilitarian might obtain equilibrium by discarding one subset of the initial intuitions, with an egalitarian reaching equilibrium by discarding a different subset. Although Rawls notes these possibilities, he refrains, wisely in my opinion, from pursuing them any further. Before we could usefully proceed to comparisons of different equilibria, much more progress would have to be made on a number of substantive issues.

There is another Rawlsian argument, however, that does appeal to empirical facts. One of the constraints he places on an acceptable theory of justice is that it should possess psychological stability, rooted in moral psychology. Rawls stipulates that knowledge about which theories possess such stability belongs among the general facts that people in his 'original position' incorporate in their deliberations, and he asserts that other things being equal they will adopt the more stable scheme of principles.[35] He then goes on to argue that his conception of justice is more stable—will generate less resentment and feeling of being unfairly treated—than the utilitarian one. But these are of course not the only alternatives. As we shall see, 'truncated utilitarianism' is seen as more acceptable than either—less wasteful than Rawls's difference principle, less unfair than utilitarianism. Moreover, even the two-way comparison of the difference principle and utilitarianism may be more difficult than Rawls allows for. If there is a choice between wastefulness and unfairness, it is not clear to me that people would overwhelmingly favour the former. This being said, Rawls offers no guidance to how any findings about stability should be incorporated into the deliberations when other things are not equal—which of course they never are.

I believe, nevertheless, that empirical studies of justice could be normatively relevant, for a different type of reason. Nobody will dispute that moral intuitions, even among well-informed and thoughtful observers, differ widely. The explanation might be, as

---

[35] Ibid. 455.

suggested above, that different theoretical approaches have
brought about different modifications in an initially shared set of
intuitions. But we might also look to the various explanations sur-
veyed in the previous section. These might provide the moral
philosopher with a different set of reasons for questioning some of
his initially held intuitions. If it turns out that some of his views
are strongly correlated with personal properties or self-interest, he
ought to take a hard second look to see if he might be subject to
bias or irrelevant influences. I do not at all mean to imply that
proof of correlation can substitute for argument. Even if one could
show that his intuitions were *caused* by self-interest or personal
properties, that would not in itself invalidate them. However, life
is short, and one cannot question all one's intuitions equally carefully. What I am suggesting, therefore, is simply that one can use
empirical findings about the determinants of subjective justice as a
heuristic in selecting which intuitions to scrutinize most intensely.
In this way, empirical findings could have a useful, if modest, role
in structuring normative approaches.

But perhaps one can think of a more ambitious role for empirical studies. In their recent work *Choosing Justice*, Norman Frolich
and Joe Oppenheimer claim to provide an empirical refutation of
Rawls's difference principle—the idea that society ought to be
organized so as to make the worst off as well off as possible. They
find that most subjects vastly prefer 'truncated utilitarianism'—the
maximization of total welfare, subject to a floor constraint on individual welfare—both to the difference principle and to uncon-
strained utilitarianism. A similar dual criticism of the difference
principle and of utilitarianism was found in the study by Yaari and
Bar-Hillel. Roughly speaking, the former theory has too much
potential for waste and the latter too little capacity for compassion
to be fully acceptable as a theory of justice.

I am two minds concerning the claims made by Frolich and
Oppenheimer. On the one hand, the idea that a theory of justice
can be refuted by experiment seems to me hopelessly naïve. On the
other hand, the fact that truncated utilitarianism is so overwhelmingly the most popular conception of justice does provide food for
thought. But I believe the function of such descriptive studies is
similar to the function of explanatory studies. Although they cannot substitute for argument, they can shape the structure and the
focus of argument. It is an interesting, perhaps remarkable, fact

that truncated utilitarianism has received virtually no attention from philosophers. It is briefly considered by Rawls, but dismissed on the grounds that the floor level of individual welfare cannot be determined from general theoretical principles.[36] I do think, however, that the wide appeal of the principle ought to induce more extensive and careful scrutiny. In the end, the principle might still have to be discarded, but in a less summary way.

The ideas underlying the preceding discussion are those of humility and fallibility. We should take careful account of the views of those who are not professional philosophers. And we should be aware of the potential biases in our own opinions. Descriptive and explanatory studies of justice can help us to focus these concerns in a better way. But, to repeat, these procedures are external to the theory itself. Although empirical studies may have a limited role in the final version of a normative theory of justice, they may be part of the scaffolding that we construct during the elaboration of the theory.

CONCLUSION

This chapter has mainly been concerned with survey and classification. I would like to end, however, on a different note, by sketching a research agenda on what I would like to call the *common-sense conception of justice*, defined as the principles of justice held by those who have given serious thought to the matter but who are not professional philosophers. In particular, I would expect these views to be widely held by lawyers, economists, and politicians, who are professional, secular all-round problem-solvers. I believe that, for the purposes sketched towards the end of the last section, we should pay special attention to the views held by such persons, because of their broad and direct experience. These common-sense conceptions are at an intermediate level of generality and abstractness. They are not intuitions about particular cases like the immorality of torturing small children, but 'high-level intuitions' such as the idea that distribution should be sensitive to ambitions but not to endowments.

I shall limit myself to issues of welfare.[37] I believe there is wide

---

[36] *Theory of Justice*, 316–17.
[37] In my *Local Justice*, 241 ff., I also sketch common-sense conceptions of rights and fairness.

consensus on the strong principle of Pareto-improvement: one should not pass up on any policy that holds out the prospect of welfare improvements for all, even if they do not improve everyone's welfare by the same amount or in the same proportion. I believe there is an almost equally strong consensus on the weak principle: one should not pass up on any policy that improves the situation for some without making it worse for anyone. The fact that, in many cases, public opinion or interest groups force problem-solvers to deviate from these principles, does not show that they do not in fact hold them.

When the issue of welfare is phrased in terms of protection of the poor, common sense holds, as indicated earlier, that truncated utilitarianism is the best principle. It would, nevertheless, be reluctant to embrace unconditional transfers to the poor. (Special principles govern support of the handicapped.) A system that offered individuals who could find work the option of living on the unconditional grant would be widely perceived as exploitative. Rawlsian concerns for the worst-off must, so to speak, be tempered not only by utilitarian concerns with efficiency but also by Ronald Dworkin's view that we should not compensate people for low ambition levels.[38] Yet Dworkin's position can also be criticized as inconsistent.[39] How can one defend the view that a low level of ambition or a high rate of time discounting are not also the products of social and genetic luck? If they are, why do they not provide grounds for compensation?

The beginning of an answer is provided by the fact that the modern welfare state is inserted into a political democracy, based among other things on the condition of publicity. To tell a citizen that he is entitled to welfare because he is not responsible for his preferences is pragmatically incoherent. One cannot at one and the same time treat the preferences of an individual as a handicap that justifies compensation, *and* treat them as a legitimate input to the political process; nor in one and the same breath treat him as moved by psychic forces outside his control, *and* treat him as rational and open to arguments. Perhaps one might justify such practices to a third party, on the grounds that it is better to let

---

[38] R. Dworkin, 'Equality of What? Part 2. Equality of Resources', *Philosophy and Public Affairs*, 10 (1981), 283–345.
[39] See notably J. Roemer, 'Equality of Talent', *Economics and Philosophy*, 1 (1985), 151–88.

irresponsible individuals have access to the political process than to cause political turmoil by excluding them. In a democratic society, however, a policy must be rejected if it cannot coherently be explained to the individuals in question. By withholding material benefits one protects the crucial values of concern and respect. Those who are able but unwilling to work should not receive support, nor should those who are able but unwilling to save be compensated for their incontinence.

Yet this austere principle is only the beginning of an answer. Applied to most contemporary societies, it would be widely and correctly perceived as unfair, because the economic and social means to form autonomous preferences are massively unequally distributed. In any society there will be individuals who for idiosyncratic reasons are deaf to incentives and who, in more serious cases, have to be supported by the state. In a society with fair background conditions the support would, however, not be offered as compensation; and the supported individuals would, like the mentally ill, be more or less randomly distributed across all social groups. Most contemporary societies do not approach this condition. They contain large groups whose members are systematically prevented, by poverty and lack of employment opportunities, from developing the mental attitude of holding themselves responsible for their actions. To treat them as if the background conditions were just, telling them that they have only themselves to blame for their failure, would be a massive piece of bad faith. As long as the influence of genuinely arbitrary features such as wealth has not been eliminated, justice may require us to count as morally arbitrary some features which would be considered non-arbitrary in the absence of the former.

The common-sense conception of welfare may, then, be stated in four propositions, each of which modifies its predecessor. (1) Maximize total welfare. (2) Deviate from that goal if necessary to ensure that all achieve a minimum level of welfare. (3) Deviate from the requirement of a minimal level of welfare in the case of persons who fall below it because of their own choices. (4) Deviate from the principle of not supporting the persons identified in (3) if their failure to plan ahead and react to incentives is due to severe poverty and deprivation.

Although Walzer and I are in broad agreement on the importance of *security* (proposition (2) above), we differ widely with regard to the context in which this value is to be assessed and implemented. Specifically, my approach differs from that of *Spheres* in three ways, related to propositions (1), (3), and (4). First, I am much more concerned with *efficiency*, a notion that is virtually absent from Walzer's book. Second, I take much more seriously the notion of individual *choice*, arguing in effect that society is under no obligation to compensate people for avoidable ills that befall them as the predictable outcome of their freely chosen behaviour. Third, I focus on *autonomy* as a condition for holding people responsible for their behaviour. These values may not be part of our 'common understandings', but I believe they are of central importance for those who have thought hard about these issues because they have been confronted over and over again with the need to make hard choices.

5

Justice across the Spheres

AMY GUTMANN

———◻◆◻———

Complex equality, Michael Walzer writes, 'requires . . . a diversity of distributive criteria that mirrors the diversity of social goods'.[1] Each social good or set of social goods—such as security and welfare, money and commodities, social office, free time, education, and political power—constitutes a sphere of justice and each sphere is governed by criteria derived from the social meaning of its good or set of goods (*Spheres*, 10). There are many spheres of justice, and principles of justice are '*internal* to each distributive sphere' (*Spheres*, 19; emphasis added).

Would a just society distribute social goods, as Walzer suggests, according to the standards of complex equality? I shall argue that, although a just society would not distribute social goods according to a single master principle, it would not do so according to the standards of complex equality either. Social justice is more complex than complex equality admits, for two reasons. First, the social meanings of some goods are multiple and the multiple meanings sometimes conflict, leading us to look for moral considerations that can adjudicate among the conflicting meanings. These moral considerations lead us beyond a search for the *real* social meaning of the good in question to moral considerations that are not internal to the sphere. The second reason is that many relevant moral considerations cut across distributive spheres. Although individual responsibility is not specific to the social meaning of any good, it is relevant to the distribution of many. When we draw upon all the moral resources at our disposal, we find that justice is complex, but not specific to each sphere.

I develop this argument in three parts. First, I defend the complexity of justice and distinguish it from the idea of sphere-

[1] *Spheres of Justice* (New York: Basic Books, 1983), 18.

specificity. Second, I show that a distributive principle is not triggered by the social meaning of a good (or set of goods) when the good has conflicting meanings. I illustrate this problem by considering the conflict between several meanings of productive employment in the USA today. Third, I suggest that there are moral considerations, which are not internal to a sphere, that we should take into account before deciding how a social good should be distributed. I illustrate this problem by showing that individual responsibility and equal citizenship are both relevant considerations in distributing medical care, but neither is specific to a sphere. Walzer himself relies upon equal citizenship in discussing the distribution of medical care, giving us yet another reason to think that complex equality should be revised to make room for interspherical standards.

A CASE FOR COMPLEXITY

Let us begin, as Walzer does, with the case for the *complexity* of social justice. Complex equality opposes the idea that social justice consists of a single master principle, whose application determines the distribution of all social goods. Justice is complex, Walzer argues, in that it consists of a plurality of distributive principles, which govern the distribution of different goods and therefore do not conflict with one another. We can develop a consistent and coherent theory of justice without a master principle.

Consider the principle of distribution according to need. Jobs, political power, honour, and fame are among the many goods that should not be so distributed. 'It would be odd', Walzer writes, 'to ask a search committee looking, say, for a hospital director to make its choice on the basis of the needs of the candidates' (*Spheres*, 25). But it makes moral sense to distribute health care, security, and other welfare goods (at least roughly) according to need. Applied to all social goods, the principle of distribution according to need would establish a kind of tyranny in society, the tyranny of the needy. Applied within a more restricted sphere—the sphere of welfare—where it reflects the social meaning of the goods whose distribution it governs, the need principle furthers justice, not tyranny.

Something similar can be said for other distributive principles. Consider the principle that probably has come closest actually to threatening tyranny across spheres in contemporary societies, the principle of distribution according to the free market. The same general reason that prevents government from distributing all goods according to need should also prevent it from letting the market distribute all goods. 'A radically *laissez-faire* economy would be like a totalitarian state', Walzer writes, 'invading every other sphere, dominating every other distributive process' (*Spheres*, 119). Distribution according to the market, understood as a generally applicable principle, establishes a tyranny of the wealthy rather than the needy. It none the less makes moral sense, Walzer argues, to reward entrepreneurial success and to distribute commodities according to market principles. The market principle should operate within limits that are set by the complexity of social justice. A just society honours constraints on market freedom so as to make room for the diverse distributive principles that are appropriate to non-market spheres. Entrepreneurs must not make so much money, for example, that they can buy political power, because political power is a separate sphere of justice, appropriately governed by principles of equal citizenship and persuasion (*Spheres*, ch. 12). Complexity ensures that no sphere is governed imperialistically, by the standards of a foreign sphere.

Justice is not only complex, according to Walzer, it is also specific to spheres. 'Social goods have social meanings and we find our way to distributive justice through an interpretation of those meanings' (*Spheres*, 19). The social meaning of a good determines its distribution (*Spheres*, 8). Market exchange is the appropriate distributive standard for commodities—like sports cars and jewellery. When we know that something is a commodity, we also know that it should be distributed by the market. Distribution according to need is appropriate to welfare goods—like health care and police protection—that we consider necessities, prerequisites to our living (almost) any kind of decent life. The social meaning of every good, David Miller writes, in the Introduction to this volume, 'triggers a particular distributive principle which we see as applying to all goods of that sort'.

There is something morally attractive and also something misleading about this picture of distributive justice. The attraction is easily stated. Social justice is complex. It is constituted by a pluralism of principles, combined into a coherent theory. We ignore this important insight of *Spheres* only at the peril of embracing a master principle. A master principle will either by tyrannical, ruling over foreign domains, or impotent, failing to do the critical work of determining how different social goods should be distributed.

'Maximize utility', still the most popular master principle, illustrates this problem. It is tyrannical when directly applied to the distribution, say, of love, education, or political power. Few utilitarians defend its direct application in these (or many other) realms. Most rely upon secondary principles, many of which turn out to be indistinguishable from Walzer's sphere-specific principles, but utilitarians say that they have the effect of maximizing utility. The mandate of maximizing utility provides little guidance in developing these secondary principles, which do the real work of distribution. Some utilitarians even argue that utilitarianism is a self-effacing principle: individuals and societies are more likely to maximize utility if they do not try to do so. Whether or not the principle of maximizing utility is theoretically defensible, it is often counterproductive as a practical guide to distribution.

There still may be abstract ideals that capture the aim of complex equality without claiming to be master principles. The freedom and equality of persons, autonomy, and other similarly abstract ideals can be consistent with the complexity of social justice as long as none pretends to serve as a general distributive principle. Put to good use, an ideal like autonomy helps us express an understanding of personhood that distributive principles may support or undermine. It may aid us in judging whether the plurality of distributive principles is consistent with a coherent understanding of human well-being. Misused, autonomy strains to take the place of more specific principles that are capable of governing the distribution of diverse social goods.

MULTIPLICITY OF MEANINGS

Nothing I say in the rest of this chapter should detract from understanding social justice as complex, constituted by a plurality of principles that are not derived from an abstract master principle. The problematic part of Walzer's theory of social justice is not its complexity but its sphere-specificity, the idea that each distributive sphere is constituted by principles *internal* to it, and those principles are in turn triggered by the social meanings of social goods. Is it unjust to distribute goods by principles that are not specific to spheres? Are all distributive principles generated by the social meaning of social goods? There is a partial truth in sphere-specificity, but taken either as a necessary or sufficient standard of social justice, it is mistaken. The partial truth is the importance of attending to the values that social goods express or serve in people's lives when we develop distributive principles. But such attention falls far short of a mandate that every social good be distributed according to its social meaning.

Suppose we begin our search for distributive principles by interpreting the social meaning of a good, in this case, productive employment in the USA. What should we do when we discover that the good has more than one meaning, and the meanings yield conflicting distributive standards? Walzer focuses on the fact that many jobs in our society are considered careers open to talent.[2] And understood as careers, they should be distributed by a process that first gives equal consideration to all qualified candidates and then tries to choose the best qualified among them, all the time recognizing the inescapable discretion of any selection process. Understood as careers, jobs constitute a distributive sphere separate from welfare. By the standards of complex equality, it would be tyrannical to distribute jobs according to need.

Yet people also *need* productive employment in order to live a decent life in our society, where the decency of our lives includes our being respected by our fellow citizens, being treated as equals. For many Americans, public standing and mutual respect depends on having productive employment. Making it on welfare—as it is commonly understood in the USA (cash, food, and housing assistance to healthy adults with low incomes)—is *not* making it, not even up to some minimal standard of equal citizenship.[3] Voting *and* earning have both long been regarded as 'attributes of an

---

[2] Most jobs in our society are what Walzer calls *social offices*: 'an office is any position in which the political community as a whole takes an interest, choosing the person who holds it or regulating the procedures by which he is chosen' (*Spheres*, 129). When the political community as a whole takes an interest in jobs, one would expect the conflict among meanings to become a matter of political dispute, as it has become in the USA, India, and many other modern societies. It then becomes all the more politically important to distribute them by publicly justifiable criteria.

[3] David T. Ellwood, *Poor Support: Poverty in the American Family* (New York: Basic Books, 1988), 5. Ellwood offers a detailed discussion of the problem of

American citizen',[4] at least for many people who have no alternative source of social standing (such as inherited wealth). When productive employment is understood to be a common precondition for the equal status of citizens, it triggers a principle of distributing jobs to all who need them. To deny any healthy person a job constitutes an injustice.

In a full employment economy, the need and qualification standards complement each other rather than conflict. But in an economy that falls far short of full employment, the two standards often compete. Perhaps the least skilled members of society should be the ones who remain unemployed, so as to satisfy fully the standard of distributing jobs according to qualification. But is this the right way to reconcile the two distributive principles? If so, it cannot be because of *the* social meaning of productive employment. The multiple meanings generate moral questions in a non-ideal society. Suppose the less qualified candidates among those who are basically qualified for a job are members of disadvantaged minorities. Would it be wrong to give preference to the less qualified candidates if their need is greater in the sense that their social standing would be significantly lower without a job than would the social standing of more qualified candidates? This question does not have an easy answer. I pose it here only to suggest that these two meanings of employment raise moral questions that must be answered before we can determine the right distributive principle for employment in our society.

There is yet another meaning of productive employment in our society. Distributing jobs to members of historically disadvantaged groups is also seen as a way of breaking the cycle of discrimination, which is perpetuated partly by racial and gender stereotyping of jobs. For example, jobs can be distributed in a way that helps equalize opportunity for blacks, the group that has been most systematically excluded from the most highly valued employment in our society. Yet this social meaning of jobs conflicts with both the other meanings. To break the racial stereotyping of jobs in this country, employment cannot be distributed to the most qualified or neediest candidates, regardless of their race. The point of pref-

welfare in the USA that supports Judith Shklar's argument that earning a living is a precondition for public standing: see Judith N. Shklar, *American Citizenship: The Quest for Inclusion* (Cambridge: Harvard Univ. Press, 1991), 1–23, 63–101.

[4] Shklar, *American Citizenship*, 3.

erential hiring on the basis of race is not to hire the most qualified candidates, according a strict understanding of qualification, or to equalize the opportunity of the neediest citizens, according to a strict understanding of need, but rather to fill social offices in a way that overcomes the racial discrimination that has been built into the job structure of our society. Preferential hiring is a temporary means of achieving a society in which it will no longer be necessary.[5] It anticipates a future when hiring the most qualified people will no longer perpetuate the racial stereotypes born of slavery and perpetuated by over a century of racial discrimination.[6]

Were jobs plentiful, and American society not plagued by a history of slavery and racial discrimination, we would not face this conflict. Because employment is scarce and many jobs are still racially stereotyped as a consequence of social injustice, the three meanings of employment conflict. Should people compete for unskilled jobs as for skilled ones? The aim, then, would be to distribute jobs, as far as possible, to the most qualified applicants.[7] Or should the neediest persons be given preference? The aim then would be to distribute unskilled jobs to those basically qualified candidates whose social standing and life-chances would be lowest without a job. This standard is unorthodox in our society, to be sure, but it is not as odd as Walzer's hypothetical example of selecting a hospital director on the basis of the needs of the candidates. Preference would be given to the neediest *among basically qualified candidates*, who then might be given on-the-job training. Or should black Americans be given preference in order to break the racial

[5] Preferential hiring entails choosing basically qualified members of a disadvantaged group (in this case, blacks) over more qualified members of more advantaged groups.

[6] Preferential hiring does not anticipate a future where each racial group is proportionately represented in each occupational category, but only one in which past discrimination stops sending signals that blacks are unwelcome in these jobs. Nondiscrimination in hiring may be insufficient to overcome the racial stereotyping of job categories—at least in a reasonably short period of time—both because those who hire are likely to be unconsciously influenced by racial stereotyping in their choice among candidates and because blacks may not even consider applying for these jobs. Racial discrimination need not take the form of prejudice by individuals or selection committees turning down qualified black candidates. It often operates institutionally. Occupations that are overwhelmingly white, due to past discrimination, send negative signals to blacks that they need not apply. Without any discriminatory actions on the part of individual office-holders, these occupations socialize citizens to believe that they are not suitable for blacks.

[7] All applicants for unskilled jobs are not equally qualified. Some people will work harder and be more productive than others.

stereotyping of jobs? Some black Americans are not as needy as some white Americans, but hiring blacks can serve the social purpose of overcoming racial discrimination, arguably the greatest injustice of American society. Our social context produces three different meanings of jobs, which in turn trigger three conflicting distributive standards.

Which standard is morally best? We cannot answer this question by deciding what jobs *really* mean in our society.[8] That's the problem, not its resolution. Jobs *really* mean careers open to talent and equal citizenship to Americans, and these things conflict under conditions of scarcity. Jobs also mean breaking the cycle of racial stereotyping. This meaning is less popular—recognizing, as it does, the enduring legacy of our history of racial discrimination and prejudice—but it does not therefore have any less claim to govern the distribution of employment here and now.[9] (Jobs in our society also mean making money, but the problem of multiple meanings is evident without adding yet another complication to it.) It would be arbitrary to pick out one meaning as *the* real one, the only one appropriate to the sphere of employment. If this is what complex equality calls for, it is not how Walzer actually argues against preferential hiring.

Walzer suggests that the conflict within the sphere of employment can be avoided by two policies. One is 'a significant redistribution of wealth and resources (for the sake, say, of a national commitment to full employment)' (*Spheres*, 154).[10] The other policy is 'reparations rather than reservation' of office, which Walzer says 'might be a better way to compensate American blacks for the effects of past mistreatment' (ibid.). With a full employment economy, jobs can be divided into two spheres with two separate, non-conflicting meanings. Understood as careers open to talent, jobs can be distributed to the most qualified candidates without

[8] David Miller, Introduction, 5–6.

[9] Walzer rightly rejects the idea that the most popular of competing social meanings should govern distribution within a sphere. He also rightly rejects the idea that popular opinion determines social meanings. He thereby opens the door not only to *interpretation* of social meanings but also to *moral argument* about which social meanings can be justified as distributive standards.

[10] Walzer argues explicitly against a quota system, not against preferential hiring *per se*. The two typically go together. Preferential hiring gives preference to basically qualified candidates from a relatively disadvantaged group over more qualified candidates from a relatively advantaged group. Preferential hiring is likely to rely on quotas, even though it is possible to do without them.

depriving any person of a job, understood as a welfare good, that is necessary to live a decent life and enjoy equal standing as a citizen. We get the best of both spheres. Add a reparations policy to a full employment economy, and preferential hiring becomes unjustified, because unnecessary. This is an ingenious resolution, but it runs up against two different problems, which suggest two different reasons why spheres cannot be kept as separate as complex equality requires.

The first problem is that the alternative to preferential hiring—full employment—may not be realizable in the short run, while preferential hiring may be. This raises a critical question for anyone who opposes preferential hiring as a short-term policy. As long as the USA does not enjoy a full employment economy, why should black Americans be made to suffer the most? In the absence of a policy of preferential hiring, this is what happens when there is unemployment in the USA. Black Americans, who are already the least advantaged group in society, suffer disproportionately to whites. This is unfair, and this unfairness is not adequately addressed by the claim of complex equality that careers, because they are careers, should be distributed according to talent, not need. We need to add an important caveat to the claims of complex equality: All goods should be distributed according to their social meanings *if* all the other goods that serve overlapping social purposes are also distributed.

This caveat is consistent with Walzer's claim that preferential hiring is a last resort, not a first one (*Spheres*, 153). If it *is* a last resort, and if we cannot now find a politically effective way to bring about a full employment economy, then (extending the logic of Walzer's own reasoning) preferential hiring may be justified for our society today.[11] In arguing against preferential hiring, Walzer opens the door to justifying it and does so by suggesting that justice is interspherical in a way not captured by his account of complex equality. If injustice is likely to prevail in one sphere, then the distributive standards of an overlapping sphere may need to be revised (temporarily) to address the injustice. The standards of ideal justice are not always appropriate to an unjust society. There is often some degree of commensurability between the social goods

---

[11] A complete defence of preferential hiring would also have to address the critic's claim that such policies backfire, and do not actually serve the needs of black Americans.

distributed by different spheres. (Spheres that are not concentric may overlap, as do the various spheres that include employment or are constituted by it.) Because many jobs satisfy needs *and* serve as careers, the distributive principles governing these ideally separate spheres cannot be determined independently from each other. Injustice in one sphere affects justice in the other.

One might call this compensatory justice between the spheres. It is not ideal justice, but it may be justice here and now, the kind of justice Walzer is committed to defending.[12] When injustice in the distribution of welfare, income, wealth, and education deprives black Americans of anything close to their fair share, preferential hiring may be justified as a way to improve their well-being. It is, to be sure, a morally imperfect way, for the various reasons that Walzer explores in *Spheres*, but it still may be the most justifiable way that stands a decent chance of being adopted.[13] Defending preferential hiring as a kind of compensatory justice between the spheres also helps explain why we readily reject it as an ideal distributive principle. It is not designed for a just society. It is, at best, a morally legitimate recourse within an unjust society.

Maybe I am too pessimistic about the possibility of bringing about ideal justice within the sphere of employment. Suppose, then, that we achieve full employment in the USA. We would still encounter a second problem that remains unaddressed by the requirements of complex equality. (I doubt that we can be *too* pessimistic about the chances of instituting a reparations policy, but reparations and full employment combined would also not resolve this problem.) Two meanings of social office would still conflict. High-status jobs in our society would remain racially stereotyped as a consequence of past discrimination, and probably would remain so for a long time to come. Because many social offices are racially stereotyped, a policy of hiring the most qualified candidates is still likely to perpetuate discrimination against blacks, especially in the short run. Racially stereotyped jobs send a signal to young black Americans that they cannot effectively compete for these jobs and that the working environments of these jobs are unfriendly to blacks, because they are so disproportionately

---

[12] See Michael Walzer, 'Justice Here and Now', in Frank Lucash (ed.), *Justice and Equality Here and Now* (Ithaca, NY: Cornell Univ. Press, 1986), 89–107.

[13] For Walzer's arguments against preferential hiring, except as a last resort, see *Spheres*, 151–4.

white.[14] Because preferential hiring breaks the racial stereotyping of jobs far more quickly than equal consideration, it may be the most effective way of achieving the non-discriminatory aims of equal consideration in the near future. This defence of preferential hiring does not fall into the trap of identifying non-discrimination with proportional representation of blacks and other disadvantaged groups in every job category. It aims at achieving a policy of equal consideration in the near future by expeditiously overcoming the discriminatory effects of job categories that have become racially stereotyped by centuries of unjust discrimination.

Advocates of preferential hiring affirm what the critics deny: that special treatment for black Americans can break the cycle of racial stereotyping that now prevents a policy of equal consideration from being non-discriminatory towards blacks. The two conflicting social meanings of jobs can be seen as competing arguments about how best to realize a shared ideal of non-discrimination in social office. The interspherical ideal of non-discrimination captures both the conflicting meanings of social office. Social justice lies not in choosing among the meanings, but rather in evaluating the details of the opposing arguments, which I can only summarize here.

On one argument, which opposes preferential hiring, open search procedures and extensive recruitment suffice to erase the effects of past discrimination, including the stereotyping of positions, within a reasonable period of time. Even if these measures do not guarantee the end of racial stereotyping for a long time to come, the moral costs of preferential hiring are thought to be too high to justify the benefits. Critics of preferential hiring also think that it may perpetuate the racist history it is designed to overcome by leading whites to believe that blacks are not well qualified for the offices they hold.

The opposing argument, which favours preferential hiring, begins by claiming that all the measures that ensure non-discrimination towards white Americans do not suffice to ensure non-discrimination towards black Americans. Preferential hiring is necessary to break the racial stereotyping of those predominantly white jobs created by centuries of discrimination. Although

---

[14] On this argument, preferential hiring should end before an occupational category is proportionately black. The aim is to hire enough blacks to break the racial stereotyping of the job category. Proportionality is not necessary to produce this effect.

preferential hiring does not insist on achieving racial proportionality in job categories, it goes far beyond the tokenism of hiring one or two blacks in every job category. It institutes a short-term policy that ends racial stereotyping, by bringing a sufficient proportion of blacks into various occupational categories to break the negative tipping effects of overwhelmingly white occupations, and thereby makes it possible to institute a policy of equal consideration in these occupations in the near future. The greater moral wrong is prolonging discrimination against blacks, proponents of preferential hiring argue, because black Americans are on the whole less advantaged than whites.

What complex equality characterizes as competing social meanings now looks more like a moral disagreement, and the moral disagreement enlists considerations that are not specific to the sphere of employment. Which policy inflicts the greater moral wrong, here and now, equal consideration or preferential hiring? This is a difficult question to answer, but complex equality begs the question by claiming that equal consideration is the real—or the ideal—social meaning of social office. At least in this case, we should expect the dominant social meaning (careers open to talent) to favour the dominant group (whites) because the opposing meaning is explicitly intended as a means of breaking the cycle of white dominance, perpetuated by a policy of equal consideration in office. (To say that equal consideration is the dominant meaning is neither to recommend it nor to criticize it.) Neither side in this conflict opposes careers open to talent as an ideal standard. Both sides favour a society in which equal consideration in employment is consistent with non-discrimination. But to resolve the conflict, both must move beyond social meanings, and attend to moral arguments. Which policy entails the lesser moral wrong? If it is a greater wrong to discriminate against the least advantaged group, then preferential hiring may be justified, provided that it can be instituted as a short-term policy.[15] This argument, which gives

---

[15] Preferential hiring was successfully instituted with an expiration date in what has been called the 'largest and most impressive civil rights settlement in the history of this nation'. *EEOC* v. *AT&T*, 365 F. Supp. 1105 (1973) at 1108. Cited by Robert K. Fullinwider, 'Affirmative Action at AT&T', in Amy Gutmann and Dennis Thompson (eds.), *Ethics and Politics: Cases and Comments*, 2nd edn. (Chicago: Nelson-Hall, 1990), 211. In a massive settlement with EEOC, AT&T agreed to a far-ranging plan that gave women and minorities preference in hiring and promotion over a six-year period. The plan achieved its goals of breaking sexual and racial

priority to improving the life-chances of less advantaged citizens in the case of moral conflict, spans several spheres of justice.

STANDARDS ACROSS SPHERES

In the context of an unjust society, justice is more interspherical than complex equality leads us to expect. There are also reasons why complex equality is not an adequate guide to the principles that should govern a just society. Some moral considerations that cut across spheres gain moral force in the context of injustice, but others take on greater moral weight as society becomes more just. The ideal of individual responsibility is one such consideration. It is not specific to a sphere. It does not arise out of our attempt to reconcile the conflicting meanings of a social good. It is part of the public culture of our society, but it is not derived from the meaning of any good. It has a moral life among spheres, and therefore does not fit well within the requirements of complex equality. The relevance of individual responsibility to the distribution of medical care illustrates the limitations of complex equality in the context of a just society.

How should medical care be distributed in the USA today? How should it ideally be distributed? Suppose we begin with what many people would take to be the obvious social meaning of medical care in our society. Medical care satisfies what most Americans (and many other people) reasonably consider a basic need, the need to live a healthy, long life. We shall return to consider a more complex interpretation of the meaning of medical care, which Walzer himself defends. The more complex meaning, however, raises the same general problem for Walzer's account of complex equality as does the simpler account with which we begin here.

If the social meaning of medical care is to enable us to live long, healthy lives, then it follows—according to complex equality—that medical care should be distributed to individuals according to their medical needs.[16] Suppose that we accept need as *the* social meaning of medical care. There still may be good reasons to question the conclusion that medical care should be distributed strictly

stereotyping, and ended on schedule. AT&T now hires and promotes by a policy of equal consideration. For details, see ibid. 211–18.

[16] David Miller, Introduction, 5.

according to need, as complex equality requires. The social meaning of medical care does not include a moral consideration that is relevant to its distribution and is also part of our common culture: people should assume some significant degree of responsibility for their own lives. We are answerable for our own voluntary actions. We do not blame other people for the consequences of those actions, nor do we expect society to compensate us for the costs of actions that we can avoid without sacrificing something that is necessary to living a good life. The ideal of individual responsibility applies to many spheres, including education, free time, recognition and punishment, divine grace, and political power. We reward students for effort as well as achievement. We punish individuals for irresponsible behaviour that harms other people. We hold people responsible for knowing what constitutes a crime. We take responsibility for the use of our free time, and do not (or at least should not) expect to be compensated for squandering it in ways that turn out to be disappointing or even painful. And so on.

We could translate all these claims about responsibility into claims about the social meaning of goods. But the translations are strained, and the strain exposes the inadequacy of basing distributive standards on sphere-specific meanings. People who make bad use of their free time should not be compensated by society. This relatively uncontroversial moral claim about distributive justice in the sphere of free time does not follow from the meaning of free time. Free time does not *mean* either compensation or no compensation for how we use our free time. In our culture, at least, it means that we may make use of our leisure time as we see fit within legal limits (which are themselves at least partly determined by moral considerations that span several spheres). The social meaning of free time is consistent with a policy of compensating people with extra free time if we use it to bad personal effect. We would still be free to use our extra free time as we wish. This proposal strikes us as ludicrous not because it conflicts with the social meaning of free time but because it violates even a minimalist moral commitment to holding individuals responsible for what we freely do with our lives.

This same minimalist notion of individual responsibility should make us hesitate before accepting the social meaning of medical care as sufficient to determining its distributive principle. Medical care meets a basic need, but need is not the only morally relevant consideration in distributing medical care (or other welfare goods). We also worry about whether it is right for people to expect their society to meet those needs that result from their voluntary taking of unnecessary risks. We think that people should take responsibility for their voluntary action. The medical needs that result from reckless behaviour may be so expensive to satisfy that society cannot then afford to meet the needs of other people who act responsibly but still suffer from misfortune. In not holding people responsible for their actions, society indirectly harms other people who act more responsibly.

This worry about responsibility takes us beyond the social meaning of medical care. A standard of individual responsibility is not internal to the meaning of medical care or welfare, more generally. It rests uneasily with the argument that, because medical care and other welfare goods serve the role in our society of satisfying needs, need is *the* relevant distributive consideration. Medical care, as most Americans understand it, satisfies our need to live a long and healthy life *even when we don't act in ways that decrease our need for it*. People who smoke and can stop, who drink excessively and refuse treatment, who voluntarily choose to climb mountains, hang-glide, skydive, or ride motorcycles, and therefore suffer from life-threatening maladies, are every bit as needy as similarly situated people who avoid these risks to their health. Is it unjust to constrain access to medical care by making it more costly to people who voluntarily take unnecessary risks with their health?[17] To do so would be to go beyond the sphere-specific principle of distributing health care according to need and to recognize that need is not the only morally relevant consideration in distributing health care.

If responsibility is relevant to the distribution of health care, then justice is not as specific to spheres as complex equality claims. We unjustifiably narrow the universe of relevant moral considerations if we do not to take responsibility into account in determining how health care should be distributed. Before determining what counts as a just distribution of medical care, we should question whether society must provide as much medical care or provide it

---

[17] To test the principled relevance of individual responsibility to the distribution of medical care, we assume that (1) medical care resources are scarce and (2) the cost constraints are imposed in a nondiscriminatory manner.

as freely to people who take voluntary risks with their health as it does to people whose medical needs result from causes that are more clearly beyond their control.

Taking individual responsibility into account as a relevant consideration does not settle the question of how medical care should be distributed. Our concern for holding people responsible for their voluntary actions leads us to ask: why should people who refuse to take responsibility for their lives (and shirk their fair share of social responsibility as well) be entitled to the same level of welfare as responsible people who suffer misfortunes beyond their control (and are willing to work but unable to find employment)? One answer, consistent with our concern for responsibility, is that a policy of imposing greater costs on what appears to be voluntary behaviour is likely to discriminate against, or disproportionately burden, already disadvantaged people in an unjust society. In a just society, however, charging higher health insurance premiums to people who smoke or take drugs is far less likely to discriminate against an otherwise disadvantaged group. Considerations of responsibility therefore carry more weight in the context of a just society.[18] Whether or not we ultimately think that the moral claims of responsibility outweigh other considerations in our society, we should recognize it as a relevant standard that is neither specific to a single sphere nor internal to the meaning of medical care in our society.[19]

Even if we cannot justify a distributive principle for our society that differentiates between responsible and irresponsible behaviour in the sphere of medical care, we still cannot fall back on need as the standard of distribution. A society should not spend everything it can to satisfy the medical needs of its members, any more than

[18] A sceptical critic of any principle based on individual responsibility would deny that any discrimination between people on the basis of voluntary and involuntary behaviour can be justified. The implications of such scepticism range far beyond health care to reliance on standards of individual responsibility in criminal law. It is impossible to *prove* that people can act voluntarily, but almost no one is willing to live with the practical implications of doing without a distinction between voluntary and involuntary behaviour.

[19] We could of course say that taking responsibility for one's health is part of the meaning of medical care in our society. But to say this is to expand the notion of social meaning to include any relevant moral consideration, whether or not the consideration is really generated by the *meaning* of a specific good. It is to Walzer's credit that he resists stretching the idea of social meaning beyond meaningfulness, thereby rendering it uninteresting.

an individual should spend all of her personal resources on medical care. Satisfaction of the medical needs of all Americans would hijack all other welfare goods, and welfare goods would hijack all quality-of-life goods. Our society and our lives would be impoverished as a result. Satisfying medical needs may have made sense as a distributive principle for some societies, but the capacities of modern medicine to maintain life are so great now as to devour all other valuable social and individual purposes. Satisfaction of need is what medical care may mean to most Americans, yet it cannot serve as a sufficient distributive principle.

Walzer also thinks that need cannot serve as the distributive principle for medical care or any other welfare good. 'Clearly we can't meet, and we don't have to meet', he writes, 'every need to the same degree or any need to the ultimate degree' (*Spheres*, 66–7). He invokes another moral consideration—equality of membership—to qualify the need principle (*Spheres*, 84). But he treats equality of membership as a sphere-specific consideration, which it is not. Like individual responsibility, equality of membership is a moral consideration that spans many spheres, as if in defiance of complex equality.

Walzer says that recognizing the underlying equality of membership is part of the twofold meaning of distributive justice in the sphere of welfare (*Spheres*, 84). 'Goods must be provided to needy members because of their neediness but they must also be provided in such a way as to sustain their membership' (*Spheres*, 78). In liberal democracies, membership means equal citizenship and the dignity of persons. But it is not only welfare goods that must be provided in such a way as to sustain equal citizenship and the dignity of persons. Income, social office, hard work, free time, education, public honour and punishment, and political power must also be distributed in such a way as to sustain equal citizenship and the equal dignity of persons. None of these spheres alone can sustain equal citizenship or the dignity of persons, but all together can. If medical care means equality of membership in the USA, so too does a minimum income, productive employment, some free time, non-discrimination in the distribution of public honours and high-status employment, due process under the law, voting rights, and a host of other civil and political liberties. Although equality of membership cannot be directly distributed to Americans, all these goods, which are necessary to its realization, can and should be.[20]

Equality of membership in the USA cannot be sustained without universal provision of medical care at a level that is widely (and reasonably) considered adequate in our society. A standard of equal membership does not tell us what medical goods and services are adequate, but it does tell us that, *whatever* level a democratic society deems adequate, it must make affordable for all its members. The lack of guaranteed medical care coverage for the working poor in the USA is clearly unjust, but it is not clear precisely how much medical care must be guaranteed to everyone. Walzer invokes democratic persuasion and decision-making—yet another manifestation of equal membership—to determine the level of adequacy. (One may defend democratic decision-making as the morally best procedure without claiming that all results of the process are justifiable.) Democratic persuasion and decision-making is a moral standard that cuts across many spheres in order to specify their boundaries as well as patrol them.[21]

Once an adequate level of medical care is provided for all members, why should people not be free to buy more medical care with their income, as long as this limited market in medical care does not undermine provision of adequate medical care for all citizens, regardless of their income? The sphere-specific answer triggered by complex equality—because medical care is not a commodity, it is unjust to buy it on the market—is deeply misleading. By supposing that the meaning of medical care resolves this issue, it directs our attention away from the complex moral and empirical consid-

[20] Although these goods can be directly distributed to individuals, what counts as an adequate distribution for supporting equality of membership depends on social perceptions (as David Miller suggests in Ch. 9). Until people regard each other as equals, equality of membership cannot be completely realized. But social perceptions also make a difference in what counts as a just distribution of many other goods. The universal distribution of productive employment may be necessary for equal welfare and membership in some societies; in others a guaranteed basic income may be an adequate substitute. Although society can distribute productive employment and income directly to individuals, the contribution of these goods to social justice depends at least in part on shared social understandings.

[21] According to Walzer, political power in a constitutional democracy *means* democratic persuasion and decision-making within constitutional limits, and this meaning therefore justifies the constitutional exercise of political power *across* spheres. (See *Spheres*, 281–311.) Political power, so understood, is inseparable from the two broader moral considerations—equal citizenship and equal dignity—that inform distributive justice in many other spheres. The distributive principle governing political power cuts across spheres, as Walzer argues, but not just because of its social meaning.

erations that are relevant to arriving at even a tentative answer.

Suppose a just society is one in which income and wealth are far more equally distributed than they now are, where everyone is guaranteed high-quality education, housing, medical care, police protection, and all other welfare goods at levels that are considered adequate by a broad, well-informed consensus of the citizenry. The citizens who support this consensus also endorse each other's freedom to buy medical care beyond what society ensures to all, provided that the limited market in medicine does not undermine the socially guaranteed level of adequacy for everyone. If the background conditions of income and welfare distribution are just, why is it not also just for this society to ensure its members the freedom to purchase extra medical care—as well as sports cars, jewellery, and hang-gliders?[22]

The answer of complex equality is that medical care is not a commodity, but sports cars, jewellery and hang-gliders are. (By the standards of complex equality, cosmetic surgery is also a commodity and therefore can be bought and sold on the market.) The freedom to buy extra medical care that holds out some prospect for improving health or prolonging life, even when it harms no one and deprives no one of an adequate level of care, gives some citizens a greater chance than others to live a healthier or longer life. But now we need to ask, if justice is consistent with some people having a greater chance of satisfying more of their desires, even their intense desires, then why is it not also consistent with some people having a greater chance of satisfying more of their needs in a way that deprives no one of an adequate level of need satisfaction? It does not suffice to say that this situation is unjust because medical care is not a commodity. We have already shown that the meaning of a good does not determine its distribution. Complex equality fails to offer reasons why justice is incompatible with a limited market in medical care, especially in circumstances where

---

[22] Similarly, if the background conditions are just, why should people be free to buy luxuries that please them but not burglar alarm systems for their homes and cars that are even safer than the legally mandated standards? The moral argument implicit in complex equality seems to be that it is an unjust state of affairs when some people are able to satisfy their needs more than others, but not when some people can satisfy their desires more than others. If it is unfair that some people can live longer than others, is it not also at least as unfair that some people can enjoy life more than others? This sense of cosmic unfairness does not translate into a requirement of justice that prevents people from differentially experiencing pleasure or satisfying their needs above a socially guaranteed level.

(*a*) income and wealth are justly distributed and (*b*) all members of society are afforded what is widely (and reasonably) considered an adequate level of medical care. If these provisos are met, it may be unjust *not* to permit people to use their income to buy medical care above the socially guaranteed level of adequacy. The freedom to buy more medical care is, after all, at least as valuable as the freedom to buy commodities, and an advocate of complex equality agrees that it is unjust to prevent people from buying harmless commodities. The claims of complex equality are insufficient to prohibit a constrained market in medicine.

What kind of society would, as a matter of principle, permit people to buy sports cars, jewellery, hang-gliders, and cosmetic surgery, but forbid them to buy additional medical care above the socially guaranteed level of adequacy? A society that is committed to the equalization of everyone's life prospects for its own sake, rather than for the sake of individual well-being. Or a society that does not trust people to care for their own needs beyond the level at which society can care for them. Or both. Although a state cannot possibly satisfy all the needs of all its members, it can outlaw a market in all welfare goods beyond what it collectively provides to all its members. This arrangement, by which no needs can be satisfied by the market, conforms to the sphere-specific reasoning of complex equality. It also deprives us of any individual responsibility for meeting our own needs beyond what we collectively secure for ourselves and each other. In addition to doubting the justice of this sphere-specific reasoning, we might worry that we would not recognize ourselves as responsible individuals in such a society.[23]

Walzer recognizes that complete autonomy among spheres is impossible. 'What happens in one distributive sphere affects what happens in the others', he writes, therefore 'we can look, at most, for relative autonomy [of spheres]' (*Spheres*, 10). In this chapter I have suggested that we should not seek the maximum degree of autonomy that is possible among spheres. There are important moral considerations—such as fairness to the least advantaged

---

[23] Or, more precisely, we might recognize ourselves as responsible, but only as *collectively* responsible for our *collective* fate, not individually responsible for any aspects of our own welfare. Why, we might also ask, should a democratic society not be free to permit a market in welfare goods above what citizens collectively provide for each other?

members of society, individual responsibility, equality of citizenship, and the dignity of persons—that span many spheres.
Although Walzer draws upon some of these considerations in his
detailed discussions, they do not find a prominent place in his
account of complex equality.

What status might these moral considerations have in a theory
of complex equality? What could be their role in regulating distributions? Fairness, individual responsibility, equal citizenship, and
the dignity of persons do not constitute the social meaning of specific goods. They are not adequately conceived as contingent cultural facts, which we just happen to hold and can readily change
at our collective will. They are not master principles, which claim
to dominate all sphere-specific distributions. They therefore do not
seem to fit comfortably anywhere in the theoretical framework of
complex equality. Yet considerations of fairness, individual
responsibility, equal citizenship, and the dignity of persons legitimately influence the way we think about distributing different
goods. They are moral considerations that make sense across a
wide range of societies, and inform our self-understanding as well
as our social understandings. They do not threaten tyranny nor do
they point in the direction of simple equality. They render many
spheres less autonomous than they otherwise would be, but they
do not obliterate their boundaries. Quite the contrary, they point
to a conception of social justice that is complex but not sphere-
specific. Such a conception would serve us well both here and now,
and into the future.

6

Politics and the Complex Inequalities of Gender

SUSAN MOLLER OKIN

In this chapter, in the context of Michael Walzer's theory of justice as complex equality, I look at the representation of women in the sphere of political life in contemporary liberal democracies. I use this term to refer to countries satisfying three criteria: all adult citizens have the right to vote, elections are held on a regular basis (or, in the case of new democracies, this is the intention), and there are at least two political parties competing for office. This is in many ways a fairly minimal definition of a democracy, as some of what I say will testify. The main questions the chapter addresses are as follows. How is the very unequal political representation of men and women a matter of injustice, and why is it a significant problem? Why are women so underrepresented in the legislatures and in high appointed office in almost all liberal democracies? And how can Michael Walzer's concepts of 'complex equality' and 'spheres of justice' help us to understand, critique, and address these issues?

COMPLEX EQUALITY AND GENDER INEQUALITY

It is important to begin with at least a brief discussion of two meanings of 'political'. In the last twenty years, second-wave feminists have put the concept of gender—by which I mean 'the social institutionalization of sexual difference'—on the agenda of both political science and political philosophy. We have challenged centuries of thinking and writing about politics as if women simply did

I would like to thank David Miller for helpful comments on an earlier draft of this chapter, and Kimberly Yuracko for valuable research assistance. This is a much altered version of a paper entitled 'Gender and Political Equality' in *Norms, Values, and Society*, ed. Herlinde Pauer-Studer, 2/1994 (Dordrecht: Kluwer, 1994).

not exist, or during which their subordination was rationalized as 'natural'. In doing so, we have contested and reconceived many conventional notions of political theory, including the concept of what is political. The feminist slogan of the 1960s, 'the personal is political', sums up briefly this broadening of the sphere of what should be considered political. We have pointed out a number of things that are ignored when politics and personal or domestic life are seen as dichotomous—as both conceptually and practically separate. First, feminist scholarship has shown that much in personal, familial, and sexual life involves relations of power and, not infrequently, exploitation or abuse. Second, attention has been drawn to the fact that it is in the supposedly non-political sphere of life that we become the persons we are, who then go out (or do not go out) into the public spheres of work and politics. Third, it has been pointed out that the imbalances of power, resources, and responsibilities between the sexes in the private sphere have been historically and are still in many respects caused and sustained by laws and other governmental action—and inaction. Fourth, the converse of this, feminists have made it clear how private or domestic differentials in power between the sexes in turn affect what men and women can and cannot do in public, including political life.[1] Thus, as a feminist theorist, I generally resist the confinement of 'political' to its narrow, conventional meaning. But because I focus much of the time in this chapter on the second and fourth points made above, I shall often use the term 'politics' in this narrower sense, having to do with governments, their members, and how they come to be in power.

As David Miller points out in the Introduction, the notion of equal citizenship plays a 'pivotal role' in Walzer's account of justice. But what does 'equal citizenship' mean? How do we know when its criteria are fulfilled? As we all know, in almost all of the liberal democracies, women have had the most important right of equal citizenship—the right to vote—for many decades now. New Zealand was the first country to enfranchise women, in 1893. Switzerland finally joined the other liberal democracies in granting

---

[1] More complete discussions can be found in Susan Moller Okin, *Justice, Gender, and the Family* (New York: Basic Books, 1989), 128–33; Frances Olsen, 'The Myth of State Intervention in the Family', *Univ. of Michigan Journal of Law Reform*, 18/4 (1985), 835–64; and Carole Pateman, 'Feminist Critiques of the Public/Private Dichotomy', in Stanley Benn and Gerald Gaus (eds.), *Private and Public in Social Life* (London: Croom Helm, 1983).

women the right to vote in 1971. But, as feminists have been pointing out for some time now, formal equal citizenship does not make for substantive equal citizenship and, in most liberal democracies, women are far from sharing political power equally with men. One very obvious indication of this—though not the only significant one, for those in appointed high political office are also overwhelmingly male—is the scarcity of elected female legislators. Since the notion of equal citizenship is so central to Walzer's theory of justice, its precepts can be effectively applied to this situation of substantive inequality.

Before I do this, though, I wish to point out that the general issue of 'malrepresentation' or 'disproportionate' representation is not only a feminist issue, which helps to explain why we can effectively use a not-specifically-feminist theory to help us think about it. In *Spheres*, near the beginning of the chapter on the sphere of political power, which he regards as the most important of all social goods, Walzer writes the following, about those who have such power:

Ostensibly, they act on our behalf, and even in our names (with our consent). But in most countries most of the time, political rulers function, in fact, as agents of husbands and fathers, aristocratic families, degree holders, or capitalists. State power is colonized by wealth or talent or blood or gender; and once it is colonized, it is rarely limited.[2]

This is clearly true. The elected and appointed office-holders, in most liberal democracies as well as in less representative forms of government, do not even begin to resemble the population at large. Walking the streets of most parts of the USA, for example, one is very much aware that it is a multi-racial, multi-ethnic, and class-differentiated society, as well as, of course, a two-sexed one—some would say, a multi-sexed one. But (even more so before the 1992 elections) whom did one see in the Senate, the House of Representatives, on the Supreme Court, in the Cabinet? Overwhelmingly, middle-aged to elderly, professional, affluent, white men. Although they are elected, and the right to vote is universal, various aspects of the electoral process, as well as other factors I shall talk about later, make the supposed representatives of the people extremely *un*representative of us in terms of virtually every demographic

---

[2] *Spheres of Justice* (New York: Basic Books, 1983), 282.

variable one could think of. What has happened to the idea, voiced long ago by Pericles, as Walzer reminds us, that '[o]ur ordinary citizens, though occupied with the pursuits of industry, are still fair judges of public matters'?[3]

Let us now take a brief look at the levels of representation of women at the national level in some liberal democracies, including some that are strongly capitalist and some with more mixed economies. These percentages of female members of national legislatures are all from the very late 1980s or the 1990s—and, in the case of countries with bicameral legislatures, I cite the percentage of women in the more popularly elected chamber. Japan has the fewest female legislators, 2.3 per cent, with France next with about 5 per cent (a figure that has remained remarkably constant since 1946, when French women were enfranchised). Then comes a group of countries, including Australia, India, Israel, Brazil, Chile, and quite a number of the smaller Latin American countries, in which women constitute from 6 to 8 per cent of the legislature. Both the USA and Great Britain were also in this group until their elections of 1992, since when the percentage in the USA increased to slightly more than 10 per cent, and that in Britain to slightly under 10 per cent. In the next obvious grouping of countries, including Canada, Italy, Spain, and Costa Rica, women make up between 12 and 15 per cent; in New Zealand, 16.5 per cent. In Austria, Germany, Iceland, and Holland, the percentage is a little more than 20, in the first two cases reflecting a sharp increase in the last few years. In Austria, the percentage of women legislators doubled between 1986 and 1990, though the reasons for this are not clear. In Germany, it seems likely that a similar increase was at least partly attributable to unification, since the percentage of women in national politics in the GDR were much higher than those in West Germany. However, this may be implausible, for the percentages of women in office in all of Eastern Europe were much higher under Communist rule than they are now. It has also been suggested that this negative change has occurred not only because the former quota systems, which ensured the representation of a wide range of groups, including women, have now been done away

---

[3] Walzer, *Spheres*, 287, citing Thucydides, *History of the Peloponnesian War*, tr. Richard Crawley (London, Everyman, 1910), 123 (ii. 40). It should of course be noted that Pericles, despite his seemingly inclusive conception of democracy, did not mean to include *women* in his definition of the ordinary citizen.

with, but also because parliaments in Eastern Europe are more powerful than previously: as the worth of such office has increased it has unfortunately become less attainable by women.

And then there are the quite remarkable Nordic countries (other than Iceland, which itself has the best representation of women of all those I have mentioned up to now). In Denmark, Norway, Sweden, and Finland, the percentages of women legislators range from 33 per cent to almost 40 per cent. Thus, these countries are actually getting fairly close to having a proportion of women in parliament that reflects their percentage in the population. Yet in most liberal democracies, the political representation of women is nothing like proportionate to their numbers.

In *Spheres*, Walzer has put forward arguments that are helpful in thinking about the continuing political inequality of women. As Miller has said, Walzer's whole argument for complex equality can be 'understood as an idea of equal citizenship'.[4] And there can be no doubt about Walzer's recognition of the importance of *political* power. 'Politics', he says, 'is always the most direct path to dominance, and political power (rather than the means of production) is probably the most important, and certainly the most dangerous, good in human history' (*Spheres*, 15). Hence the need for constraints, checks and balances, limits on political monopoly, and for the wide distribution of political power. However, Walzer only briefly applies his most relevant concepts, 'separate spheres' and 'complex equality' to the subject of the political underrepresentation of women. I shall expand on how the fundamental principles of his argument might be applied to it, and shall argue that the fulfilment of Walzer's criteria for a society that is just in respect of its distribution of political power *must* directly address issues of gender. A just society, I shall conclude, must work towards the reduction and eventual elimination of the division of labour on the basis of sex, and must also, for the interim, utilize mechanisms to ensure much better political representation of women than occurs under current methods of candidate selection and systems of voting.

In Walzer's *Spheres*, we can find helpful ways of thinking about the political inequalities of gender. I shall pass over the more communitarian tendencies in the book—his arguments that principles

---

[4] Miller, Introduction, 3.

of justice should be based on the 'shared understandings' of each culture—which, as I have explained elsewhere, have many problems, from a feminist point of view.[5] I shall focus instead on Walzer's other criterion for justice, 'separate spheres' or 'complex equality', which requires that inequalities in any one sphere do not spread to others. Walzer's work is unusual among mainstream contemporary theories of justice in paying any attention at all to women and gender. In *Spheres*, he uses largely non-sexist language, insists that the family constitutes a significant 'sphere of justice', and makes specific references to power imbalances between the sexes and discrimination. Moreover, if we separate Walzer's 'separate spheres' framework out from his 'shared meanings' arguments, which I think is quite possible, it has considerable force as a tool for feminist criticism. In particular, like Rawls's insistence on the fair value of political liberty,[6] it constitutes a potentially powerful critique of the paucity of women representatives in liberal democracies.

In Walzer's chapter 'Kinship and Love', he clearly states both that women (and children) are often oppressed and dominated within families, and that women's exclusion from many other social and political spheres is a case of what he calls 'dominance'— the translation of an inequality within one sphere of life into others. Walzer recognizes that the family 'imposes what we currently call "sex roles" upon a vast range of activities to which sex is entirely irrelevant', and that these sex roles are reproduced in the larger world outside the family (*Spheres*, 240; see 239–42 *passim*). While Walzer rather underestimates the effects of sex roles on the domination of women *within* the family, he certainly does not neglect their influence outside of it. 'The family itself', he writes, 'must be reformed so that its power no longer reaches into the sphere of office' (*Spheres*, 239).

I wholeheartedly concur with this conclusion. Its urgency was made clear in the USA during the recent 'Zoe Baird/Kimba Wood' affair. In this case, two married women with children were

---

[5] Regarding relations and inequalities between men and women, not only are social meanings often not shared but, rather, deeply divisive. Even where they do appear to be shared, this is often the outcome of the dominance of some groups over others, the latter being silenced, rendered incoherent, or co-opted by the more powerful. For a fuller critique, see Okin, *Justice*, 62–8.

[6] For a discussion of this, see Okin, 'Gender and Political Equality', *Vienna Circle Yearbook*, 2/1994.

successively considered for the position of Attorney-General in the Clinton administration. Before Baird was nominated, she revealed that she and her husband, seeking care for their baby, had illegally hired an undocumented alien couple as household workers. When this became public, extremely negative public reaction soon made it apparent that her confirmation to the nation's highest legal office was doomed. The opposition to Baird, in my view, had some clear legitimacy; she and her husband, though burdened by a greater conflict between their professions and their parental responsibilities than many parents, were also a lot more affluent than most, and surely had no need to break the law in order to have their son properly cared for. It should be noted, though, that Baird, a top executive, would have been far less likely to require as much household help as she did (and therefore to have trouble finding it without resort to illegality) if she were a man, especially one married (as she was) to an academic, with demanding but *flexible* working hours. As Anthony Lewis commented on the whole affair, in his *New York Times* column, 'It's Gender, Stupid'.[7]

The real gender injustice in the situation occurred in the next stage, however: Judge Kimba Wood, the next person to be considered for nomination, had also hired non-registered aliens to care for her children. The important difference was that she had done so only at a time when this was legal. Nevertheless, fears of a resurgence of the bad publicity surrounding what had become known as 'the nanny problem' meant that Wood's nomination was rapidly scotched. President Clinton did fulfil his promise to appoint a woman as Attorney-General; notably, as a never-married woman without children, Janet Reno was immune from 'the nanny problem'.

What is the pertinence of this sorry tale to the issue at hand? As Walzer argues in his chapter on 'Office', there is an appropriate range of relevant qualities for any office, and justice requires that selection committees take care not to consider irrelevant characteristics: 'abilities that won't be used on the job, personal characteristics that won't affect performance, and political affiliations and group identifications beyond citizenship itself' (*Spheres*, 145–6). But Wood was deprived, on account of her sex and parental status, of the opportunity to compete on fair terms for the

---

[7] *New York Times* (2 Feb. 1993), A15.

office she sought; her relevant merits were drowned out by the likelihood of entirely undeserved 'bad publicity'. The child-care problem she (and Baird) encountered is quintessentially a problem faced by wives or mothers who also seek positions of political (or indeed other) influence. Professional and highly paid women are by no means immune from the inequitable distribution of family work, of which I shall say more later. Men who are husbands and fathers, and who seek political office, are far more likely than women office-seekers to have spouses who support their aspirations in innumerable ways, material and non-material; thus they are far less likely to be encumbered by 'nanny problems'. Moreover, unlike the women who aspire to high office, their image is often enhanced by their being 'family men'. Very rarely is it asked of *them*, how can they have both families and high-powered careers?[8]

As I have suggested, Walzer clearly perceives this problem, which is still endemic to our gendered society. At one point, he signals the extent to which women are still excluded from 'the sphere of recognition as it is currently constituted' and, as I have mentioned, he calls for reform of the family so as to separate, as complex equality requires, any imbalances of power within it from the sphere of office (*Spheres*, 252, 240–1). Unfortunately, though, his suggestions as to what might be done about this are not developed in any detail. He rejects as 'degrading' one of the possible solutions that a less egalitarian thinker might turn to—the hiring of domestic servants to care for the homes and children of those who could afford them, enabling the women who would otherwise be doing most of this work to enter professions, including politics. He also disapproves of daycare, calling it the 'abandon[ment of children] to bureaucratic rearing', and remarking that the communal care of young children is 'likely to result in a great loss of love', except in a small, close-knit society such as the kibbutz (*Spheres*, 52, 179–80, 233 n., 238).[9]

How, then, *does* he think the work that is now almost entirely done by women within the household would be done in a society

---

[8] Emily Stoper, 'Wife and Politician: Role Strain among Women in Public Office', in M. Githens and J. Prestage (eds.), *A Portrait of Marginality* (New York: Longman, 1977), 320–38.

[9] Parts of this and the next paragraph are paraphrased from my arguments in *Justice, Gender, and the Family*, 114–17.

that aims to preserve justice between the sexes? He spends very little time on this, but what he does say is quite revealing. First, society's hard, and especially its dirty, work should be shared—'at least in some partial and symbolic sense, we will all have to do it'—and he stresses the special importance of such sharing within households. Second, though only in a footnote, he suggests that there is no reason parents should not share in caring for their children (*Spheres*, 174–5, 233 n.). While I disagree strongly with Walzer's dismissal of the value of daycare—I think daycare differs just about as much in quality as care by individual parents—I think that his quickly held-out solutions do constitute part of the way in which the injustices of the gender-structured family can be done away with. The sharing he suggests, so long as it is complete and real, not just 'partial and symbolic', is necessary (though not sufficient) if Walzer's separate spheres criterion for justice is to be met, if the inequalities of families are not to carry over into all the other spheres, including the crucial sphere of political power. But, given the history of gender, we know that equality between the sexes, whether within or outside of families, is simply unlikely to happen. Only legal, political, and social changes can bring it about.

WHY MUST WOMEN BE PRESENT IN POLITICS?

I shall now consider why it is such an important matter of justice that women share in political office, both appointed and elected, and that they not only be women, but women many of whom have had the experience of raising children in a fairly 'hands-on' way, as well as at least some who have had the experience of juggling paid work and the demands of family without vast quantities of paid help.[10] We first need to consider, in a general way, what it really takes to be able to 'represent' someone effectively. There have been many answers to this question put forward by scholars of politics, though until fairly recently they have been mainly concerned not with the actual members of supposedly representative bodies, but with who needed to have the right to *vote*, in order for a legislature to be representative. After all, it has been only in the twenti-

---

[10] Ideally, of course, we should also have in office men who have been equal or primary participants in their children's rearing, but so far such men are very rare.

eth century that most countries have given up the myth that legislators elected by the upper or middle classes could represent the
interests of the working class. Still, even those who have found
unacceptable the representation of one class by members elected by
another have often found nothing wrong with women's being represented by members elected by men.[11]

These days, few people would defend the position that some categories of people can adequately be represented without having the
right to vote. Certainly, in *Spheres*, Walzer condemns as quite
unacceptable in a democracy the situation existing throughout
much of Europe in the late twentieth century, in which long-resi-
dent 'guest workers' are denied citizenship, and with it political
rights. He writes: 'The determination of aliens and guests by an
exclusive band of citizens (or of slaves by masters, or women by
men, or blacks by whites, or conquered peoples by their con-
querors) is not communal freedom but oppression' (*Spheres*, 62).
But with the first issue of representation, 'Who needs the vote?' settled, the next arises: 'Who is able to get elected?' For having the
right to vote, or even actually voting, though related to being represented, surely does not necessarily ensure it. As we have noted,
the situation common to many liberal democracies now is that all
adult citizens, male and female, rich, middle class, and poor, have
the right to vote, but the members of the legislatures they elect are
overwhelmingly comprised of fairly or very well-off, highly educated, middle-aged or older, white men.

Numerous radical critics of modern liberal democracies have
charged them with being, in effect, oligarchies, on account of the
class membership of their legislators and other office-holders. But
most of these critics have had nothing to say about the extraordi-
narily low numbers of women present in their governments.
Thinkers who have not considered that members of one *class* could
adequately represent members of another have, then, not usually

[11] James Mill argued in his *Essay on Government* (1820) that broadening the suffrage was essential, because human nature was such that people tend to exploit each
other whenever possible and that government therefore must be broadly representative. Yet he went on to say that women could safely be represented by men,
because husbands and fathers could be relied upon to protect the interests of their
female relatives. Equally convinced that *women's* suffrage was a question entirely
separate from democracy, Thomas Jefferson said, at the time of the founding of the
USA: 'Were our state a pure democracy there would still be excluded from our
deliberations women, who to prevent depravation of morals and ambiguity of
issues, should not mix promiscuously in gatherings of men.'

applied the same reasoning to sex. Sometimes it is because of the lingering idealized vision of families as having but a single interest. This myth operates, in some cases, to make people think that the underrepresentation of women is less serious than the underrepresentation of those of a minority race. Very recently, in a review article about Thurgood Marshall, I found a comparison between him and his perspective on the kinds of issues that come before the Court, and that of the most recent appointee to the Court, and its second female member ever, Justice Ruth Bader Ginsburg. Ginsburg's career has largely been devoted to combating sex discrimination, much as Marshall's was to combating racial discrimination. But in spite of their similar commitments to battles against discrimination, the reviewer said:

Sitting around the conference table with the other justices, she will be much likelier than Marshall to be proceeding from the same basic assumptions about how well the society is functioning. Genuine empathy for feminism, moreover, might be easier to come by on the Supreme Court than it was for Marshall's issues: every justice has blood ties to women (two of them now *are* women), only one does to blacks.[12]

There are several odd things about this passage. One is the curious neglect of a phenomenon I shall return to later, that sometimes members of groups do little or nothing to represent the predominant interests of those groups. The sole current black Supreme Court Justice, Clarence Thomas, has rapidly accumulated a record of positions on cases that are far from favourable to most African-Americans. His very conservative politics render *his* 'blood ties' to other blacks notoriously weak when it comes to his judicial reasoning. Second, and more important for the subject at hand, masses of historical evidence shows us that the very fact of their familial ties with women has influenced many men in the direction of trying to control them as tightly as possible, and to promote their interests only in so far as this does not conflict with the perceived interests of men. The notion that men can be *relied* upon to empathize with and adequately represent women because they are the sons, fathers, and husbands of women is a widely promoted but ridiculous myth. If it were true, there would have been far fewer feminist causes to fight for.

[12] Nicholas Lemann, 'The Lawyer as Hero', *The New Republic* (13 Sept. 1993), 36.

Hanna Pitkin has said that essential to representation is 'acting in the interest of the represented, in a manner responsive [to the represented]'.[13] A strong case can be made that people with very different life experiences cannot represent each other adequately—and that this applies to men and women living in any society that places great salience on sexual difference. This is sometimes because they simply do not *see* things that are obvious from the other's point of view; sometimes because they see them very differently. Part of my own very deep conviction about this comes from my experience as a scholar who is also a woman, a feminist, and the mother of two children. When I find almost every political theorist and philosopher, from the Greeks to the present, at the same time assuming and ignoring virtually all of the work that women do, or else taking it for granted that the division of labour and inequality between the sexes is natural, I, like many other feminist scholars, notice it. But generations of male scholars, and even the occasional male-identified female scholar, simply did not, or chose not to, take any notice.[14] This kind of disregard, unconscious though it may be, seems to me the very opposite of the 'responsiveness' that is needed for representation.

I would like now to try to schematize some of the reasons why justice requires that the percentage of women elected to political office be more or less proportional to the percentage of women in the population. I shall suggest three reasons, both pointing out

---

[13] *The Concept of Representation* (Berkeley, Calif.: The Univ. of California Press, 1967), 209.

[14] The scholarly neglect of women's work is by no means a thing of the past. An article I read fairly recently about the post-divorce economic situations of families rested on the assumption that a family with one parent and two small children could live on less income than a family with two parents and two small children. Taking care of children is costly, either in time or money or both. A two-parent family has the option of one parent's staying home to take care of the children while the other earns the family's income, or both parents' working, and using some of that combined income to pay for child care. The single parent is in a very different situation: in order to earn, he or (usually) she must pay for daycare, which may consume a very large proportion of her earnings. In order to take care of her children costlessly (in terms of money, that is to say), she must forgo wagework. *Because* her family has one fewer member, it requires more income, because each adult member of a family is, potentially at least, an asset, in terms of work—paid or unpaid—whereas each child is, financially and in terms of time, a cost. This is just one small example, typical however, of mistakes in many fields that arise from the simultaneous assumption and neglect of a great deal of the work that women do.

possible objections to them and commenting on the extent to which I think they are valid, and why.[15]

First, the unequal representation of the sexes is particularly unjust in the sphere of politics because of the enormous impact of political power on other spheres of our lives. As Walzer puts it, political power 'is not simply one among the goods that men and women pursue; as *state power*, it is also the means by which all the different pursuits, including that of power itself, are regulated'. Those with political power can (and do) allow or prohibit, spend or withhold, regulate, redistribute, facilitate, or block—in areas of our lives crucial to us all.[16] Thus the gross underrepresentation of women in the ranks of the politically powerful in nearly all liberal democracies constitutes a distinct injustice. It seems clear, on the face of it, given that women vote in approximately the same numbers as men, and that they have just as many interests (counting both self-interests and other-regarding interests), that, when they hold high political office in far smaller proportions than men, complex equality is being violated. As Anne Phillips puts it: 'The obstacles that deny certain people the chance of election are as undemocratic in their way as the laws that once excluded them from the right to vote.'[17]

Some have argued, in response to such charges of injustice, that the absence or relative absence of women from various occupations, including politics, might be simply a matter of women's preference for doing other things, but several facts undermine this theory. First, as I have already suggested and shall return to later, the family obligations assumed by women are a considerable impediment to gaining and holding high-level political office. Second, it is notoriously more difficult for women to raise money when running for office (a fact of far greater importance in some countries, like the USA, than in others, where campaign spending is better controlled).[18] Third, women were still excluded from many

---

[15] The discussion in the next few paragraphs draws on arguments made by Anne Phillips, in *Engendering Democracy* (Cambridge: Polity Press, 1991), and by Helga Maria Hernes, in *Welfare State and Woman Power* (Oslo: Norwegian Univ. Press, 1987).

[16] For Walzer's arguments that political power is 'the most significant and dangerous form that power can take', see *Spheres*, ch. 12, esp. pp. 281–5.

[17] *Engendering Democracy*, 65.

[18] See e.g. 'Women's Campaigns Fueled Mostly by Women's Checks', *Congressional Quarterly Weekly Report* (17 Oct. 1992), 3269–73.

of the relevant occupations, or their necessary educational and training programmes, within living memory.[19] Fourth, there is still a great deal of discrimination against women in the professions and in other traditionally male occupations that are often the launching pads for successful political careers. These four factors considerably weaken the argument that women simply *prefer* to opt out of powerful positions, whether in or outside of politics. In both cases, injustice, rather than choice, has to provide at least a large part of the explanation. Complex equality is being violated, since women's less advantaged position in the spheres of both family and workplace is undercutting their opportunity for fair representation in politics.

Second, women's image—as well as women's interests—suffers from the scarcity of women in positions of political power. As Virginia Sapiro writes: 'Women and men continue to think of politics as a male domain because the empirical truth at this moment is that politics *is* a male domain. People of both sexes find governance by women odd, remarkable, extraordinary, and even inappropriate.'[20] It seems likely that the presence of substantial instead of token numbers of women in a legislature or on a high court would change some of the ways in which other women are perceived and treated. Walzer refers briefly to this type of claim, as 'a strong argument' for the democratic allocation of political power—the argument from respect, it might be called. 'There is, indeed,' he says, 'a prudential argument for democracy: that the different companies of men and women will most likely be respected if all the members of all the companies share political power' (*Spheres*, 284). Even if women in office do not in every way resemble most women, surely their very public presence there, as women, is likely to lessen the occasions on which women are made to look or sound ridiculous in advertising, to be seen primarily as sexual objects, and so on? And surely women in high political office, like women in influential positions in other professions, also serve as important role models for other women, who are

[19] Prominent examples of this are Harvard Law School, which did not admit female students until 1953, and did not allow anyone to study part-time until 1989; and Cambridge University, whose formal conferral of degrees on women post-dates the Second World War. On this subject see e.g. Virginia Woolf, *Three Guineas* (London: Harcourt Brace Jovanovich, 1938).

[20] Virginia Sapiro, 'When are Interests Interesting? The Problem of Political Representation of Women', *American Political Science Review*, 75 (1981), 701–16.

otherwise likely to assume that it is pointless to aspire to such positions? In this respect too, complex equality is currently violated, to the extent that women's underrepresentation in politics affects perceptions of them in many other spheres of life.

The third and most radical argument is, as Anne Phillips has expressed it, 'that men and women are in conflict and that it is nonsense to see women as represented by men'.[21] Like Phillips, I think that, in its most bald form, the claim is misguided, but I agree with a modified form of it. The bald form has two serious weaknesses. One is that it is both simplistic and false to imply that men and women are in conflict about *everything*. There are some apparently 'women's issues', of which one of the most obvious is abortion, on which some women and men disagree very strongly with other women and men. On such issues, it makes no sense to say that only women can represent women, if what is meant by that is 'represent the views or opinions of all women'. The other weakness of the 'total conflict' claim is that there are some men in high-level politics who are enthusiastic and reliable supporters of causes that have benefited women and, on the other hand, there are some women in high political office who have little or no concern about issues of great importance to many women. (Margaret Thatcher's decision, as Secretary of State for Education to cut out free milk for children at primary school is one striking example.)

What this reveals about the importance of women's proportionate *presence* in the various spheres of political life is that when female politicians are in a small minority, they are often unwilling to speak 'for women', or to be seen as associated with what they perceive as 'women's issues'. One reason for this is the desperate attempt some such women make to assimilate to the male norm, sometimes called 'Uncle Tomism'. Nancy Kassebaum, one of only two women then in the US Senate said, a few years ago, that she describes herself 'not as a woman senator, but as a United States senator'.[22] The reluctance of some women politicians to espouse

---

[21] *Engendering Democracy*, 63.

[22] Quoted in *Radcliffe News* (summer 1992), 4–5. Unfortunately, this type of behaviour is not irrational since 'there is evidence that a woman's desire to represent women, if voiced, would be a drawback in campaign politics. In a recent experimental study, a pro-equal rights male defeats an anti-equal rights male by 28 percentage points, but a man who says nothing on the subject defeats a woman who runs as a representative of women by 32 percentage points.' Sapiro, 'When are Interests Interesting?', 711.

women's issues (or, as in this case, even to be willing to identify themselves as women) appears to change in a positive direction when they are not in such a small minority. Again, though male and female politicians do not divide neatly on how they stand on issues, even those of particular concern to women, it seems that the women are more prepared to stake political capital on such issues than the men who also support them. An example of this happened recently in the US Congress, where a bipartisan group of pro-choice women members coalesced to make their support for President Clinton's health-care reform dependent on its including the availability of government-financed abortions and the equal treatment of women's with men's health concerns.[23] Some of the pro-choice men in Congress expressed support, but did not join them in taking a firm stand on the issue. It may well be that there is a 'numbers threshold' beyond which women are prepared to speak up for the interests of their sex.[24] It seems wise to conclude, with Phillips: 'Getting more women elected may be a necessary but is certainly not a sufficient condition for the success of policies that favor women.'[25]

The modified version of the claim that the conflict between men and women renders it 'nonsense' to regard men as the representatives of women is this: that women need to be *present* in high-level politics, and not simply to have their interests represented by men, both because they do have some distinct interests, as women, and because their experience as women can bring a different perspective to bear on many issues.[26] Very few men have much experience of the day-to-day care of young children, the sick or handicapped, or the old; far fewer men than women have been raped or subjected to serious domestic violence; no man has ever been pregnant, whether intentionally or not; few men have had to juggle the demands of wagework and parenthood to the extent that many women do; few men are single parents (especially single parents living in poverty); comparatively few have been sexually harassed. The list, of course, could be much longer. The point is that a vast number of issues that legislatures, high courts, and executive

---

[23] *San Francisco Chronicle* (14 Sept. 1993).   [24] *Engendering Democracy*, 70.
[25] Ibid. 70. Sapiro comes to the same conclusion in 'When are Interests Interesting?', 712.
[26] This modified version is argued both implicitly, and sometimes quite explicitly, in Phillips's *Engendering Democracy*. See e.g. pp. 65–6. On women's distinct interests, see also Sapiro, 'What Makes Interests Interesting?', 703–4.

branches of governments make decisions about every day are experienced very differently by most women than they are by most men. Many of them, indeed, are experienced differently *because* of decisions that have been made in the political realm. Of course, because of the extent of class, race, occupational, and sexual-orientation biases that also exist in most, if not all, liberal democracies, the women who reach the top levels of politics are, in some of the above-mentioned respects, not representative of *all* women. But they are, at least in some respects, more likely to be able to represent them than men are. In sum, we do not even need a very precise definition of 'representation' to argue that women are not nearly equally represented in most liberal democracies, and that complex equality is seriously violated by this situation.

WHY ARE WOMEN SO UNDERREPRESENTED AND WHAT IS TO BE DONE ABOUT IT?

How can we try to ensure that women are more proportionately represented in politics—to alleviate the injustice of the male domination of political life, to use Walzerian terms? We have seen that complex equality is a far-off dream in most liberal democracies for women, whose inequalities within the other spheres of their lives clearly extend themselves into the crucially important sphere of political power. While carefully arguing for complex equality, Walzer does not give much guidance about what we are to do about its violations. Are we to try to erect barriers between spheres, so as to prevent monopolies from transgressing the lines between them? If this fails, or proves unfeasible, are we to intervene within spheres, to try to reduce or eliminate the monopolies that seem unable to be contained? Let us take a look at the potential of each tactic as a way to alleviate the political domination of women by men.

First, I should stress that I do not think there are any easy or quick solutions. We need to take two basic approaches, since there are two major reasons for women's present underrepresentation: the role of gender in personal and domestic life, which spreads into the spheres of both wagework and politics, and the specifically *political* obstacles that women face in trying to achieve political power. Confronting the first means intervening within a sphere—

on the grounds that its inequalities seem unable to be contained. Confronting the second is more a matter of trying to block the spread of inequalities from sphere to sphere, by compensating for the disadvantages that women bring into their competition for political power.

As we have already seen, the role of gender in personal and domestic life is a major factor inhibiting women's equal political representation. This includes women's socialization, caring roles, time demands, and underrepresentation in occupations that are considered to 'qualify' one for political office. It includes the widespread expectation that they will move in order to promote their husbands' careers but that the reverse is an aberration, public (especially media) attitudes about mothers with careers, especially careers in politics, and so on. Married women, especially those with children, are less likely to be engaged in continuous or full-time wagework than are men, but numerous studies have shown that, in the USA at least, in heterosexual households where both adults work full-time, the woman does, on average, at least twice as much of the unpaid 'family work' as the man does.[27]

It is important to note here that not only do women tend to have less time, which is of course crucial to high-level political involvement, but that the demands on women's time—especially as parents and carers for the sick or elderly—are less predictable than the demands on men's time. Even in occupations with relatively flexible hours, it makes an enormous difference being the one who almost always drops everything and runs off to deal with some emergency, whether a child's illness or a broken pipe. Many male politicians have wives who are full-time home-makers, or who adjust the hours and other demands of their work to the needs of their husbands' political careers. But very few female politicians are endowed with similar husbands. Indeed, it was disturbing to read in the *New York Times* US Senator Diane Feinstein's claim that she cannot get her husband to stop leaving his wet towels on

[27] See e.g. Barbara Bergmann, *The Economic Emergence of Women* (New York: Basic Books, 1986), ch. 11; Suzanne M. Bianchi and Daphne Spain, *American Women in Transition* (New York: Russell Sage, 1986), 213–40; Philip Blumstein and Pepper Schwartz, *American Couples* (New York: Morrow, 1983), 144–8; Kathleen Gerson, *Hard Choices: How Women Decide about Work, Career, and Motherhood* (Berkeley, Calif.: Univ. of Calif. Press, 1985), 170; Arlie Hochschild, *The Second Shift: Working Parents and the Revolution at Home* (New York: Viking, 1989).

the floor.[28] Of course, she *could* get him to stop; if she never picked them up, he would start to fall over them, and would eventually find he had nothing to dry himself with. But it is one of women's unfortunate burdens from the past that they often still consider themselves responsible for taking care of other people for no good reason, when these others are perfectly able (though they may not be perfectly willing) to take care of themselves.

Thus unequal gender practices and expectations within households, founded on traditional notions of differences between the sexes, translate into inequality in the spheres of both the workplace and political life, greatly inhibiting the extent of equality that women in liberal democracies have been able to achieve in these spheres. I have argued at some length, in *Justice, Gender, and the Family*, that there is a cyclical process at work, reinforcing the dominance of men over women, from home to the workplace to the political arena, and thence back home, only to start all over again. Anne Phillips and Carole Pateman are two among many feminist political theorists who have developed this point.[29] The implication for women in politics has been put strongly by British politician, Shirley Williams, who said that until there is 'a revolution in shared responsibilities for the family, in child care and in child rearing', there will not be 'more than a very small number of women . . . opting for a job as demanding as politics'.[30]

In order to fix this part of the problem of women's political inequality, we need to keep trying to break down the division of labour between the sexes, and to rethink and reorder (though not eliminate) the public/private dichotomy. Of course, different public policies in different liberal democracies—especially those having to do with such things as child-care provisions, working hours, and various aspects of family law—make it in some places more and in others less easy for their citizens to alter the traditional division of labour.

But there is a chicken-and-egg problem here. How are we going to get these changes to happen until there are more women— including women whose lives are more representative of women's

---

[28] Marion Burres, 'Even Women at Top Still Have Floors to Do', *New York Times* (31 May 1993), A11.

[29] Phillips, *Engendering Democracy*, esp. 95–101; Pateman, *The Sexual Contract* (Stanford, Calif.: Stanford Univ. Press, 1988), esp. ch. 6.

[30] Elizabeth Holtzman and Shirley Williams, 'Women in the Political World: Observations', *Daedalus*, 116 (1987), 25–33.

typical experiences—with political power? But how are more women going to achieve positions of political power until there has been more reduction of the inequalities in the realm of domestic life? Present inequalities in the various resources necessary for political power help to perpetuate the public and private inequalities that in turn sustain the unequal distribution of resources. Complex equality is clearly being violated, yet the changes in domestic life that might reduce the violations are not happening fast at all. This problem has led some feminist theorists, notably Iris Marion Young and Anne Phillips, to look to more directly *political* ways to increase women's representation.[31]

This is a response to the other reason for women's underrepresentation in politics in most liberal democracies: the political obstacles, in the more conventional sense of the word. This includes election procedures, and those whom Anne Phillips refers to as the 'male selectorates who guard the gateways to political life'.[32] The recognition of these problems leads to the advocacy of solutions that, though they would be considered extremely controversial—virtually unthinkable—in some countries, are already practised with some success in others. What I am referring to is the development of mechanisms at various stages of the selection and electoral processes, which take account of present differences between the sexes, and gender inequality, and thus 'ensure a new proportionality between the sexes in those arenas within which political decisions are made'.[33] Phillips's advocacy of such measures results from her conviction, based on a number of studies, that political factors in themselves have a great deal of effect on the extent of women's presence in politics. She makes it clear, however, that she regards the adoption of such mechanisms as a temporary (though probably long-term temporary) measure: 'I regard the emphasis on sexual differentiation as necessary, but transitional, for I do not want a world in which women have to speak continually as women—or men are left to speak as men.'[34] Indeed, her eventual

---

[31] Phillips, *Engendering Democracy*, esp. ch. 3; Iris Marion Young, 'Polity and Group Difference: A Critique of the Ideal of Universal Citizenship', *Ethics*, 99 (1988–9), 250–74, and *Justice and the Politics of Difference* (Princeton, NJ, Princeton Univ. Press, 1990).

[32] Phillips, *Engendering Democracy*, 80.   [33] Ibid. 7.

[34] Ibid. She adds, however: 'each of us knows that [this transition] will last out our life'.

aim, like mine, is to achieve a world in which sexual difference is of virtually no political or social significance.

Before we look at the various mechanisms that might facilitate the better representation of women as a group, it is important to mention two problems with the general idea of group representation. One is that people belong to many groups, have many aspects to their identity—sex, class, religion, ethnicity, and so on—and often it is not clear that any one of them is definitive of the person. Even if this were not so, there might still be cause for concern that such group representatives might think of themselves as representing *only* those groups. Do we not expect, or at least hope, that our representatives, while representing us, also try to think and act out of more general concern? As Phillips says, this latter concern is less of a real problem with women, who form a majority of the population in most liberal democracies and who have a wide range of opinions and interests, than it is with special-interest groups representing small numbers of people.[35] Also, women's interests are often closely connected with those of children, and thus they represent the welfare of a significant majority of the population.[36]

What, then, are some of the specifically political mechanisms that facilitate the more proportionate representation of women? One is proportional representation, in its various forms.[37] Non-PR systems, with single-member constituencies, favour those popularly perceived as 'less risky' choices—the kinds of politicians people are used to. But faced with a multi-member constituency, with a number of candidates to vote for, people are more likely to go for some of the 'riskier' ones; if they do not, as Phillips says, 'it begins to look odd if they are all of them the same'.[38] The same is likely to happen with the party list version of proportional representation, where the electoral district is a multi-member one, the party ranks

---

[35] Phillips, *Engendering Democracy*, 69.

[36] On this, see also Okin, *Justice, Gender, and the Family*, esp. chs. 1, 7, and 8.

[37] It is noteworthy that a recent book, which compares PR of various kinds with other electoral systems, has no index entries for class, race, religion, ethnicity, gender, or women. Instead of being concerned with how well-represented members of such groups are under different electoral systems, it is preoccupied with the extent to which political parties are proportionately represented, as well as with other issues, such as governmental stability. Rein Taagepera and Matthew Soberg Shugart, *Seats and Votes: The Effects and Determinants of Electoral Systems* (New Haven, Conn.: Yale Univ. Press, 1989).

[38] Phillips, *Engineering Democracy*, 80.

its chosen list of candidates and the voter chooses a party rather than a person. All else being equal, and especially if the parties are even-handed in choosing and ranking candidates of both sexes, this can increase the numbers of women elected. It can help to make legislatures more representative of their electorates, in other ways too—race, religion, ethnicity, class, and sexual orientation.[39]

Recalling some of the statistics I cited earlier can help us to see that there is a fairly strong, though not absolute, correlation between proportional representation and the proportional representation of *women*. There are some countries without PR, such as Canada and New Zealand, that have much higher percentages of women in their parliaments than some with PR, such as Israel. Nevertheless, a cross-national study done by Pippa Norris of twenty-four liberal democracies, published in 1985, showed that the election of women was strikingly more closely correlated with PR than with other factors, such as attitudes about sexual equality and socio-economic differences between the sexes.[40] And all of the countries in which women have a strong presence in legislatures have PR with party lists, which seems to allow much more scope for equalizing the sexual composition of the legislature. While proportional representation can bring with it other problems, such as political instability, as Anne Phillips concludes: 'In terms of the "mirror" effect of reflecting the population, . . . some form of proportional representation wins hands down over first-past-the-post systems.'[41]

In the Scandinavian countries, where women have so much more presence in national politics, not only is proportional representation the rule, but most of the political parties have adopted a female quota (typically 40 per cent) of women in all elected offices within the party, and on their lists of candidates for local and national elections—much as the German SPD has recently committed itself to. What explains the fact that this has happened in just a few countries? Several explanations have been given: it is probably related to the strength of the women's organizations within the social democratic parties and to the greater focus on

[39] Ibid. P. Norris, 'Women's Legislative Participation in Western Europe', in S. Bashevkin (ed.), *Women and Politics in Western Europe* (London: Cass, 1985), E. Vallance, *Women in the House* (London: Athlone, 1979).

[40] Norris, 'Women's Participation'.

[41] Phillips, *Engendering Democracy*, 81.

traditional political power by Scandinavian feminists than those in many other countries. It may also be due in part to the fact that the strong social welfare systems of the Scandinavian countries since the Second World War have to some extent broken down the public/private dichotomy and made women's position a more explicit public concern; women were objects of public policy long before they became major makers of it in significant numbers.[42] The welfare systems of the Scandinavian countries have also lessened women's dependence on men, which is likely to have the effect of giving them more power in their private lives.[43]

Thus, the very unusual extent of women's representation in Scandinavian politics is probably caused by a mixture of the two possible solutions to their underrepresentation in other countries that we have been considering. First, in these countries the assumption by society of more of the responsibility for welfare, especially that of children, has helped to erode the public/private dichotomy and, with it, the corresponding inequality between the sexes. Second, and, as has been suggested, partly due to the effects of the first on women's political clout, specific political mechanisms have been put into place in a largely successful attempt to equalize women's representation, by blocking the spread into politics of whatever inequality remains in the other spheres.

What hope of greater political equality for women does any of this give those of us from the liberal democratic countries where women's presence at the highest levels of government is still so out of proportion to our numbers? The bad news is that the prospects of the USA or Great Britain changing its electoral systems to proportional representation or of its major political parties adopting quotas on the Scandinavian model for female candidates seem extremely unlikely.[44] If we cannot even get an Equal Rights Amendment passed, in the USA, how likely are we to get a Constitutional Amendment passed that would change the electoral

[42] This is argued in Helga Maria Hernes, 'The Welfare State Citizenship of Scandinavian Women', in K. B. Jones and A. G. Jonasdottir (eds.), *The Political Interests of Gender* (London: Sage Publications, 1988).

[43] See Okin, *Justice, Gender, and the Family*, ch. 7, for arguments about the relationship between power and economic dependence in families.

[44] The British Labour Party has recently adopted a policy whereby, when candidates are being selected for parliamentary elections, the shortlists must be made up entirely of women in half of all the marginal constituencies. However, this policy remains controversial even within the party, and it remains to be seen whether it will prove to be effective in increasing the number of women MPs.

system in order to equalize the numbers of women and men in political office (as well as making Congress 'mirror' the population more closely in other ways)? In these countries, there seems to be little concern that elected officials mirror their constituents. But the good news is that, even without any such changes, things finally seem to be changing slightly in the right direction; women *are* winning more national level elections, despite all the obstacles I have been talking about. So this most obvious, public instance of gender injustice, which is so intimately connected with many of the other, less visible, instances of it, is finally beginning to change. If the current, painfully slow changes in family responsibilities continue, it seems that we can look forward to at least some reduction of the complex inequalities that still so strongly affect the political representation of women.

7
Money and Complex Equality

JEREMY WALDRON

Money has a chapter all to itself in *Spheres of Justice*, but its importance pervades the book.[1] For money is a solvent of complex equality: an institution that enables people to cross each and all of the boundaries that Michael Walzer discerns between the distributive spheres of different goods.

Money is not the only threat to those boundaries. Nepotism is another kind of threat: in communities where nepotism flourishes, the distribution of family membership is permitted to determine the distribution of office or employment. But it is money above all that symbolizes the collapse (or absence) of boundaries between various goods, and the interpenetration of one good's meanings and those associated with others. For money represents not merely the possibility that *this* good or service will be traded for *that* good or service; such a possibility is present as soon as people grasp the concept of exchange. Money institutionalizes the idea that anything might be traded for anything, and that a given pair of traders do not even have to have in mind the particular goods they want to end up holding or enjoying as the upshot of the series of transactions they are currently initiating. To trade something for money is to put oneself in a position to deal with *anyone* in the future who might be holding *any* good one might conceivably want, provided only that such a person also relishes the opportunity to deal with others in this universe of potential traders (provided, in other words, he has reason to accept one's money).[2]

---

[1] Michael Walzer, *Spheres of Justice* (New York: Basic Books, 1983), ch. 4.

[2] The result is, in Max Weber's words, 'a tremendous extension of the area of possible exchange relationships. . . . [M]onetary calculation means that goods are not evaluated merely in terms of their immediate importance as utilities at the given time and place and for the given person only. Rather, goods are more or less systematically compared, whether for consumption or for production, with all potential future opportunities of utilization and gaining a return, including their possible

Another way of stating this is that money is an *abstract* measure of exchange value—abstracted more or less comprehensively from any of the concrete uses to which specific goods might be put or, indeed, from any particular exchange in which a specific good might feature. As such, it stands to Walzerian boundaries in a posture of utter contempt, for it embodies the very principle of their transgression. Money is indeed the universal pander—a sly, all-purpose go-between in what, on Walzer's account, are illicit dealings among goods of different spheres that properly speaking should have nothing to do with each other.[3]

THE SOCIAL MEANING OF MONEY

We must be careful how we describe the affront of money to the meanings of particular goods. One of my claims will be that the account given in *Spheres* mischaracterizes the nature and extent of money's antipathy to the integrity of social meanings. (The other claim will be that it is, bluntly, wrong to *denigrate* money on the basis of this antipathy: there is ground for celebration, not lament, in the fact that the rise of money represents the passing away of the sorts of meanings Walzer cherishes and of the primitive social, economic, and political conditions in which alone they can be sustained.)

utility to an indefinite number of other persons who can be brought into the comparison insofar as they are potential buyers. . .'. *Economy and Society*, ed. Guenther Roth and Claus Wittich, 2 vols. (Berkeley, Calif.: Univ. of Calif. Press, 1978), i. 80–1.

[3] Cf. Georg Simmel, *The Philosophy of Money*, tr. Tom Bottomore and David Frisby, 2nd enlarged edn. (London: Routledge, 1990), 385: 'Money, more than any other form of value, makes possible the secrecy, invisibility and silence of exchange. By compressing money into a piece of paper, by letting it glide into a person's hand, one can make him a wealthy person. Money's formlessness and abstractness makes it possible to invest it in the most varied and remote values and thereby to remove it completely from the gaze of neighbours. Its anonymity and colourlessness does not reveal the source from which it came to the present owner: it does not have a certificate of origin in the way in which, more or less disguised, many concrete objects of possession do.' (The immediate context of these remarks is Simmel's discussion of bribery.) According to Walzer, this slyness and secrecy is a mark of the dishonesty that attends all violations of the spheres of different goods (*Spheres*, 98). Simmel's point about anonymity was anticipated in part by Karl Marx, in *Capital*, i, tr. Ben Fowkes (Harmondsworth: Penguin Books, 1976), ch. 3, p. 205: 'Since every commodity disappears when it becomes money it is impossible to tell from the money itself how it got into the hands of its possessor, or what article has been changed into it. *Non olet*, from whatever source it may come.'

According to Walzer, the danger with money is that it tends to become what he calls a 'dominant' good—a good whose possession enables the individuals who have it to command a wide range of other goods (*Spheres*, 22). A person who has money can buy a better house, an exotic vacation, a fancy car, and well-tailored clothes; but he can also secure a better education for his children, buy a place in a privately protected community, influence the outcome of an election, change the editorial tone of a newspaper, and endow a university chair. In a market economy, powers and pleasures like these are distributed not according to any inherent meanings of their own, but in a way that patterns the existing distribution of money. Many years ago, in a criticism of such patterning—a criticism which I understand served as an inspiration for Walzer's idea of complex equality—Bernard Williams spoke about the way the meaning and distribution of a good such as health care is distorted by the influence of money:

Leaving aside preventive medicine, the proper ground of distribution of medical care is ill health: this is a necessary truth. Now in very many societies, while ill health may work as a necessary condition of receiving treatment, it does not work as a sufficient condition, since such treatment costs money, and not all who are ill have the money; hence the possession of sufficient money becomes in fact an additional necessary condition of actually receiving treatment. Yet more extravagantly, money may work as a sufficient condition by itself, without any medical need, in which case the reasons that actually operate for the receipt of this good are just totally irrelevant to its nature.[4]

In the latter case—cosmetic surgery, for example—the arts of the medical profession are prostituted to the whims of those who can find no other luxury on which to lavish their wealth. In the former case, by contrast, those in genuine need—those afflicted by disease or injury—find that their condition is no longer treated as a reason for medical care at all; the issue is always 'How much can you pay?'

So long as money is dominant, it matters tremendously who has it. It seems to be Walzer's view that, if money were confined to its own sphere and did not determine the distribution of anything else,

---

[4] 'The Idea of Equality', in his collection *Problems of the Self: Philosophical Papers 1956–1972* (Cambridge: Cambridge Univ. Press, 1973), 240. See also *Spheres*, 9 and 323 n. 7.

we would not have to worry about the maldistribution of wealth between rich and poor (*Spheres*, 107). The rich could wallow in coin and banknotes like Walt Disney's Uncle Scrooge, while the poor would enjoy a variety of social goods, each according to its meaning, to which enjoyment their lack of money would make little or no difference. I shall not attempt to evaluate this as a thesis about social justice; other contributors to this book are addressing that issue.[5] Instead, I want to discuss the conception of money which underlies Walzer's view.

Walzer believes it is important to confine money to its own sphere, and not allow it to determine who gets what other goods. In principle, however, when money is used to buy something, that is *not* to be regarded as a foray out of its own proper sphere. The social meaning of money, if it has a social meaning, is precisely that it is exchangeable for other goods. That is what money is for. Indeed, revelling in money for its own sake (as though it had its own inherent meaning), rather than using it to buy things, is what should be regarded as odd and deviant from the point of view of social meanings.

The other side of this coin (so to speak) is that it may be a mistake to regard money as *a good* (i.e. as one good among others) on a par with food, health care, education, political office, etc. I think money should be regarded as a representation of the commensurability of the meanings and values of other goods, not as a good with meaning or value in itself.

Admittedly, the matter is complicated.[6] The history of money consists in the gradual emergence of practices of regarding certain objects as nothing but symbols of exchange value and of ignoring or downplaying any intrinsic utility associated with those objects themselves. Until recently that process has been imperfect; and to the extent that it is imperfect, money-objects do have meanings of their own on a par, logically speaking, with the meanings of the goods that money can buy. If silver coin is also used routinely as jewellery, then to that extent its status as money is undeveloped and every transaction in which it is involved retains an element of barter. To buy political office with silver in those circumstances would be to commingle the social meanings of office and adornment in a direct

---

[5] See e.g. Chs. 5 and 10.
[6] There is an excellent discussion in Simmel, *Philosophy of Money*, ch. 2: 'The Value of Money as a Substance'.

way, and not only in the indirect, abstract, and symbolic manner of a specifically monetary transaction.

Today, however, we are way beyond that in our money economy. For us, coin and banknotes have almost no intrinsic value, and no meaning of their own apart from the abstract representation of potential exchange. One might, I suppose, use pennies as ballast or roll up a $20 note to snort cocaine. But when we use them *as money*, they function purely as markers of exchange value. Indeed, since the dissolution of the gold standard, they have even ceased to be markers of the exchange value of anything in particular.[7]

Certainly money is a concrete object—though some developments in the modern economy of electronic credits are taking us in the direction of treating money as an abstract representative of abstract value (as opposed to a concrete representative of abstract value). But its concreteness is uninteresting except to the extent that its particular features (the inscription 'TWENTY DOLLARS') and its provenance (having been manufactured under the auspices of the Federal Reserve Bank) connect it with currency as an official institution.[8] Ultimately what matters to us is the concreteness of the institution and the security of the guarantees it issues, not the concreteness of coins or notes as such.[9]

In one place, Walzer acknowledges that it may be wrong to say that money is a good, like other goods, which should be confined to its own sphere: 'In theory at least, free exchange creates a market through which all goods are convertible into all other goods through the neutral medium of money' (*Spheres*, 21). He thinks,

---

[7] Karl Marx, however, denies that money ever ceases to be an object in its own right. The money-commodity necessarily has a 'dual' use-value: 'Alongside its special use-value as a commodity (gold, for instance, serves to fill teeth, it forms the raw material for luxury articles, etc.), it acquires a formal use-value, arising out of its specific social function.' (*Capital*, i, ch. 2, p. 184.) On the one hand, Marx is insisting that the specific exchange-facilitating aspect of money is a *social* use-value; and on the other hand, he believes that it is only by virtue of money's being a valuable object in its own right, and on that basis susceptible to private ownership, that the social function of exchange becomes privatized in a capitalist economy. (See ibid., ch. 3, p. 229.)

[8] It ought to be significant, surely, for Walzer's account, that money—or at any rate, paper money—is a public institution, sponsored and sustained by the state.

[9] Thus when Georg Simmel writes that '[t]he activity of exchange among individuals is represented by money in a concrete, independent, and, as it were, congealed form' (*Philosophy of Money*, 176), it is the stability of the institution that is referred to, not the hardness of the coin or the resilience of the paper.

however, that the reality is radically at variance with that rather optimistic suggestion: 'Money, supposedly the neutral medium, is in practice a dominant good, and it is monopolized by people who possess a special talent for bargaining and trading—the green thumb of bourgeois society' (*Spheres*, 22). I believe Walzer is right to notice that money is not 'neutral' with regard to social meanings. But he is wrong to attribute it to money's dominance as a good in its own right. The 'neutrality theory' that he criticizes is certainly implausible. One gathers that 'neutrality' is supposed to imply that the distributions resulting from market transactions will reflect rather than undermine the social meanings of the goods that are exchanged:

For each bargain, trade, sale, and purchase will have been agreed to voluntarily by men and women who know what that meaning is, who are indeed its makers. By definition, then, no *x* will ever fall into the hands of someone who possesses *y*, merely because he possesses *y* and without regard to what *x* actually means to some other member of society. The market is radically pluralist in its operations and its outcomes, infinitely sensitive to the meanings that individuals attach to goods. (*Spheres*, 21)

The reason why this 'neutrality' view is hopeless is indicated by Walzer a few lines later when he writes: 'free exchange leaves distributions entirely in the hands of individuals, and social meanings are not subject, or are not always subject, to the interpretative decisions of individual men and women' (*Spheres*, 22). That is precisely the point: money is not a good which has begun to dominate other goods; rather money is the embodiment of the practice of individuals' transgressing the boundaries of other goods. That money is directly and necessarily corrosive of social meanings in Walzer's sense is not a matter of one good's dominating another, as opposed to remaining in the sphere of its own meaning. It is a case of social meanings being abolished altogether, and with them the spheres and boundaries that make sense of Walzer's talk of dominance and monopoly.

COMMODITIES VERSUS COMMUNAL GOODS

It is, of course, a caricature to imply that when Walzer speaks of 'the boundary to the proper sphere of money' (*Spheres*, 98), he has in mind Uncle Scrooge wallowing in his coin and forgetting that he can spend it. Instead, what Walzer seems to have in mind is that some goods can and should, and others cannot and should not, be sold or exchanged with one another.

What is the proper sphere of money? What social goods are rightly marketable? The obvious answer is also the right one; it points us to a range of goods that have probably always been marketable, whatever else has or has not been: all those objects, commodities, products, services, beyond what is communally provided, that individual men find useful or pleasing, the common stock of bazaars, emporiums, and trading posts. It includes, and probably always has included, luxuries as well as staples, goods that are beautiful as well as goods that are functional and durable. Commodities, even when they are primitive and simple are above all commodious; they are a source of comfort, warmth and security. . . . No doubt, every culture has its own characteristic set of commodities, determined by its mode of production, its social organization, and the range of its trade. But the number of commodities in every set is always large, and the standard way of sorting them is market exchange. (*Spheres*, 103–4)

What are we to make of these tautologies? First, if there is in every society a large array of goods (call them *commodities*) that can be freely traded in markets and thus exchanged back and forth for money, then those goods must be an exception to Walzer's general thesis that all goods are endowed with specific social meanings. We have already conceded Walzer's claim that market exchange dissolves the distinctness of social meanings, inasmuch as it is part of the concept of *the social meaning of a good* that it is *not* at the mercy of the sort of individual decisions that market economies involve. Commodities must therefore exist in a sphere beyond meanings—or rather, not in a sphere at all, but in a sort of vacuum that is the complement of the spheres of those goods whose meanings remain secure and distinct from one another. Talk of the sphere of money, the sphere of the market, or the sphere of commodities, is just a way of characterizing that complementarity.

What Walzer says about this contrast, between commodities, on the one hand, and goods with spheres of their own, on the other, is instructive in part for the light it casts on his conception of social meanings. Commodities, for the most part, are individualized possessions, material things; and

things are our anchors in the world. But while we all need to be anchored, we don't all need the same anchor. We are differently attached; we have

different tastes and desires; we surround ourselves, clothe ourselves, fur-
nish our homes, with a great variety of things, and we use, enjoy, and display the things we have in a great variety of ways. (*Spheres*, 104)

The implication is that where there is difference—where a culture
allows 'individual men and women to choose for themselves the
things they find useful or pleasing and to define themselves and
shape and symbolize their identities over and above the [social]
membership they share' (*Spheres*, 106)—*social* meanings are inappropriate. Where there is individual difference, commodities hold
sway.

    More subtly, Walzer says that market relations imply that there
are certain goods that do not belong to any *specific* person in virtue
of their social meaning. Although such things are private goods—
that is, although they belong at any given time to some particular
person or other—it does not really matter to whom in particular
they belong. Walzer develops this into an intriguing substantive
about the way such goods are to be distributed:

Commodities don't come with proper names attached, like packages from
a department store. The right way to possess such things is by making
them, or growing them, or somehow providing their cash equivalent for
others. . . . [M]arket morality (in, say, its Lockeian form) is a celebration
of the wanting, making, owning, and exchanging of commodities. They are
indeed widely wanted, and they have to be made if they are to be had. . . .
Things can be had only with effort; it is the effort that seems to supply the
title or, at least, the original title; and once they are owned, they can also
be exchanged. So wanting, making, owning and exchanging hang together;
they are, so to speak, commodity's modes. (*Spheres*, 104–5)

The contrast here seems to be with goods whose production is
social or communal. What is individually produced—'all those
objects, commodities, products, services, beyond what is communally provided' (*Spheres*, 103)—is, so to speak, apt for exchange.
The public provision of a good, however, has a communal or social
meaning, and that meaning must be protected and vindicated
against the vicissitudes of individuals, markets, and money. The
integrity of social meanings—and their concomitant inviolability
by individual exchange decisions—is supposed to correspond to
their social provenance. What *we* produce together has a meaning
(and thus a distributive destiny) that is *ours* (i.e. intrinsically social)
and it is not to be undermined by the hubris of any individual

trader. Only those goods that are privately produced should be left to the mercy of exchange.

Unfortunately, this contrast—between what the community provides (public goods with social meanings) and what individuals provide (mere commodities, beyond the realm of meanings)—will not work, for three reasons. First, in modern societies, public provision is seldom independent of private provision, or of the markets and commodity forms in which private goods circulate. The public provision of monumental buildings, national defence, arts endowments, roads, earthquake relief, and welfare—all of this is made possible by governments' *taxing* economic activity in the private sector. The expenditures (which themselves often take the form of contracts with private firms operating in the market-place) are made by the state in money form; the state is in a position to spend this money only because it levies taxes and raises loans (again, in the financial market-place); the taxes are paid by citizens in the form of money; and their extent and incidence is calibrated according to the extent of the market transactions in which they are engaged (sales taxes, income taxes). Money, and the market activities on which money supervenes, are implicated in public provision from start to finish.

Walzer uses the example of Civil War conscription—where the rich could purchase exemptions for $300—to illustrate how repugnant it is to have people discharge public service in cash rather than kind. 'It was a bad business in a republic, for it seemed to abolish the *public thing* and turn military service (even when the republic was at stake!) into a private transaction' (*Spheres*, 99). But this a case of the exception that proves the rule. Wartime conscription—together perhaps with jury service—is virtually the only example of the state's discharging its functions by exacting service rather than money from its citizens. Since the dawn of the modern era, states have relied for the most part on cash rather than in-kind contributions. This too is a matter of social meanings: the importance of being able to provide one's support to the state in money rather than kind is part and parcel of the modern state's emergence out of feudalism.[10]

---

[10] Weber, *Economy and Society*, ii. 964, points out that a money economy is indispensable for sustaining legal/bureaucratic administration and the sphere distinctions (e.g. between office and property) that that involves: 'According to historical experience, without a money economy the bureaucratic structure can hardly

It follows that the state, in its capacity as public provider, has an intense interest in the health of the market economy. Quite apart from concern for the individual prosperity and well-being of their constituents, political leaders know that a slump in the private economy can severely curtail their ability to deliver public goods and services.

Secondly, even for those elements of public provision that depend on citizens' services rather than citizens' money, the public aspect will seldom exhaust the meanings that are implicated in the situation. For there is also the meaning of the good or service to the individuals whose contributions it comprises—or at least the meaning to them of their contributions. The time and energy that a young Israeli has to devote to compulsory military service may have one meaning for the society; but few young people in Israel are so single-mindedly patriotic that the official meaning would wholly coincide with the meaning of that time and effort *for them*.

Partisans of the state's view may protest that the public meaning, in this case, represents also the intrinsic meaning of the good. To this, however, we may respond as Robert Nozick responded to Bernard Williams's original point about health care:

Williams says (it is a necessary truth that) the only proper criterion for the distribution of medical care is medical need. Presumably, then, the only proper criterion for the distribution of barbering services is barbering need. But why must the internal goal of the activity take precedence over, for example, the person's particular purpose in performing the activity? . . . If someone becomes a barber because he likes talking to a variety of different people, and so on, is it unjust of him to allocate his services to those he most likes to talk to?[11]

Nozick's point is that what we call the 'internal goal' of an activity should not necessarily have priority over the contingent goals

avoid undergoing substantial internal changes, or indeed transformation into another structure. The allocation of fixed income in kind from the magazines of the lord or from his current intake—which has been the rule in Egypt and China for millennia and played an important part in the later Roman monarchy as well—easily means a first step toward appropriation of the sources of taxation by the official and their exploitation as private property.'

[11] Robert Nozick, *Anarchy, State and Utopia* (Oxford: Basil Blackwell, 1974), 234. Walzer responds only in part to these points in *Spheres*. He argues (p. 88 n.) that there might be societies in which haircuts mattered so much that the communal provision of barbering services based on barbering need *would* be morally required. But he does not address the point about the separate meanings that such provision might have for the barbers.

of the individuals who engage in the activity. Individuals create meanings of their own for their lives and agency. Since almost all state activities depend upon individual activities, whether in kind or through money—a point, by the way, which is *not* undercut by the truth of the converse proposition—it follows that almost any form of public provision is likely to engage conflicts of meaning as between the purpose aimed at in the public provision as such and aims which are nurtured by the individuals who find themselves having to contribute, one way or another, to the fulfilment of these public purposes.

I am not trying to make the conservative or libertarian point that it is always wrong to override individual meanings for the sake of social meanings. Maybe the careerist meaning for an ambitious young Israeli of those three years from age 18 to 21 *should* be over-ridden by their social meaning as potential contributions to national self-defence. I do want to insist, though, that these conflicts can only be settled by political argument not definitional fiat. It is this point, I think, that Walzer misses. Although he acknowledges there are sometimes hard choices to be made, he believes nevertheless that certain individual goods and services simply *belong* to the society as a matter of social definition. '[A]t some level of taxation, if not necessarily at prevailing levels, the political community can't be said to invade the sphere of money; it merely claims its own' (*Spheres*, 120). I do not share this confidence that, at some point, social and individual meanings disentangle themselves into neat and unequivocal principles of distribution.

The points just made have to do with the character of one's contribution to public provision. A third point has to do with the meaning of what is provided. Sometimes what we provide collectively, as a state or as a public, are goods which differ in kind from market goods. They may be contingent public goods like roads, monuments, and national defence, or they may be inherent public goods like culture or language.[12] This is not true, though, of all or even most government provision. Many of the goods that modern governments provide count as private goods—goods that might practicably be (and in fact ordinarily are) produced privately and enjoyed or consumed privately. If the government provides housing for poor families, for example, it is providing for them the very

---

[12] For the idea of contingent and inherent public goods, see Joseph Raz, *The Morality of Freedom* (Oxford: Clarendon Press, 1986), 198–203.

good that most people provide privately for themselves on the basis of market activity. It is not part of the ethos of housing provision that people should not need to provide this good for themselves. (Even modern socialists do not look askance at private housing in the way some of them look askance at, say, private education.) On the contrary, welfare provision, particularly in the USA, is predicated on the hope and expectation that *most* families will be able to provide this good for themselves on a market basis, that those who are currently receiving public assistance will not need it for long, and that interim public provision is necessary, at most, only to ensure that every family is housed on *some* basis or other.

If this is true, then the general claim which we are considering in this section—concerning the distinctive meaning of communally provided goods and concerning the link between such social meanings and distributive principles—must be abandoned. What is evident in the case of housing (and I think also in most other cases of welfare provision) is that the fact of *our* aiming *collectively* at a certain distribution—e.g. housing for every family—is not matched by any sense that the good in question, namely housing, *has* to have a communal rather than a market character. The distributive principle to which we give our allegiance in cases like this is determined more by our sense of people's *need* for the sort of good in question, rather than by any sense of the meaning of the good itself or that that meaning should dictate the basis on which the good is provided.

BLOCKED EXCHANGES

So far I have criticized Walzer's abstract account of 'the proper sphere of money'. He appears to be on slightly firmer ground when he presents a concrete list of what he calls 'blocked exchanges', things that are not to be traded for money, 'limits', as he puts it, 'on the dominance of wealth' (*Spheres*, 100).[13]

The list of goods whose social meanings are said to preclude their being exchanged for money, comprises the following: (1) human beings; (2) political power; (3) judicial decisions and legal

---

[13] For a helpful discussion, see Ch. 8 by Judith Andre.

services; (4) basic liberties, like the freedoms of speech, press, religion, and assembly; (5) marriage and procreation rights; (6) the right to emigrate; (7) exemptions from military service, jury duty, and other forms of communally imposed work; (8) political office and professional standing; (9) basic state services like police protection and primary and secondary education; (10) anything, when the exchange is born of desperation; (11) prizes and honours; (12) divine grace; (13) love and friendship; and (14) anything whose sale, existence, or possession is illegal.[14]

It is difficult to imagine anyone reading this list and remaining sceptical about Gilbert Ryle's notion of a 'category mistake'.[15] It is supposed to be a list of *goods*, each of which has a social meaning of its own and a concomitant distributive principle that would be distorted or undermined if its exchange for money were permitted. Many of the items, however, are better understood as rights. Now Walzer suggests at the beginning of this part of his discussion that rights may never be sold for money: rights 'stand outside the cash nexus' and are 'proof against sale and purchase' (*Spheres*, 100). But he cannot mean this as a general proposition. 'Inalienable rights' is not a redundancy; property rights are the obvious exception; and legal theorists spend a lot of time studying which sorts of rights can be dealt with on a market basis and which cannot.[16] I think we can assume that he means to refer to constitutional rights. But though he describes the American Bill of Rights as 'a series of blocked exchanges' (*Spheres*, 100), it is surely more sensible to regard it simply as a list of actions that must not be performed by the government, whether that performance is elicited by money or not. The wording of the First Amendment, after all, is not 'Congress shall not accept money as an inducement for abridging the freedom of speech'; it is, 'Congress shall make no law abridging the freedom of speech.' (I shall return to this point in the next section.)

---

[14] The list is found at *Spheres*, 100–3. Walzer notes (p. 100) that in many ways it mirrors the topics of the other chapters of the book.

[15] See his *The Concept of Mind* (London: Hutchinson, 1949).

[16] For four approaches which testify in different ways to the complexity of the issue about the marketability of rights, see: Guido Calabresi and Douglas Melamed, 'Property Rules, Liability Rules and Inalienability: One View of the Cathedral', *Harvard Law Review*, 85 (1972), 1089–1128; Richard Tuck, *Natural Rights Theories: Their Origin and Development* (Cambridge: Cambridge Univ. Press, 1979); Diana Meyers, *Inalienable Rights: A Defense* (New York: Columbia Univ. Press, 1985); and Margaret Jane Radin, 'Market-Inalienability', *Harvard Law Review*, 100 (1987), 1849–1937.

Sometimes what an item's presence on Walzer's list of blocked exchanges connotes is that rights of certain imaginable kinds— particularly certain Hohfeldian privileges—are not to be brought into existence. When Walzer says, for example, that one 'cannot purchase a license for polygamy' (*Spheres*, 101), his point is surely not that licences for polygamy have their own social meaning and must be distributed accordingly; it is rather that there are to be no licences for polygamy. Similarly, when he says that 'exemptions from military service, from jury duty, and from any other form of communally imposed work cannot be sold' (ibid.), he is not saying that these goods (exemptions) are to be gained by other means, in the way (for example) that love and friendship are gained; but rather that for the most part these exemptions should not exist at all.

Conversely, for some of the other items on the list, the point is not that certain things must not be bought or sold, but that a level of minimum provision is to be assured. This must be what Walzer means, for example, when he says that the services of defence attorneys are not for sale, or when he includes police protection or education on the list.

In one case at least, the nature, meaning, or existence of goods or rights is not what is in question at all. The ban on 'desperate exchanges' is a ban that presumably applies to *all* goods; the ban is triggered by the spirit and motivation of the exchange transaction, not by the meaning of the good that is in question. I do not question the idea that 'trades of last resort' need special scrutiny and may be coercive; but it is odd to find them on a list of goods that are supposed to have a sphere of their own. Maybe Walzer means to refer to the subsistence goods that are likely to be the subject-matter of desperate exchanges. But here we come up against the point I made at the end of the previous section. Goods like food, clothing, and shelter are, for most people, readily obtained in the market-place and quite properly obtained in that way. It is only when someone is in desperate straits that we are worried about the trade-offs she might make to secure these goods. The goods themselves do not have a sphere apart from the market.

The final heading on Walzer's list—'criminal sales'—is a particularly bewildering rubric, under which we are given a number of disparate examples: blackmail, heroin, fraudulently described goods, adulterated milk, guns, unsafe cars, murder contracts. No purpose is served by this conglomeration. Sometimes it is certain ways of doing business that are referred to (fraudulently described goods); sometimes it is matters of quality (unsafe cars, adulterated milk); sometimes it is genuine contraband (drugs, guns); sometimes it is prohibited actions (murder contracts); and sometimes it is transactions (like blackmail) whose logical category, for these purposes, remains a matter of academic dispute.

The only uniting principle for item (14) seems to be that the boundaries of the 'goods' in question are patrolled by the law. That raises a broader issue: how are the *other* exchanges on the list blocked? The main list conceals a disconcerting variety of answers. Sometimes the answer, even for items other than those grouped under heading (14), is the law (together, presumably, with the social norms that the law reflects)—the ban on buying and selling slaves or political favours, for instance.

In other cases, legal blocks seem irrelevant: 'Sex is for sale, but the sale does not make for a meaningful relationship' (*Spheres*, 103). The point here seems to be that, whether or not there is a legal ban on prostitution, one *cannot* buy love or friendship, in some psychosocial rather than normative sense of 'cannot'. Now if the point is that it simply cannot be done, then one is left unclear about what, exactly, is wrong with trying and why some sort of Johnsonian refutation—'We thought it could not be done, but look, it turns out that it can'—would be precluded. What mistake are people making in seeking their own standards of meaningfulness through exchange?

The response may be that life in a community involves sharing certain social and cultural meanings with one another. To attempt, for example, to court love with money would be to show that one did not understand the world one had in common with the person one was pursuing. Certainly, that *may* turn out to be the case. My point about Johnsonian refutation, however, is that in fact we live in a community many of whose meanings and boundaries are far from settled, so that we are often not in a position to say a priori what can (satisfactorily) be exchanged for what until we have attempted the exchange and experienced the quality of enjoyment or relationship that results. One way of looking at money is as the medium in which these essays are made. Far from being the corrosive solvent of pre-existing spheres of meaning, money may be conceived as a tool that we use in the modern world to pursue experiments in exchange—to probe and test which boundaries between goods are permeable or dilapidated and which are not. After essaying some allegedly blocked exchange, we may want to conclude that the result is awful and that the boundary-crossing should never have been attempted. But that is not the only prospect. We may surprise ourselves and find that the integrity of the good has in fact survived its immersion in the market-place: think of those who have met their true love through a dating service. Or we may find that the transaction has changed the character of the good we thought we were dealing with, but that the change is not necessarily for the worse; the new good may just be *different*. Goods and their meanings change, we know, and this may turn out to be one way that dynamic occurs. I wish Walzer had offered some examination of these alternatives. Unfortunately, in *Spheres*, that task is sacrificed to an entirely artificial sense, conveyed by his list, that a given good is statically and categorically either exchangeable for money or not.[17]

PROHIBITIONS AND BLOCKED EXCHANGES

I want to return now to the point I made earlier when I was talking about rights: it may be important to distinguish between an outright ban on something and a rule that some good or service may not be exchanged for money. Consider, for example, the following two kinds of blocked exchange: (A) murder for money, i.e. contract killing; and (B) sex for money, i.e. prostitution. The two differ sharply, not only as sex and death differ, but in the sense in which an exchange may be said to be 'blocked'. In a block of type (A), an exchange is blocked because one of the items being exchanged is banned. Murder is illegal, so *a fortiori* the procurement of murder by money is illegal. The block follows the ban. In a case of type (B), by contrast, it is precisely the exchange that is blocked, not the activity itself. In a liberal society that neither frowns on nor prohibits fornication, sex between consenting adults,

---

[17] For a particularly sensitive discussion—one that keeps faith with social complexities and social possibilities—see the account of surrogate parenthood in Marjorie Maguire Shultz, 'Reproductive Technology and Intent-Based Parenthood: An Opportunity for Gender Neutrality', *Wisconsin Law Review* (1990), 297–398, esp. pp. 336–7.

even strangers, is fine. It is only the use of money to secure consensual sex that is condemned; *free* love is OK. True, this example is ideal-typic. Societies that prohibit prostitution are rarely untroubled by the prospect of sexual promiscuity where no money changes hands. But we might imagine a society in which that was true. Logically speaking, a ban on prostitution in those circumstances would be quite different from the situation presented in case (A): for, in case (A), murder for free (even murder for love) is forbidden.

Walzer's discussion is commonly thought to be focused on cases of the second sort, blocked exchanges of type (B). Thus Richard Arneson writes:

> I take it to be a datum of commonsense morality that we ought to be left free to engage in some activities or not as we wish, but not to engage in them for a price. Similarly, there are some goods that we should be left free to transfer to others if we wish, but not to buy or sell. In these respects there should be limits on the permissible scope of market exchange activity.[18]

He cites Walzer as having made this point particularly clearly in the passage we are picking over. In fact, it is surprising how few of the items on Walzer's list of blocked exchanges actually fit this description.

Some are clearly cases of type (A). The 'long series of criminal sales' (*Spheres*, 103) that Walzer groups together as item (14) fall into this category: one cannot sell one's services as an assassin because murder, even for free, is illegal; and one cannot sell secrets to the enemy, because espionage of any sort, even espionage unbought and given out of devotion to a principle, is banned.

Other goods fall into category (A) because they amount, in effect, to a ban that is non-negotiable. Rights are a good example. One's basic constitutional rights are, as Walzer himself stresses, rights to negative freedom—i.e. rights not to be prevented from speaking, worshipping, emigrating. As such they amount to a requirement that certain actions (viz. the prevention of speech, worship, emigration, etc.) not be performed by the government. Now if an official is bound by such a categorical requirement, he may not attempt to make it conditional, by negotiating a money price for

---

[18] Richard J. Arneson, 'Commodification and Commercial Surrogacy', *Philosophy and Public Affairs*, 21 (1992), 133.

observing it. In these cases, then, what the alleged block on exchange amounts to is that certain actions simply must not be performed, for *any* reason (including someone's failure to pay money to secure their non-performance). Once again, the block on exchange follows the ban, rather than vice versa.

The same applies to rules that require the positive performance of certain actions or the positive provision of certain services. A School Board is mandated to admit local children to its schools; it may not fail to do so, and it certainly may not fail to do so on the ground that an insufficient payment has been forthcoming from the children's parents. This is true, too, of police services and welfare entitlements: the police must give their services to all who need them, and welfare officials must pay welfare cheques and food stamps to those whose circumstances entitle them. Walzer is right to stress that they may not charge for these basic services, but he is wrong to identify this prohibition with anything specific to money or exchange. The reason for the ban on charging for these services is that the services are mandated—*period*—so that the option which would be implicit in the charging of a price is ruled out. The block follows the mandate.

Walzer cites bribery (of a judge or a politician) as an example of a blocked exchange. This too is more like case (A) than case (B)—though the judge example is an interesting one. Suppose that, in litigation before a court, justice clearly requires a verdict for the plaintiff. Then the presiding judge *must* find for the plaintiff; the judge is like a welfare official confronting a clear case of entitlement; the plaintiff, as it were, has a right to the verdict. Having reached that conclusion about the merits, the judge is not then entitled to decide for the defendant, and so of course it follows *a fortiori* that he is not entitled to decide for the defendant on account of a payment the defendant has made or on account of the failure of the plaintiff to make such a payment.

If one thought that judges and officials had what Ronald Dworkin has called 'strong discretion',[19] one might be tempted to assimilate this example to case (B) rather than case (A). At least in a hard case, one might say that a judge had discretion to decide for the plaintiff or for the defendant; but that, though he was free to make either of these choices, he was required not to exercise that

<hr />

[19] *Taking Rights Seriously*, revised edn. (London: Duckworth, 1977), 32–3.

freedom in response to a payment. We could therefore accept Walzer's concept of blocked exchanges for such cases, provided we were prepared to swallow this very controversial theory about the nature of official discretion. We could say: 'This official may decide the matter before him any way he likes, only he may not decide it for money.' I believe, however, that this seriously distorts our sense of what is bad about bribery. Our concern about bribery is more often that a payment may lead the judge or the official to *the wrong decision*, than that there is something intrinsically wrong about money changing hands.

I do not want to claim that there are never cases of type (B). Surely in some cases it is the exchange as such that we care about. However, we may care about exchange for reasons that Walzer does not consider. Think, for example, of the issue of surrogate motherhood (a type of situation that rose to prominence in the public mind some time after *Spheres* was published). In recent years, many childless couples have resorted to surrogacy arrangements: typically, the husband impregnates a third person, who in return for a substantial cash payment bears his child to term and, shortly after the birth, surrenders the baby to the couple who paid her. Some of our misgivings about such arrangements may have to do with the breach of norms of monogamy: to that extent the situation is like case (A). Some of our misgivings may be exactly of the kind Walzer indicates: a concern about the contamination of conception, gestation, and childbirth with base monetary motives. In addition, there is at least a concern about the *contractual* aspect of these arrangements—and in particular the possibility, highlighted in recent litigation, of whether and how to *enforce* surrogacy contracts. Thus sometimes when we do 'block' such exchanges, it is as much out of compunction about enforcement—having to tear screaming children from their surrogate mothers' arms—as about the monetary aspect *per se*.

The example is a caution against working with an overly simple account of what it is for an exchange to be blocked. We must bear in mind all the different ways in which the law might check or restrict a transaction. A contract judged immoral (like prostitution) or otherwise undesirable (like surrogacy) might be banned and perhaps entering into it might be made a criminal offence. Alternatively, the contract may be permitted, but treated as unenforceable. If it is enforceable, it may be enforceable only for money damages and not by specific performance. These different styles of 'blocking' an exchange testify to the fact that, even in cases of type (B), respecting Walzerian boundaries may be rather more complicated than Walzer himself suggests.

I hope all this is not striking the reader as pedantic. There is a good reason for asking whether the blocked exchanges that Walzer enumerates are analysed better under heading (A) or heading (B). If they are better understood under heading (B), then Walzer can cite them as examples of our uneasiness about exchange, an uneasiness which might be based on a concern to uphold the boundaries between goods. But if, as I have argued, the blocked exchanges are better analysed under heading (A), then what is really going on has nothing to do with the integrity of the boundaries between goods. It is purely a matter of the existence of certain social rules and requirements. When we ban murder contracts, it is not because we want the practice of assassination to be kept free of the taint of money. When we ban bribery, our aim is not to prevent the cash nexus from polluting the sphere of arbitrary or unjust decision-making. In both these cases, we are simply imposing a social rule, and insisting that it may not be broken for any reason. 'For any reason' certainly includes 'for money'; but that is hardly the essence of the matter.

If Walzer's list shows anything, it shows that we are not an unregulated society. Sociologically, it is interesting to observe that the triumph of money and exchange is not identical with the triumph of *laissez-faire*. Though money 'answereth all things', it answereth only the things that are otherwise permissible, and the list of social prohibitions and social requirements may be very long. That point is not new, of course: among others, Emile Durkheim noted that the ascendancy of contract in modern society was accompanied by a growth, not a decline, in social regulation. One might think that the more we become an exchange-based society, the less role there is for social rules, obligations, and controls.

But it is very evident that, far from diminishing, [social action] grows greater and greater and becomes more and more complex. The more primitive a code is, the smaller its volume. On the contrary, it is as large as it is more recent. . . . To be sure, it does not result in making the sphere of individual activity smaller. We must not forget that if there is more regulation in life, there is more life in general. This is sufficient proof that social

discipline has not been relaxing. One of its forms tends, it is true, to regress
... but others, much richer and much more complex, develop in its
place.[20]

THE FEAR OF COMMODIFICATION

I doubt that anything that has been said so far really addresses the
widespread sense of unease that many people feel about a world in
which everything is for sale, everything has a money price, everything is dealt with in the market-place. Even if they do not express
the point in terms of Walzerian meanings and boundaries, many
people have grave misgivings about the idea of 'universal commodification'.[21]

I have not dwelt on this aspect of the matter so far, partly
because Walzer himself has surprisingly little to say about it.
Unlike other critics of commodification, he believes

it's not implausible to hold that every valued thing, every social good, can
be represented in monetary terms. It may be that a series of translations
are necessary to get from this valued thing to that cash value. But there is
no reason to think that the translations can not be made; indeed, they are
made every day. Life itself has a value, and then eventually a price (different conceivably for different lives)—else how could we even think about
insurance and compensation? (*Spheres*, 97)

Still, he concedes that the monetization of everything can seem
'somehow degrading':

Consider the definition of the cynic attributed to Oscar Wilde: 'A man
who knows the price of everything and the value of nothing.' That definition is too absolute; it's not cynical to think that price and value will
sometimes coincide. But often enough money fails to represent value; the
translations are made, but as with good poetry, something is lost in the
process. (Ibid.)

---

[20] Emile Durkheim, *The Division of Labor in Society*, tr. George Simpson (New
York: The Free Press, 1933), bk. i, ch. 7, p. 205.

[21] The phrase is taken from Radin, 'Market-Inalienability', 1859, who is at pains
to distinguish her opposition to commodification from Walzer's: see ibid. 1858 n.,
and Radin, 'Justice and the Market Domain', in J. Chapman (ed.), *Nomos XXI:
Markets and Justice* (New York: New York Univ. Press, 1986), 179–83.

Is it possible to say anything in general about what this something is?

One set of worries about the prevalence of money values and market prices has to do with the substitution of quantitative for qualitative values. '[O]ne of the major tendencies of life—the reduction of quality to quantity—achieves its highest and uniquely perfect representation in money', writes Georg Simmel.[22] People worry about a bleaching or a flattening of the qualitative valuation of things. Objects which, in a non-monetized society, might strike us as tasty, beautiful, richly coloured, well-crafted, or having the historical properties of an heirloom, now strike us only as costing $8.99, or whatever.[23] I believe this apprehension is in fact far-fetched. The pastry and the *cappuccino* I buy each morning for breakfast have a price, but for all that, they are valued by me for their taste and stimulation. I do not think of myself as consuming a certain amount of money as I enjoy them, though I know that without a money economy—linking me impersonally and indirectly to coffee growers in Sumatra—there would be no possibility of my enjoying them. When I go from café to café in Berkeley to find the one that serves the best *cappuccino*, the fact that what I am looking for costs money does not distract me from the qualitative search. I hope the point is as obvious as it is banal; but it needs to be made as an initial response to those who lament the loss of qualitative value in a market economy.

Still, the worry bears a little more scrutiny than this. According to Simmel,

The fact that more and more things are available for money and, bound up with this, the fact that money becomes the central and absolute value, results in objects being valued only to the extent to which they cost money and the quality of value with which we perceive them appearing as a function of their money price.[24]

There is something to this. People like to show off that they have 'expensive' things; often, however, such display depends on a perceived correlation between price and quality, rather than an obliteration of quality altogether.

---

[22] Simmel, *Philosophy of Money*, 280.
[23] Cf. Marx, *Capital*, ch. 3, p. 204: 'In their money form all commodities look alike.'
[24] Simmel, *Philosophy of Money*, 279.

Simmel's account perhaps better captures what goes on among 'commodities traders' than what goes on among consumers. The interest of someone who buys coffee futures in Chicago may be quite different from the interest of a consumer: the former cares about quality only to the extent that it affects price. For him, a ton of coffee is just an opportunity to make a profit on resale. But the effect of this on the world of values needs to be analysed carefully. On the one hand, we have learnt from experience (of the Soviet Union, for example) that a world without commodities markets is a dystopian world, in which manufactured goods are produced poorly and haphazardly and exotic goods made available only to a few. On the other hand, there seems no reason to infer that the treatment of goods in such markets taints or affects the qualitative character of their eventual enjoyment. Margaret Radin suggests that there is a sort of Gresham's Law or 'domino effect' whereby the commodification of any good undermines the qualitative valuation of all goods; and I assume she would claim too that the commodification of a good at any stage of its production or distribution undermines its qualitative valuation at all later stages.[25] In fact, however, it is surprising how easy it is for people to keep these things straight. The markets in which commodity transactions take place are understood by all their participants to be secondary markets (none the less significant to them for that), which depend empirically as well as logically on the existence of primary markets in which the same objects are traded as use-values. Those who deal in coffee futures probably do so with a *cappuccino* in their hands, and they enjoy their beverage to the full even as bags of coffee beans appear on the VDUs in front of them as just so many rows of numbers.

So what, then, *is* the content of our shock at finding that something we thought of as unique, personal, inalienable, or irreplaceable has a value expressible in money terms? The reduction of quality to quantity is a superficial answer. At a deeper level, what is indicated is a radical multiplication of qualities. Just when we thought we were focusing on this *one* good with its own qualities, we find in effect that its price summons up an image of the

---

[25] Radin, 'Justice and the Market Domain', 173–5. See also Walzer's claim (*Spheres*, 119–20) that market relations are 'expansive' and that 'a radically *laissez-faire* economy would be like a totalitarian state, invading every other sphere, dominating every other distributive process'.

qualities of each and every other good that also has a price. An object that can fetch $100 in the market-place is now associated with all the other objects that one could *buy* for $100 in the market-place. Far from being eliminated, qualities pour in on every side. Someone who finds that an antique vase in her attic has a market value suddenly sees in it not just ceramic, floral, and heirloom qualities, but vacation qualities, symphony-subscription qualities, college-education-for-the-children qualities, and so on. The price on the vase stands as representative of every other quality of every particular good or service which might be exchanged for the money that the vase could fetch at auction. In this sense, the early Marx was right to observe:

Because money can be exchanged not for a particular quality, for a particular thing or human faculty but for the whole human and actual objective world, from the point of view of its possessor it can exchange any quality for any other, even contradictory qualities and objects; it is the fraternization of incompatibles and forces contraries to embrace.[26]

This of course takes us straight back to Walzer's concerns about the infection, through money, of any one sphere of goods with ideas, qualities, and meanings associated with others.

At the level of rhetoric, this 'universal confusion . . . of all natural and human qualities' can sound disturbing and profane.[27] Is nothing sacred? Is nothing to be just what it is, and not immediately call to mind the cornucopia of objects it might be sold for? But it may be worth dwelling on the other side of the matter—on the value (indeed, in some cases, the ethical value) of this interpenetration of qualities.

One account is given by Ronald Dworkin in his discussion of the role of market values in a theory of distributive justice.[28] In a modern society people have different conceptions of the good, different views about what gives value to life, and thus different preferences for goods and services. It follows that the problem of justice

[26] *Economic and Philosophical Manuscripts of 1844*, in Karl Marx, *Early Texts*, tr. David McLellan (Oxford: Basil Blackwell, 1972), 182.
[27] For an exaggerated view of the importance of rhetoric in these matters, see Radin, 'Market-Inalienability', 1877 ff.
[28] 'Liberalism', in Stuart Hampshire (ed.), *Public and Private Morality* (Cambridge: Cambridge Univ. Press, 1978), esp. 128–36; see also 'What is Equality? II. Equality of Resources', *Philosophy and Public Affairs*, 10 (1981), 283–345.

cannot be expressed in terms of how a *given stock* of goods is to be divided up, for one of the issues that people in society must settle among themselves is what the nature and quality of the divisible stock of goods is to be, what products available labour and raw materials should be used to produce, and 'which activities should be prohibited or regulated so as to make others possible or easier'.[29] In this situation, it would be, Dworkin reckons, a kind of moral failing for someone to insist stridently on the particularistic importance of their own projects and preferences, and the particular goods that those require, without considering what other goods the existence or production of *these* ones precludes. (An example, though a limited one, of this failing is the 'nimby' syndrome that people adopt as a way of obstructing the provision of public goods like roads, airports, and shelters for the homeless. To insist reflexively, 'Not in *my* back yard', is to refuse to make commensurate the value of one's own preferences and the value of those preferences represented in the public project at issue.) It would be wrong, therefore, to refuse to contemplate the market price of one's activities or satisfactions:

The market, if it can be made to function efficiently, will determine for each product a price that reflects the cost in resources of material, labor and capital that might have been applied to produce something different that someone else wants. That cost determines, for anyone who consumes that product, how much his account should be charged in computing an egalitarian division of social resources. It provides a measure of how much more his account should be charged for a house than a book, and for one book rather than for another.... These measurements make a citizen's own distribution a function of the personal preferences of others as well as his own, and it is the sum of these personal preferences that fixes the true cost to the community of meeting his own preferences for goods and activities. The egalitarian distribution, which requires that the cost of satisfying one person's preferences should as far as possible be equal to the cost of satisfying another's, cannot be enforced unless those measurements are made.[30]

Of course, this is not all that markets do, and they seldom do it perfectly. But I have quoted this passage from Dworkin at length to illustrate the positive contribution that thinking in money terms may make to our responsible discharge of social obligation. One

---

[29] Dworkin, 'Liberalism', 130.   [30] Ibid. 130–1.

treasures the quality of one's backyard for the particular pleasure that it is; but it is important also to know, in general terms, what others in the community are forgoing to preserve that yard. Since the answer to this question is not always that they are forgoing *a yard* (for themselves), but that they are forgoing all the other uses to which that land might be put, a Walzerian guarantee that yards must never be compared with anything but yards is a recipe for blinkered selfishness and social irresponsibility.

Beyond this ethical point, there is also the progressive aspect of money to be considered. In the early work from which I have already quoted, Karl Marx described money as a 'perverting power ... the enemy of man and social bonds that pretend to self-subsistence'.[31] But even in 1844, his attitude to this enmity was far from unambiguous. Money is also 'the externalized and self-externalizing species-being of man ... the externalized capacities of humanity'.[32] If I look at a piece of land and see only the ties that have bound me and my family inalienably to that plot and to its subsistence-possibilities for generations, then I necessarily view my or our relation to the rest of humanity in a very limited aspect. *All* we are for others is growers (and perhaps sellers) of potatoes in these climes and in this soil; all other relations are unthinkable. Money, however—i.e. putting a price on the land—is, in Marx's marvellous phrase, 'the galvano-chemical power of society'.[33] With a price and the possibility of sale, there are thousands of things that this land can do, thousands of things that I and my family can do, thousands of ways in which we can participate in the species-life of humanity as a whole. It is here that the great apotheosis of modernism in *The Communist Manifesto* becomes relevant. Old established industries are dislodged by new ones that work up raw materials from here, there, and everywhere. 'To the great chagrin of Reactionists', Marx writes, the cosmopolitan character of capitalist production liberates people to find new relations with their fellows—as humans, not just as neighbours, brothers, or traditional partners.

In place of the old wants, satisfied by the productions of the country, we find new wants, requiring for their satisfaction the old products of distant lands and climes. In place of the old local and national seclusion and

---

[31] Marx, *Economic and Philosophical Manuscripts*, 182.
[32] Ibid. 181.   [33] Ibid.

self-sufficiency, we have intercourse in every direction, universal inter-dependence of nations. . . . All fixed, fast-frozen relations, with their train of ancient and venerable prejudices and opinions are swept away, all new-formed ones become antiquated before they can ossify. All that is solid melts into the air, all that is holy is profaned, and man is at last compelled to face with sober senses, his real conditions of life and his relations with his kind.[34]

True, Marx has the gravest misgivings about the fetishism that might make this seem the achievement of money and commodity circulation acting on its own.[35] But there is also an older fetishism that binds us to objects by their traditionally conceived meanings. That bondage must be done away with if humanity is to realize the full extent of social possibility. I believe that our propensity to elaborate the process of exchange without regard to traditional boundaries—the propensity evinced in our use of money and our indifference to Walzer's meanings—is one of the major solvents of those bonds.

[34] Karl Marx and Friedrich Engels, *The Communist Manifesto*, tr. Samuel Moore (Harmondsworth: Penguin Books, 1967), ch. 1, pp. 83–4. (Though the order of the two passages is reversed in this excerpt, the meaning is not affected.)

[35] Compare Marx, *Capital*, i, ch. 3, p. 188: 'It is not money that renders the com-modities commensurable. Quite the contrary. Because all commodities, as values, are objectified human labour, and therefore in themselves commensurable, their val-ues can be communally measured in one and the same specific commodity, and this commodity can be converted into the common measure of their values, that is into money. Money as a measure of value is the necessary form of appearance of the measure of value which is immanent in commodities, namely labour-time.'

8

Blocked Exchanges: A Taxonomy

JUDITH ANDRE

In *Spheres of Justice* Michael Walzer lists fourteen 'blocked exchanges': things which in the USA cannot be bought or sold.[1] He does so out of concern about domination; although his title refers to justice, his target is oppression rather than inequality as such. It lessens domination, Walzer argues, to recognize different spheres—aspects of life in which different principles of distribution are appropriate. Separating these spheres limits the power any one person can acquire; the greatest wealth, for instance, should not be able to buy human beings, political office, criminal justice, and so on.

In fact, of course, money is vastly powerful. If not human beings, it can buy us servants; if not political office, the attention of elected officials; if not criminal justice, the best lawyer in the country. And everyday, it seems, there is more and more that money can buy. Some of the new commodities are inventive: singing telegrams, time-share apartments; even the mortgage itself can be sold. Other new commodities, actual or suggested, are more frightening. In some European countries—Germany for instance—kidney sales have been reported: for a few thousand dollars people have had one kidney surgically removed and implanted in

This is an expanded version of an article with the same title that first appeared in *Ethics*, 103 (1992–3), 29–47. It is repr. by kind permission of *Ethics* and the Univ. of Chicago Press. Original material © 1992 by the University of Chicago. All rights reserved. I began this chapter during a year as Fellow with the Harvard Program in Ethics and the Professions, and completed it during a residency with the Virginia Foundation for the Humanities and Public Policy and a Rockefeller Fellowship with the Institute of Medical Humanities, University of Texas Medical Branch. I am grateful to Amy Gutmann for her encouragement and suggestions.

[1] *Spheres of Justice* (New York: Basic Books, 1983), 100–3.

someone else's body.[2] Richard Posner and William A. Landes have proposed a market in babies in the USA.[3]

Walzer would impede this march towards commodification. His list of blocked exchanges is rough and unorganized, suggestive rather than conclusive. It includes: human beings; political power and influence; criminal justice; freedom of speech, press, religion, and assembly; marriage and procreation rights; the right to emigrate; exemptions from military service, jury duty, and other communally imposed work; political office; basic welfare services like police protection and education; desperate exchanges, such as those involved in accepting dangerous work; prizes and honours; divine grace; love and friendship; criminal acts. He believes the list is complete, but leaves open the possibility that it is not. His general position is that different kinds of goods carry with them different criteria of distribution.

Walzer is not alone in wanting to limit the market. Several theorists have offered other approaches to restricting it. Margaret Jane Radin, for instance, distinguishes personal from fungible property: personal property is bound up with one's being the person one is; it is valued for its own sake and cannot be replaced with money alone. Laws may therefore, she contends, prohibit its sale.[4] Elizabeth Anderson argues not just from the nature of the goods in question but also from the nature of commerce, and claims that some good things cannot survive therein. Only those things should be for sale 'whose dimensions of value are best realized within market relations'. That is not true of gifts, shared goods, ideals, and objects of need, all of which require other kinds of social relations.[5]

Walzer, Radin, and Anderson each offer us a single principle with which to bound the market. Radin's is broad and basic: protect human flourishing by shielding non-fungible property from the full force of the market. Walzer, too, works from a broad and basic

[2] 'Kidneys for Sale: The Issue is Tissue', *Newsweek* (5 Dec. 1988), 38. Cf. 'Kidney, Cornea Sale Flourishes in Brazil', *The Washington Post* (12 Oct. 1981), A22.

[3] 'The Economics of the Baby Shortage', *Journal of Legal Studies*, 7 (1978), 323.

[4] 'Market-Inalienability', *Harvard Law Review*, 100 (June 1987), 1849–1937. In an earlier article she argues that personal property should also be privileged against government control; i.e. the government needs more justification to take, redistribute, or control it: 'Property and Personhood', *Stanford Law Review*, 34 (1982), 957–1015.

[5] Elizabeth Anderson, 'The Ethical Limitations of the Market', *Economics and Philosophy*, 6 (1990), 179–205.

principle—lessen oppression by using different grounds for distribution in different spheres of life—but he also lists in detail what belongs outside the sphere of money. Anderson's perspective is in one sense plural, since markets have a number of characteristics (impersonality, self-interest, want-regardingness, etc.) each of which might be destructive of different things. Yet, ultimately, she too is working with a single principle: protect from the market those things to which it is essentially inhospitable. Mark Nelson takes a somewhat different approach: he lists ten examples of blocked exchanges, and derives from them nine principles. The principles are only loosely related to one another.[6]

In this chapter I present a new approach, neither a list (whether of blocked exchanges or of unrelated principles) nor a single overarching principle, but a set of logically related considerations—a framework for thinking about the issue. Once we understand what a sale is, and look closely at Walzer's useful list, we find that there are a number of distinct grounds for blocking exchanges. Divine grace, for instance, should not be sold because it cannot be, and pretending to do so is a fraud. The right to marry should not be sold because it should be inalienable. Criminal justice should not be sold because a bribed decision is not justice at all.

Perhaps every intermediate principle I uncover here could in turn be explained by Walzer's, Radin's, or Anderson's accounts; I do not try to settle that here. Since much theory works directly from examples, organizing those examples should help us evaluate any theories, whether by Walzer, Radin, Anderson, or someone else. Let us begin with some background. We can be confused by a mental picture of a sale as primarily a physical exchange. We imagine one person handing another an object, say a pencil, while the second hands the first money. Now we all know that this change of physical relationship, of what object is in whose hand, is neither necessary nor sufficient to a sale. What is essential is that a set of rights, duties, and liabilities[7] pass from one person to the

---

[6] Mark Nelson, 'The Morality of a Market in Transplant Organs', *Public Affairs Quarterly*, 5 (1991), 63–79. Nelson considers one principle, then notes an exception to it and formulates a principle to account for the exception. To that in turn there is an exception; and so forth.

[7] I will use this phrase and similar ones to indicate a full Hohfeldian set of legal statuses: claim-rights, duties, privileges, powers, liabilities, and immunities. See Wesley Newcomb Hohfeld, 'Fundamental Legal Conceptions as Applied in Judicial Reasoning', *Yale Law Journal*, (1913–14), 16–59, and 26 (1916–17), 710–767.

other. The transfer depends on words or symbolic actions, and these may or may not include a physical exchange.

When we buy a physical object or a piece of land, we acquire a set of legal rights and duties concerning it, and the previous owner has the money we once had. (The legal statuses include, for instance, the right to use what is owned, the rights to its fruits, liability for upkeep and taxes, and so on.[8]) After the sale, each party has something the other had before: the rights, privileges, liabilities, and so on, which are constitutive of the legal status of ownership, transfer without alteration to the buyer; rights over a sum of money pass unchanged to the seller.

Once we understand this, we see something else crucial: nothing can be sold unless someone has certain prior legal relationships to it. Ownership admits of degrees; I can own a sewing machine more completely than I can own historic buildings, for instance, since the law allows me to do whatever I want to the machine but not to the building. Not every set of rights, duties, and so on, concerning an object, constitute ownership. Full ownership includes the privilege of using something, a claim to state assistance in excluding others, and the right to alter and destroy what is owned. Some subsets of the rights which constitute full ownership also count as ownership; I will not try to explore the precise boundaries of the concept here.

Nothing can be sold, then, unless rights over it can and do exist. Nor can anything be sold unless it is possible to separate those rights from the person who has them. *Unobjectionable* sales concern rights which not only can exist but morally may; and which it is not only possible but proper to separate from the owner. This supplies four different grounds on which an exchange might be blocked; and of course there is a fifth, for possibly something which is appropriately owned and given should nevertheless not be sold. Some people believe this about blood and kidneys.[9] The same

---

[8] The *locus classicus* is A. M. Honoré's 'Ownership', in A. G. Guest (ed.), *Oxford Essays in Jurisprudence* (Oxford: Clarendon Press, 1961), 107–47. His list includes rights to possession, use, management, income, capital, security, transmissibility, and others. In 'Full Ownership and Freedom' I develop what I think is a more ordered list.

[9] There is a different set of questions about ownership, having to do with language, which is beyond the scope of this chapter. I have an exclusive right to the use of my kidney, and the law will help keep away anyone who wants to take it without my consent. Whether we should call that relationship ownership, whether we should call our bodies property, is a question I do not address here. I will use

can be said of certain actions, such as sex (which, done for money, becomes prostitution) and judicial decisions (which cease being just). In this chapter I identify these considerations, flesh them out, and organize them logically. I do not try to refine them or defend them.

WHAT CANNOT OR SHOULD NOT BE OWNED

Some things by their nature cannot be owned

Some of Walzer's blocked exchanges concern things over which legal rights are not possible. The clearest examples are friendship, love, and divine grace.

Friendship and love: an essential element in friendship is spontaneous mutual appreciation; love is a matter of joy in the other's presence (at least occasionally) and concern for their welfare. These attitudes cannot be willed. The law cannot guarantee that they continue. That is not to say the law is helpless; it could punish breach of promise and adultery, and the fear of punishment might lead to some curbing of desire. But the connection would be contingent and indirect. The essence of friendship and love is an inner attitude beyond the reach of the law. Of course one could have legal rights to their simulacra, to companionship or service, but those are not the same thing.

Divine grace: by definition no one can have legal rights to the pleasure of God or gifts from God. An omnipotent God is beyond the reach of the state. It is meaningless to talk of protecting with force one's status before God. The reason one cannot sell divine grace is that one does not own it to begin with. Again, however, we could have a legally constituted right to simulacra, to the performance of certain actions by priests. Failure to perform and interference with performance could be punishable to law. But whether these actions bring with them grace is not up to human beings.

If we move from secular to ecclesiastical law, things get murkier. Some churches hold that holders of particular offices have special powers. The church decides who holds those positions, and then

the language of ownership for convenience but I mean the words only to refer to legal states of affairs.

God has promised to work through these people in special ways. In such a case the church claims control over a conduit of divine grace and indirectly over the grace itself. (There may be theological objections to this picture, but I want to set those aside.) What is claimed here *is* a kind of ownership, and therefore the later questions of how these offices can and should be transferred can sensibly be asked.

From this discussion we can formulate a general principle: nothing can be owned unless it is something over which laws can be effective. Affection and divine grace are not ownable because our having them is not subject to law. (We might also ask why anyone would bother to forbid a market which is impossible anyway. The answer must have to do with our fear of simulacra, which are quite possible and are degradations of something important and good.)

There is a second way in which things can be not-ownable: the use of some things cannot be confined to any individual or group. Some public goods are by their nature non-exclusive: the air we breathe, the climate of trust in which we operate, quiet. To some of these things we can have enforceable rights, and conceivably those rights could be owned and sold. But since those rights are not rights to exclusive use, nor to alteration or destruction, they do not constitute ownership.

Some things could be (fully) owned, but should not be

Human beings: people should not be owned. The Kantian reasons are familiar: people have purposes (and, neo-Kantians might add, feelings and desires) and these must be treated as valuable in themselves. Persons can and must take responsibility for some of the shape their lives take; respect demands that they be allowed to. Ownership makes the subjective lives of others into means only.

In fact, it might seem that people not only should not be owned, but that they cannot be. Power over objects is direct: we can pick them up, move them, change them, destroy them. But power over people is ordinarily indirect: we influence their choices. Legal power over people is usually a matter of threatened punishment. The justice system does sometimes physically restrain or confine people, but the system would not work unless most people were dissuaded from even trying to break the law. Nevertheless, this picture is misleading, not in what it says about the way law influences people, but in what it suggests about owning objects. Property is not a relation between a person and an object, it is a relation among people about that object. Something is legally mine only if I can call in the police to keep others from taking it. Titles to diamonds, like titles to slaves, are effective because threat of legal punishment influences the choices people make.[10]

In slavery, of course, people were owned. A set of legal arrangements existed between people about other people. Because even an owned person makes choices, the slave-owner had to use different means of control than a tractor owner would; he had to influence the choices that the slaves made. The law, too, punished actions by slaves (and of course tractors perform no actions); there is a difference in property laws about machines and those about people. But a major element in slavery was that other people—non-owners—could not interfere with what a slave-owner did, and could not legally help the slaves escape. The state did not (much) limit what the owner could do, and did limit what non-owners could do about it.[11]

People, then, can be owned. In fact many rights over others falling far short of slavery have been called property rights. Some arise from contract; employers and employees have rights over one another. Some arise from status: parents can make many decisions about their children, and in turn children (through representation) have enforceable rights to support and proper treatment. Alimony has been called one spouse's property right in the other. In all of these cases people can use some of the power of the state to persuade others to act. Perhaps these arrangements should not be called property rights at all. But questions of language aside, these other rights over persons help us define by contrast what should *not* exist: no one should *fully* own—have a complete legal right to dispose of—any other human being.

Public goods: although they disagree about details, most political theorists agree that some public goods should be beyond private control, for reasons of efficiency, justice, or community. Earlier I spoke of public goods that cannot be privately owned, like quiet;

[10] As well as the lack of legal recourse for a thief, who could not call in the law to keep others away, nor sell a stolen object and depend on keeping the proceeds.

[11] This of course differed from regime to regime. For a comprehensive study of slavery in many different cultures, see Orlando Patterson, *Slavery and Social Death* (Cambridge, Mass.: Harvard Univ. Press, 1982).

here I refer to things that could be but should not be privately owned. I use the term public goods roughly and stipulatively, to include those things that are preconditions of community life, such as defence and roads, as well as those that preserve community resources, like wetlands that protect biological diversity and forests that maintain the ozone layer. Furthermore some of the necessities of individual life—food, water, and shelter—need to be publicly available, but the prohibition here is against full ownership not of any particular loaf of bread but of the whole supply.

Art and historical objects partially constitute the life of the community, and some of these need to be kept from total private ownership. A Rembrandt, the original Declaration of Independence—these must be protected. If they go into private ownership, then it cannot be full ownership: the person who paid money for the sake of private enjoyment should not have the right to deface or destroy it. Furthermore, some things which merely adorn community or private life also should be kept public, things like beaches and parks.

The general principle here is that, for the good of the community, the individual ownership of some things must be limited or prohibited. Obviously there is a great deal of debate about what specifically falls under this principle, far more than I can address here. My purpose is only to identify the principle and relate it to others. So far I have named two major categories of blocked exchanges: those things which, by definition, cannot be owned (subject to legal control); and those things which should not be, for their own sake (e.g. human beings) or for ours (e.g. public goods).

WHAT CANNOT OR SHOULD NOT BE ALIENATED

Some things cannot be alienated

To alienate, to make other, refers to several different things. In one sense, something is alienable if it can be disconnected from the person it is now connected with and yet go on existing. In this sense we can alienate land—transfer its ownership to someone else—but not our memories. In another sense, to alienate something means simply to cease to have it, whether or not another acquires it. When Jefferson wrote of inalienable rights, he meant rights which not only could not be transferred to another person, but also could not be lost. One party might be able to alienate an object which another party could not. Honours, for instance, can be refused, but once given and received the award cannot be cancelled *by the recipient*. Once a Nobel laureate, always a Nobel laureate. But the committee who awarded the honour could withdraw it, as they do when they discover fraud.

Few of the things about which market theorists worry are incapable of alienation. Nothing, for instance, on Walzer's list belongs here. His list concerns exchanges which have threatened to happen, and need to (continue to) be obstructed. Or, as in the case of divine grace, realms in which we fear counterfeit and deception. There seems to be nothing of either kind to fear here.

Some things could be alienated but should not be

Natural rights may be inalienable, but legal rights are not. They can be lost, and conceivably they could be transferred to another. Much of Walzer's list belongs in this category: things that not only should not be alienable for money, but should not be alienable at all. We should not be able to sell our freedoms of speech, press, religion, and assembly, our right to emigrate, to marry, to procreate—but neither should we be able to renounce them or give them away. The general principle is that persons should be in some respects invincibly armoured against the state and other potentially oppressive agents.[12] This principle derives from an understanding of basic human flourishing—of the independence needed for moral growth, the privacy needed for intimacy. It also assumes the equal worth of all persons.

Something similar is true of our welfare rights to education and to police protection. It is not just that we should not be able to sell them; we should also not be able to lose them or transfer them to another. The general principle is that states should provide everyone with what is essential for life and growth. That principle in turn appeals either to general beneficence, to the preconditions of genuine democracy, or to the just distribution of what communal efforts make possible. Principles of justice and democracy also

---

[12] The transfer of marriage rights may be forbidden on additional grounds. Suppose someone does not want to marry; should she be able to hand over her particular right to a friend who wants to be bigamous?

apportion some duties equally. No one can fulfil another's military duty, for instance.

All of these restrictions on alienability have to do with our rights against the state and our duties toward it. Again, I do not try to refine or defend the principles at stake. Instead I want to identify objections to alienability *qua* alienability and separate them from objections to alienation for gain.

WHAT SHOULD NOT BE CHANGED FOR GAIN

When there is no objection to giving some particular thing away, we may still object to its being given in return for something—particularly when what we gain is money. We may be concerned here either about (*a*) the entity sold or traded, such as babies; or (*b*) those who are doing the exchanging—objections to a market in organs fit here. Finally, sale strictly so-called (as opposed to barter) raises specific questions. Does money make an exchange for gain worse? What is so filthy about filthy lucre?

Some markets mistreat what is sold

Babies can be given away. True, not even parents can simply transfer to someone else their legal rights concerning a child. All adoptions must be approved by the state. But parents (unless they have lost their own rights) can decide whether to release a child for adoption, and often to whom. In these ways, not absolute but not trivial, parents can give children away. And they could do so in return for gain.

Many people hold that doing so would be trafficking in human beings, a form of slavery. But the rights and responsibilities transferred from birth parents to adoptive parents are very different from what was transferred among slave-traders. The state barred itself and others from interfering with most of what slave-owners did to their slaves; the primary purpose of the laws was to protect the owners. Laws respecting parental rights primarily seek the welfare of the children. Slaves are said to be owned because there is so little restriction on what may be done to them. Children cannot be said to be owned.

But at least two legitimate worries about a market in babies arise. One has to do with consequences: new incentive structures have unpredictable results. But there is a quite different objection, independent of whether the effects of the market would be good: is it right to treat babies as a crop? First, let us consider the concern about results. When something acquires exchange value, people have new reasons to acquire and protect it. A market in babies would not change the motivations of adoptive parents, since babies would be what anthropologists call terminal commodities: once acquired, rights over children could not again be traded. Adoptive parents' motives would be what they are now, desires to love and be loved, to nurture, to pass on one's name, perhaps to be cared for in one's old age and remembered after death. (Note that some of these desires treat the child as an end, some treat it as a means.)

Biological parents, however, would have new reasons for what they do. Some would begin pregnancies simply for what they could gain from trade. One result, the one emphasized by market theorists, is that the supply of babies would be more likely to match demand. Even the 'perfect' market, however, has results beyond itself. In this case there would be more babies available for adoption. Perhaps more of these would be 'desirable'—healthy white infants—but perhaps not; people who turn to this livelihood are likely to be desperate, quite possibly sick or users of drugs. In either case the number of 'less desirable' babies that go unadopted would be likely to increase.

No one knows for sure; economic analysis is partly made up of speculation. But it is worth noting some of the other situations in which altered incentives have had unexpected results. One is the story of tobacco in America in the seventeenth century. For the Indians tobacco had ceremonial value; for the Europeans it had exchange value. Once tobacco could earn money (or copper or guns) more of it was grown. Tobacco exhausts land, and new fields have to be begun every few years, so the demand for tobacco created a demand for land—and that led to conflict and violence.

One reason, then, to hesitate about giving babies—or anything else—exchange value is that doing so alters incentive structures, a change with unforeseeable results. Some consequences could hurt children, those conceived to be traded as well as those who result from miscalculation or misfortune. Yet powerful as this objection is, it does not seem to capture our real concerns. There is something stubbornly untranslatable in our objection to treating babies as commodities. Even if we could be sure that no one would be worse off, and everyone better off, human beings may not be treated simply as means.

Kant said that human beings should not be treated 'as a means only'. But the phrase needs unpacking,[13] since people are virtually always useful to one another, and paying attention only to that usefulness can be morally unproblematic. We can ask someone the time of day, or stand so that he blocks the sun from our eyes, without doing anything wrong. 'Treating someone as a means only' is not just an ignoring of someone's intrinsic value, but a denial of it. Affirming their intrinsic value includes acknowledging their worth; allowing them to be, to function, and to grow; and fostering all of that. Endangering, hurting, and destroying people are obvious cases of treating them as if they had no intrinsic value.[14] Failure to acknowledge their worth is a more complicated subject. Not-attending-to implies 'you are worthless' in some situations, but not in others. Richard Wasserstrom gives a vivid example: a newspaper reported that 'all the children in town' took part in a festival, when only the white children had participated. A factory that puts waste in local water and never asks whether the waste is dangerous treats its neighbours as if they did not matter, even if it turns out that the waste is harmless.

Treating someone 'as a means only', then, should be understood as actions inconsistent with valuing that person in themselves: harm, coercion, deception, and those actions that imply that someone has no value in himself or herself. With that clarification, let us return to the question of markets that demean what is sold, using as our example a market in babies. Exchange value is a particular form of instrumental value. Like other forms of instrumental value it coexists easily with intrinsic value; recognizing exchange value does not eliminate an appreciation of something's intrinsic value. The dealer in Oriental rugs or in Renaissance paintings may fully appreciate the beauty of his stock. But the decision to sell something is a decision about its whole future, made purely on the grounds of gain to the seller. If the 'stock' is babies, the state might hedge the transaction with safeguards, and the birth parents might

---

[13] My treatment is neo-Kantian rather than an exegesis of Kant himself.

[14] Strictly speaking this is true only if nothing else is gained by the harm, force, or deception. But it *is* true then, and my purpose is only to illuminate the connection between these wrongs and the failure to treat people as ends.

choose the buyer carefully. But if you conceive a child you do not mean to keep, you may be forced to let it go to an unsatisfactory home—or keep it where it is unwanted. You have done something with profound implications for another person's future, and your most important motivation had nothing to do with that person's welfare. You have treated a human being as a means only.

Now in most actual cases of contracted motherhood[15] the biological mother has been confident that there is a family eager and able to care for the child; although these women would not have conceived unless money were offered, neither would they have done so if a home were not available. It is just because their motivations are mixed that we are unclear how to respond. If they believed they were not endangering the baby, then *they* were not treating it as if it had no intrinsic value. Yet a publicly sanctioned market in babies, of the kind for which Posner argues, would allow conceptions where neither the mother nor the father intended to raise the baby. Whether or not that ever happened, providing the legal space for it would be tantamount to approval of it.

In any case, my purpose here is not to resolve the dispute about contracted motherhood, but to isolate and explicate one kind of objection to markets. A different example of the objection arises for scholars. We study and write for many different reasons; in part we want a secure job and the respect of others, but we also do it for the sake of the subject itself: we want something important to be better understood.[16] Inevitably, though, work earns rewards, and the reward can become too important. The more we shape our work to earn money or attention, the more uncomfortable we (should) become; when the pursuit of money or glory dominates, then the work we do has been demeaned. (I give more attention later to the ways in which actions change their meaning when done for money.)

---

[15] I owe this term to Sara Ann Ketchum. As she points out, 'surrogate' mothers are just mothers who have agreed to transfer their rights over their children to others, usually the biological father. 'Selling Babies and Selling Bodies', *Hypatia*, 4 (1989), 116–27.

[16] We also want to be its author; this is a desire for personal worthiness. Some might call that an admixture of egoism; I would not, but that is a subject for another day.

Some markets are bad for seller and buyer

The suggestion of a market in human organs excites similar opposition. Yet a part of a human being is not a human being; treating hair, for instance, as a commodity is not treating a human being 'as a means only'. But fears about altering incentive structures, mentioned above because of consequences for the object of exchange, also fit here; if money can be made from selling organs, a lot more of them will be offered. That would seem to be good for those who need transplants, but not unequivocally; people offering their organs for profit would have a reason to conceal facts making their organs unsuitable. Beyond that, we all know that those most likely to submit to painful and invasive surgery, and to accept the risks involved, will be the poor. In contracted motherhood in the USA poor women offer their wombs and their babies, rich women pay for them. In other words, we wonder about endangering buyers and exploiting sellers.

Besides the question of unfair treatment of one party, objections to exchange sometimes concern the nature of the relationship involved. In *The Gift Relationship*[17] Richard M. Titmuss argued that a gift relationship is superior to a commercial one, since gifts essentially involve concern for other people, while the market demands only rational self-interest. He held that putting something on the market destroys the 'deeper freedom' to give what is priceless.[18] Defending this position, Peter Singer talks about changes in social understanding: 'The idea that others are depending on one's generosity and concern, that one may oneself . . . need the assistance of a stranger . . . [that] we must rely on the good will of others rather than the profit motive—all these vague ideas and feelings are incompatible with the existence of a market in blood.'[19]

Some of these concerns are easier to specify and to remedy than others. Diseased and defective organs can often be identified and

---

[17] (New York: Pantheon, 1971).
[18] Peter Singer, 'Altruism and Commerce: A Defense of Titmuss against Arrow', *Philosophy and Public Affairs* 2 (1973), 312–20, and 'Freedom and Utilities in the Distribution of Health Care', in Gerald Dworkin, Gordon Bermant, and Peter G. Brown (eds.), *Market and Morals* (Washington, DC: Hemisphere, 1977), 163–4; cited in L. Lomasky, 'Gift Relations, Sexual Relations and Freedom', *Philosophical Quarterly*, 33 (1983), 250–8.
[19] Singer, 'Altruism and Commerce'.

discarded.[20] Exploitation and injustice are far trickier to deal with; the philosophical literature on these issues is large. The same is true of claims about lost freedom,[21] and of fears about changes in social relationships and in cultural climate. In this chapter I only locate those concerns; I do not refine or defend them.

Money adds particular problems

The objections I have identified so far apply to barter as well as to sale. But sale—exchange for money—creates several particular problems. Money is a peculiar thing. By definition it is highly abstract and makes a fully ordered set with no highest number; its distribution tends to be highly uneven, and based on limited characteristics. Each of these dimensions has ethical implications.

First, prices are fully ordered: every price is either equal to, less than, or more than every other price. Everything priced is commensurable: this diamond ring is worth 4,000 roller skates; that airplane cost twice what this house did. Should rights over babies be put on the market, a child would know that she cost, say, about what a second car for the family would have cost. She might also know that she cost more, or less, than other children. One moral danger, then, is an erosion of our sense of the uniqueness of what once was 'priceless'.[22]

Secondly, money accumulates. It is a form of power, as are physical strength, talent, legal status, and social standing. Like these, money begets more power: markets can be cornered, resources bought, political influence cultivated. But unlike most other forms

---

[20] Public discourse is overly optimistic about this. HIV, for instance, is not reliably detectable until months after it has been contracted. Furthermore this solution is possible only when we are talking about organs. If someone conceives a baby *in order to* sell it, then discovering its medical problems only reveals the problem. It solves nothing.

[21] I examine this issue in detail in 'Full Ownership and Freedom' (MS).

[22] It is not my purpose in this chapter to evaluate these possibilities. For further discussion see Nancy C. Hartsock, *Money, Sex, and Power* (New York: Longman, 1983), 98 and elsewhere; Eric Mack, 'Dominos and the Fear of Commodification', in John W. Chapman and J. Roland Pennock (eds.), *Markets and Justice* (Nomos XXXI) (New York: New York Univ. Press, 1989), 198–225, esp. 217; Jan Narveson, 'The Justice of the Market: Comments on Gray and Radin', in ibid. 271; and Margaret Jane Radin, 'Justice and the Market Domain', in ibid. 165–97, esp. 171. Many have argued recently that we humans are far too arrogant about the differences between ourselves and the non-human world. But the thrust of those arguments is almost always to give greater status to the non-human rather than less to the human.

of power, money can be accumulated endlessly: there is no highest number. Furthermore, preserving it is relatively simple; money does not rot, it takes up no room, and it can often be guarded more efficiently than objects.

Thirdly, money accumulates unevenly. Not only do some people have vastly more than others, they collect it through various combinations of good fortune, hard work, and native ability. Moral desert is at best one of the factors at work. Perhaps luck, effort, and ability are good reasons for allowing someone to travel more widely and live more comfortably than others can. But it is not clear that they justify a greater chance at surviving disease or at establishing a family.

Fourthly, money is purely instrumental. Assigning a monetary value to something emphasizes its instrumentality, and makes it more likely that that thing be treated simply as a means. Fifthly, money provides diminishing marginal utility. $100 means less to a Rockefeller than to a postal clerk. And some things, perhaps, should cost us roughly equally.

The abuse of indulgences illustrates some of this. Suppose we accept for a moment some theological presuppositions: that after death people will suffer for a while in purgatory until, purified, they are allowed into heaven; and that voluntary penance on earth can reduce time in purgatory. Suppose we accept, too, that a church can designate that some actions are equivalent to others: that saying certain prayers, for instance, reduces purgatory time as much as 100 days of penance would. From here it is an easy step to rewarding certain helpful actions with indulgences, actions such as cleaning the sacristy or embroidering vestments. And after that comes the fall: what is more helpful than money? Why not reward contributions to the church with indulgences? (On this interpretation the church did something it should not have done, rather than claimed to do something it could not have done. The second question raises quite different issues.) The church should not have sold indulgences because money is too far removed from the sphere of personal desert to which indulgences are properly attached. A financial cost is not the same as cost in sincere prayer or bodily service.

Another example is the legal obligation to serve one's country. No kind of contribution would cost everyone exactly equally; time means more to some people than others, physical effort comes more or less easily. Still, time and effort burden people more equally than monetary expense does. So we forbid buying one's way out of service, in order to make more equal demands on each person.

If we turn to what should not even be owned, much less transferred to others, money darkens that picture, too. Is it worse to sell slaves than to give them away? Yes, other things being equal, and for some of the reasons just given. If it is degrading to be owned—to be fully subject to the will of another—being priced adds insult to injury: the slave is one commodity among others, worth perhaps less than a house and more than a horse. Furthermore, the slave being sold is treated as 'a means only'. In an auction or purely commercial sale, the seller must yield to the highest bidder or the first offer. The decision about the slave's new owner, one which deeply affects the slave, is not made for the sake of the slave. Seller and buyer need only be moved by their own self-interest.

WHEN ACTIONS ARE FOR SALE

When contracts, promises, and agreements to act involve money, we sometimes use the language of sales: 'He sold his talents to Exxon'; 'MGM has bought her next two performances'. This is especially true when we disapprove of what happened: 'She sold out', 'The senator has been bought'. From Walzer's list, the following concern actions done for money: 'desperate exchanges' such as dangerous or degrading work, 'selling' political power and influence, public office, and criminal justice, and agreements to break the law.

Are agreements to act a form of sale?

I would argue that these transactions are not really sales: the 'seller' does not hand over, unchanged, a bundle of legal rights and liabilities which had made him an 'owner'. Others, however, hold that these agreements are a kind of sale: that, for example, when a ballplayer signs with a team, he sells it exactly what it can then sell to another team: rights over the use of his time.

In opposition I would note, first, that it is often a struggle to say clearly what has been sold. Time? Effort? Ability? Freedom?

(Honour?) Second, whatever has been sold was not originally 'owned' in the same sense that land and licences are. Third, there is not just a trade in legal statuses. Typically the employee must now seek the employer's goals, and the employer must provide for and protect the employee. None of these obligations existed before the initial agreement was struck. Compare this with the sale of a house, or of a player's contract: the new owner now has exactly those rights and liabilities which the previous owner had. In contrast, most of the legal rights, liabilities, and so on that result from contracts of service arise *de novo*. They do not pre-exist the arrangement and thus are not transferred from one party to the other.

Finally, the courts treat contracts for personal service quite differently than they do sales. When a *sale* is held to be valid, the seller must relinquish what she sold. But when the courts enforce a *contract of service*, the 'seller' (the person who received money) is rarely required to do what he promised to do (although he will have to make recompense of some kind).

I think the attractiveness of the 'sale' paradigm reflects the extent to which exchange theory, and neo-classical economics, operate as unchallenged assumptions. Note, for instance, the persistent tendency to think of gifts as disguised sales. However, I need not settle the disagreement here. Whether agreements to act are really sales or only metaphorically so, certain interesting questions arise within them, and only within them.

The moral considerations

Before presenting the questions specific to the 'sale of actions', let me note that many of the problems I have identified in ordinary sales also crop up here. We block employment contracts for dangerous and degrading work out of fear of injustice and exploitation, the same reasons for which we block the sale of organs. Most contracts for service which are blocked, however, are blocked for a different reason. They concern actions, and actions inherently involve purposes. When something is done for money, it is done for a different purpose than it otherwise is, and the change in purpose can change the nature of the action. To use an example of Eric Mack's, sexual love is not simply a 'fee-free version' of prostitution.[23] Many interactions change so radically when they are

---

[23] 'Dominos', 198–211.

done for money that they need new names. Take the court system: a judge whose decisions have been bought is no longer dispensing 'justice', because he or she is no longer deciding on the basis of evidence and law.

The new institution—criminal injustice, let us call it—is inferior to the one it replaces. Of course the judge has broken promises and broken the law, which adds to her wrongdoing; but it is not just the fact of her promise that matters, but its substance as well. Criminal justice, ideally, treats people equally; in it (again, ideally) people determine their own futures by the choices they make.[24] Bribery destroys all this.

The special characteristics of money highlight some of what has been lost. For one thing, since money accumulates so unevenly, no kind of equality before the law survives. For another, one's fate before the law depends not on one's conformity to it, but on the luck and effort which brought one money. Those qualities which lead to wealth, even the most admirable of those qualities, are only a subset of what makes people worthy. The same is true of democratic office. When the person in office is chosen by the voters, the office is democratic; when the person in office is chosen by people with the most money, the office is not.

Sex is a borderline case of this kind of essential change. Sexual interaction expresses many things, among them desire, affection, love, or commitment. The lovers may be set on exploitation, mutual reverence, pleasure, determined dedication, or some combination of these and other purposes. All of this informs what they do and what they experience. In commercial sex the partners need to care only about themselves. Each wants one thing—money, satisfaction, domination—and each agrees to give what the other wants. Neither needs to care about the other. Objections to prostitution assert that sexual interaction should not be a meeting of mutually self-interested parties, treating one another only as means to their own ends. Objectors hold that mutual concern is central to sex as it should be, and that any arrangement which makes mutual concern unnecessary and unlikely should not exist.

Divine favour is something else which would not be what it is if it could be bought. I suppose a deity is imaginable who looks with

---

[24] See Herbert Morris, 'Persons and Punishment', *The Monist*, 52 (1968), 475–501.

favour upon the wealthy,[25] or upon those who support the divine work with the most money. But that could not be the God of the Judaeo-Christian-Islamic tradition, loving all equally, responding to purity of soul.

Respect is another interesting case. On the face of it, we cannot respect someone because of the amount of money she has. Yet in a way we do; we can certainly be impressed. And we might well respect the effort and ability which brought her wealth. Still, that would not be respecting her for her money, but for what the money represents. And it is hard to imagine one person paying another for respect; one would get instead respectful actions, what MacIntyre calls simulacra, not the same thing at all. And so for prizes and honours: they represent accomplishment and merit. If they could be bought, they would represent something else: the luck, particular effort, and specific abilities which give one wealth. When a prize is bought, it is not really a prize at all.

Prohibitions on doing something for pay, then, usually concern actions whose very nature changes when money motivates them. Our language suggests that it is the presence of money which contaminates the interaction. Almost always phrases like 'X is for sale', when they are not literally true, are pejorative. My analysis suggests that it is not so much the presence of money as the absence of other things to which we object; but that is not quite the whole picture. Take, for instance, a recent article praising Jimmy Carter for his work in conflict resolution. In saying 'For Carter the presidency has a "Not for Sale" sign', the writer implicitly criticizes Ronald Reagan, who accepted a million dollars for a brief appearance in Japan. The implicit criticism was not just of a former president's doing nothing, but of his using his office for self-interest.

We use terms like buying and selling, then, partly to lament the extinction of something good, but also to rebuke the substitution of self-interest for the other, preferable, motives. If what Reagan had received were a priceless netsuke I suspect there would have been less outcry. Money seems to us the capital occasion for selfishness, because—I think—of its pure instrumentality. Desire for money has no admixture of appreciation of something's intrinsic value, as would desire for an exquisite carving.

[25] Calvin's God, I believe, rewarded the worthy with prosperity. The wealth was a sign, not a cause, of divine favour.

SUMMING UP

Questions about the proper scope of the market will always be with us. Money is so powerful that the borders between its domain and others will always need defence. At the beginning of this chapter I described a number of perspectives which have been offered to help us draw the border clearly. Margaret Jane Radin protects non-fungible property from the full force of the market; Michael Walzer limits the market in order to lessen oppression; Elizabeth Anderson analyses market relations (impersonality, self-interest, and so on) and shows that some good things cannot survive within them. Mark Nelson derives a number of loosely related principles from a set of examples.

The perspective I offer here is more complex. There are many reasons why some sales cannot or should not take place. The questions we need to ask include the following:

1. The possibility of ownership: Is it possible for this entity to be controlled by legal arrangements? (Divine grace and friendship cannot be.)

2. The morality of ownership; i.e. exclusive control: Is this the kind of thing which may legitimately be controlled? (No person should be completely subject to another.) Is this the kind of thing which may legitimately be kept from others? (Public goods should be available to all.)

3. The possibility of alienation, i.e. separation: can this thing be separated from the person to whom it now attaches? (Moral rights cannot be lost.)

4. The morality of alienation: Should it be possible for anyone to lose this? (Basic civil rights should be inalienable.)

5. The impact of the market on what is exchanged: Does exchanging this thing for gain endanger or demean it? (Some babies conceived for sale would suffer; some would be treated 'as means only'.)

6. The impact of the market on buyer and seller: Does exchanging this thing for gain exploit, endanger, or demean anyone? (Commercially obtained organs may be contaminated; sellers are poor and desperate.) To what extent does the market relationship of mutual self-interest crowd out other relationships of mutual concern?

7. The way money shapes an interaction: Everything priced is commensurable. (Can we retain an understanding of a child's immeasurable worth if the child was purchased?) Money is unevenly distributed; accumulating it depends upon luck, work, and ability. (Should civic duties be distributed upon different criteria, perhaps equally?)

8. The fact that accepting money essentially changes some actions: Does allowing people to do this for the sake of money destroy something of value (democratic office, prizes, criminal justice) or replace a desirable institution with a less-desirable or bad one (prostitution)?

I doubt that any single principle or perspective can synthesize all these questions. Yet they are more than simply a list. They form a logically related set which can help us think in an orderly way about the questions which steadily confront us.

Many people have pointed out to me that these questions are double-sided. A relationship can be *improved*, for instance, by being commercialized: money can counter social prejudice and bring it about, for example, that racists sell to and behave civilly towards minorities. The positive side of commodification could be approached through the same taxonomy with which I have here sketched the negative side.

POLITICAL IMPLICATIONS

It is the state, ultimately, which must confront the question of which exchanges to honour and which to block. Ownership and sale are legal facts, and as such made possible by state power. Many governments, for instance, do not allow private ownership of heroin and do not enforce contracts for prostitution.

If no single perspective comprises the various reasons for which exchanges should be blocked, it is unlikely that any single consideration will settle the role of government. Walzer's concern for 'complex equality' leads him to conclude that the state needs to protect the boundaries between spheres, but not to intervene within them. Complex equality, in turn, is meant to prevent domination, to prevent anyone from 'grinding the faces' of others. Put more positively, Walzer is concerned with democratic self-respect, an attitude not 'dependent on any particular social position . . . [but having to do with] one's sense of oneself . . . [as] a full and equal member, an active participant'. The 'deepest purpose' of distributive justice is to make self-respect possible (*Spheres*, 277–8).

David Miller, in his Introduction, suggests that these grounds should lead Walzer to approve, in some cases, political intervention within spheres and not just at their borders; and, conversely, that the borders themselves need not always be guarded. The taxonomy I have given suggests that Miller is right; furthermore, that reasons other than those of justice need to figure in a state's decisions about commerce.

What cannot be sold

For one large class—those things which by their very nature cannot be owned or cannot be alienated—it would seem that no action is necessary. What cannot be done need not be prohibited. But the situation is not so simple: perhaps the object cannot be sold, but people can still be deceived.

We worry considerably about some of these deceptions: about claims to offer divine favour in return for money; about false friends; about honours awarded for the wrong reasons; about corrupt judges. Of course the government has the responsibility to govern its own institutions, and so to regulate judges and other officials. In addition, the state has some natural role whenever money is involved; one of its purposes is the regulation of commerce, and embezzlement, fraud, and bribery are crimes. This means that Walzer is not quite right in saying that believers 'cannot be protected from fraud' (*Spheres*, 245). The slick preacher who uses donations for personal rather than religious use can go to jail. Other offenders of this kind, however, are beyond the law. The fund-raising minister who uses donations *as he said he would*, even if that means a Rolls Royce for every member of his family, cannot be touched. Nor can the fair-weather, fair-fortune friend.

The law has to be limited in these cases of obvious abuse. First, the conceptual point: religious claims by their very nature cannot be settled by vote, nor by political bargaining. Secondly, the Walzerian, normative point: religion should be kept largely independent of political power because religion is an independent source of meaning and self-affirmation. It has often been a sanctuary for the disenfranchised and the persecuted. Walzer points out the slow steps by which Americans recognized, and built, a wall separating church and state.

But though the law must be limited, society has more scope. As Mill realized, social pressure is fearsome. When honours are corrupted, exchanged for money, or for favours, then gossip, public outcry, and organized resistance can come to the rescue. When friends are false, other friends may sound a warning. When religion grows corrupt there is likely to be a reformation or an expulsion. None of this works faultlessly or painlessly; I only want to say that, where the state cannot reach, society retains powerful weapons. And just as the state needs to be circumscribed even at some cost, so it is good that social pressure is limited. As Walzer could point out, social spheres need to be kept somewhat separate. Otherwise goods like the ability to choose one's friends and beliefs would be in danger. Privacy and autonomy would bow beneath the tyranny of social acceptability.

What should not be sold

The state has a more obvious role in the case of things which could be sold, but should not be. My first category of this kind concerned what should not be owned in the first place. Recognizing that people should not be fully subject to the control of others, we have outlawed slavery and indentured servitude. This is a fine example of keeping Walzerian spheres separate: the proper domain of commerce is what is properly subject to human control.

The domain of commerce should also be limited to what other human beings (non-owners) may properly be excluded from. The decision to make schools, police protection, and so on generally available may again count as guarding boundaries: basic physical safety along with the chance for intellectual growth, it might be thought, should not depend on one's skill and luck in the market. But no general argument is available here. Different goods might be kept public for different reasons. Few of our roads charge tolls, almost none are privately owned. Suppose the purpose behind that is to make trade more efficient and to lessen barriers to newcomers. That might be considered intervention *within* commerce, to improve it on its own terms and to establish some equity. (Antimonopoly laws have the same purpose.)

The second category of things which could be sold but should not be is that which should be inalienable; civil rights are a clear case. If we say, as I did, that in these respects people should be 'invincibly armoured', the metaphor resembles Walzer's bounded spheres. And of course he talks quite explicitly about many of these basic rights. The decision to marry belongs to the couple, not to the state, nor to their parents. This is the sphere of intimacy. Similarly religion and the press need to be protected from the state.

The third category is that which should not be exchanged. The first reason for forbidding exchange is danger to the participants. Besides the complete prohibitions mentioned earlier (kidneys, for instance), regulations like food and drug laws fit here. (What may not be exchanged is *unapproved* food.) And when the state forbids certain actions, like offers of unsafe employment, out of fear of exploitation, that too is motivated by a desire to protect people. Are these rules at the boundaries of 'spheres', or within them? The answer is not clear. Complete prohibitions (say, of the sale of kidneys) seem to act at the boundary of the sphere of money, but what sphere is protected is not obvious. Safety and health do not seem like spheres. And regulations (say of food or workplace safety) seem to operate within a sphere. Perhaps, however, these prohibitions could fairly be described as means of protecting a sense of equal citizenship. They all keep disadvantage in the market from damaging or destroying the rest of one's life.

Finally there are areas where markets put our shared understanding of something at risk. Should children be given a price? Should blood be considered a commodity? Here it is a little clearer that boundaries are being protected: not only is the domain of commerce limited, but neighbouring protected domains can be described: family life, perhaps, and a health-care-providing gift-exchange network.

In the end, however, Walzer's 'complex equality' seems to me more properly 'complex inequality'. The separation of spheres helps keep any person or group from being dominant in all; it also helps, a little, to ensure that no one is subordinate in all. But it is not just social arrangements that make defeat in one area so often lead to defeat in another. People are complex emotional, social, cognitive wholes, who can find themselves in downward spirals: one failure breeds others. We get discouraged, we lose our footing, we turn away from our friends. What is important, as I think Walzer suggests, is that there be a fundamental dignity and decency which it is hard to lose. As he puts it, the powerful should not be able to grind the faces of the powerless; but I would say even more, that there needs to be some fundamental social understanding which inhibits the least powerful from self-loathing and self-destruction: from grinding their own faces. Although I agree that simple equality is rarely what is needed for its own sake, and that preventing tyranny is an important part of what is needed, I do not think that alone will answer. In recent work Walzer has begun to address these questions.[26]

The taxonomy I have presented, therefore, indicates that there are reasons for states to intervene within spheres as well as at their boundaries; furthermore, as Miller suggests, that the idea of equal citizenship does some work that the metaphor of bounded spheres does not. I conclude as well that Walzerian dominance is not the only threat to self-respect and that self-respect is not the only reason for prohibiting exchanges.

[26] Michael Walzer, 'Exclusion, Injustice, and the Democratic State', *Dissent* (Winter 1993), 56.

9

Complex Equality

DAVID MILLER

My aim in this chapter is to develop and explore Michael Walzer's notion of complex equality as a way of bringing together the potentially conflicting ideas of distributive justice and social equality. In Walzer's *Spheres of Justice*[1] we have the materials out of which may be constructed understandings of these notions that are quite different from (and, I believe, superior to) those to be found in the mainstream of political philosophy. I do not claim that my reading of Walzer is absolutely faithful to his intentions, for, as I indicate below, there is some ambiguity, especially in his conception of equality. I intend rather to develop more explicitly certain conceptual theses implicit in Walzer's work, and, in the second half of the chapter, to examine the empirical plausibility of some of these theses.

SIMPLE AND COMPLEX EQUALITY

The idea of complex equality can perhaps best be introduced by contrast with ideas of simple equality. I call an idea of equality 'simple' when it holds that equality requires the equal possession or enjoyment of some advantage X. A society is egalitarian, on this view, when all its members are equal in respect of X; that is, they equally enjoy the stuff or the condition represented by X. There are as many notions of simple equality as there are plausible contenders for the X in this formula: candidates include property, income, opportunity, rights, resources, capacities, and welfare. In

I am grateful to members of the Nuffield Political Theory Workshop for discussion of the issues raised in this chapter, and especially to Jos de Beus, Simon Caney, Adam Swift, Robert Van der Veen, Michael Walzer, and Andrew Williams for their written comments on earlier drafts.

[1] (New York: Basic Books, 1983).

recent political philosophy there has been a fierce debate as to
which of these objects of distribution best captures our intuitive
sense of what it means to treat people equally, or to show them
equal concern. The debate is about 'equality of what?'[2] But
although the participants disagree about how the blank in the formula should be filled in, they agree that the formula itself is an adequate way of representing the ideal of equality.

I do not mean to suggest that simple egalitarians always advocate the unconditional application of the ideal of equality that they
favour. Having defined the ideal, very often they go on to say that
we may have to sacrifice equality to some extent in order to promote rival values such as individual choice or social utility. Indeed,
as I shall later argue, there is a tendency to convert simple equality into a form that makes these trade-offs less acute—for instance
into some version of Rawls's principle that the advantages of the
worst-off group in society should be maximized. But this has the
effect of obliterating the value of equality itself. If when we talk
about equality we are really talking about the Rawlsian difference
principle, then what intrinsic value is there in the equal distribution of our favoured X? Simple egalitarians begin by proclaiming
a radical principle, such as equality of resources, and then go on
to qualify it in such a way that it becomes difficult to see what is
distinctively egalitarian about the final outcome. So if we are
inclined to think that equality does indeed have a value of its own,
not reducible to other values such as the relief of poverty, we
should not begin by looking for some version of simple equality as
a way of expressing that value.

Complex equality requires us to adopt a different starting-point.
We should abandon the search for some favoured characteristic X,
the equal distribution of which would realise equality. Instead we
should envisage social equality arising as a by-product of many
separate distributions, each of which is in itself inegalitarian, in the
sense that individuals enjoy different quantities of X, Y, Z, and so
forth.[3] So here equality does not refer to the way some identifiable

---

[2] See A. Sen, 'Equality of What?' in *Choice, Welfare and Measurement* (Oxford:
Blackwell, 1982) and G. A. Cohen's mirroring of this title in 'Equality of What? On
Welfare, Goods, and Capabilities', in M. Nussbaum and A. Sen (eds.), *The Quality
of Life* (Oxford: Clarendon Press, 1992).

[3] I later qualify this assertion, however, when I claim that complex equality does
in fact require one form of simple equality, namely equality of citizenship (see
n. 16).

good is distributed, but describes the overall character of a set of social relationships. How is it possible, though, for relationships of this kind to be regarded as egalitarian in nature? I shall argue, following Walzer, that a society whose distributive practices are radically pluralistic—recognizing many irreducibly different kinds of social goods, each having its own criterion of just distribution— may achieve an overarching equality of status among its members. This idea of a fundamental equality of status (whose meaning I shall attempt to elucidate shortly) yields the best interpretation of social equality.

Now it might seem that in making this claim I have merely added another candidate—namely status—to the list of contenders for X in the 'equality of X' formula; that what is being offered is really just another version of simple equality. However, such an appearance is misleading, as I shall now try to show. Simple equality is about assigning shares of some good to each of a number of persons. It is a distributive ideal applying to individuals. In some cases, such as equality of income, what it requires is that our institutions should be arranged so that an equal share of X is directly distributed to each person. In other cases, such as equality of welfare, we cannot directly distribute X; however, we can attempt to distribute some other good Y so that, taking account of each individual's propensity for converting Y into X, the correct distribution of Y produces an equal distribution of X. Thus, if we know how each person converts income into well-being, we can in principle arrange to have income distributed in such a manner that everyone's level of welfare is equalized.

Equality of status, in the sense in which I shall understand it, is not in this way an ideal specifying distributions to individuals. Let us say provisionally that equality of status obtains when each member of society regards him- or herself as fundamentally the equal of all the others, and is regarded by the others as fundamentally their equal. It should be obvious that status in this sense is not a good that can be directly distributed equally. There is nothing one can hand out to individual people in the way that one can hand out titles to income or property. Nor does it seem likely that there will be some other good Y, the appropriate distribution of which will lead to equality of status. For it is not a question of how each particular individual converts Y into X, as it was in the case of income and welfare. Rather, in so far as a certain distribution of Y may contribute to or detract from equality of status, it must do so by way of social understandings. That is, given the way that other kinds of goods are distributed in the society we are considering, and given the way that Y is understood in that society, the distribution of Y that is being proposed may be seen as helping to establish equality of status, or as having the opposite effect. The link between the distributed item and the egalitarian outcome here depends not on features of individuals, but on a shared social understanding of the relevance of one to the other. This is why, on the complex egalitarian view, equality must be conceived as a characteristic of social relations, not as a property of distributions to individuals.

Complex equality not only gives us a different understanding of the ideal of equality itself; it also differs from simple equality in the way that it conceives the relationship between equality and distributive justice. On the simple view, the relationship is a conceptual one: the principle of equality could equally well be described as the principle of egalitarian justice.[4] Pinning down the appropriate X in the 'equality of X' formula is also determining what (egalitarian) justice requires in respect of the distribution of X. Now a simple egalitarian might go on to argue that justice is a more complex notion than this appears to suggest, and that (for example) departures from equality should be regarded as just when these reflect the voluntary choices of all the individuals concerned. He would then arrive at a formula such as this: justice in the distribution of X = equality in the distribution of X, unless inequalities in the distribution of X arise by voluntary choice. Here the conceptual link between justice and equality is retained, but given a slightly more subtle expression. Either way, equality as a social ideal is subsumed conceptually within justice. There is no particular problem in understanding why equality should be valued; it is simply (part of) justice.

Matters stand differently in the case of complex equality. Here equality and distributive justice are each conceived as free-standing social ideals, and the link between them is an empirical one. Justice comprises the various criteria that govern the allocation of social

---

[4] This assimilation is particularly clear in G. A. Cohen, 'On the Currency of Egalitarian Justice', *Ethics*, 99 (1988–9), 906–44, and in R. Dworkin, 'What is Equality? Part 2: Equality of Resources', *Philosophy and Public Affairs*, 10 (1981), 283–345.

goods; it is a distributive notion. Equality is a predicate of the whole society within which many just distributions occur. The argument of the complex egalitarian, of course, is that by ensuring that justice is done within each particular sphere we may achieve overall equality, but this is not asserted as a matter of conceptual necessity. The claim is a broadly sociological one. We can conceive (as Walzer does) of a counter-example in the form of a society in which goods are always allocated according to relevant criteria but in which certain individuals outstrip the rest along all dimensions, thereby creating an élite and destroying social equality (*Spheres*, 20). A defence of complex equality requires us to show that such counter-examples will not occur in practice. I shall consider some of the issues this raises later in the paper.

So far I have endeavoured to explain the difference between simple and complex ideals of equality without giving any grounds for preferring the latter. Let me now give some reasons for rejecting simple equality. The first is the elusiveness of the X in the 'equality of X' formula. We are invited to consider in respect of what does it matter fundamentally that people should be treated equally. On close inspection it turns out that none of the candidates proposed meets this condition; each is open to serious objection.[5] We may legitimately suspect that there is *no* single ground of equal treatment that is of paramount importance; instead, our concern for people is irreducibly multifaceted. We are concerned in one way that their opportunities should be equal, in another way that their resources should be equal, in yet another way that their welfare should be equal, and so forth. Where these concerns clash, there is no more basic currency in terms of which they can be reconciled.[6]

A defender of simple equality might argue here that the failure of the quest so far does not imply that we will never find a single basic currency which is adequate to express our commitment to equality. But now consider a second difficulty. Suppose for the sake of argument that we succeed in identifying an X which fits the 'equality of X' formula and which captures our basic concern for equality: it matters fundamentally to us that people should be equal in their shares of X. Suppose also, however, that starting

---

[5] I have argued this in the case of some of the main contenders in D. Miller, 'Equality', in G. Hunt (ed.), *Philosophy and Politics* (Cambridge: Cambridge Univ. Press, 1990).

[6] See Cohen, 'Currency', esp. 921.

from an equal distribution of X, it is possible to engineer a strongly Pareto-improving change, i.e. to move to a situation in which shares of X are unequal, but in which everyone has more of X than in the original condition of equality. If we are fundamentally concerned about people's shares of X, how can we fail to applaud a change which increases everyone's share of X while at the same time breaking the equality?[7] In particular, should we not endorse the equivalent of Rawls's difference principle applied to X, namely the principle that we should maximize the minimum quantity of X enjoyed by anyone in our society regardless of the degree of inequality that that outcome requires?[8]

A simple egalitarian might try to fend off this objection by emphasizing the conceptual relationship that is assumed to exist between justice and equality. Pareto-improving inequalities in the distribution of X might be *justified*, all things considered, but this does not show that they are necessarily *just*. But here we must test the strength of the postulated link between justice and equality. There is one obvious connection of this sort, namely the requirement of justice that all those who are equal in the relevant respects should be treated equally. But this is plainly a formal condition and implies nothing about what are to count as relevant similarities and differences. Why should we suppose that justice requires equality in any more substantive sense than this? If, instead of taking it for granted that the principles of justice we aim to discover must be principles of equality, we were simply to consider a number of distributive questions and ask what justice required in the case of each, we would find that the criterion of just distribution varied according to what it was we were being asked to distribute. In particular, *desert* is often a relevant criterion of just distribu-

---

[7] This is the line of thought pursued to telling effect by J. Raz in *The Morality of Freedom* (Oxford: Clarendon Press, 1986), ch. 9, who argues that many so-called principles of equality are better construed as principles of entitlement (i.e. principles asserting that everyone has a right to a certain level of X). I have examined the limits of this argument in 'Equality after Raz', forthcoming in S. Caney and A. Williams (eds.), *Joseph Raz's Political Philosophy*.

[8] An egalitarian might attempt to meet this challenge by asking *why* inequalities in the distribution of X are needed in order to raise the minimum to its highest point. An argument of this form is presented in G. A. Cohen, 'Incentives, Inequality, and Community', in S. M. McMurrin (ed.), *The Tanner Lectures on Human Values*, xiii (Salt Lake City: Univ. of Utah Press, 1992). But Cohen does not assert that Pareto-superior inequalities are impossible; his argument is that they are not compatible with the existence of a certain kind of community. So equality is saved here by invoking community as an independent value.

tion—indeed there are some goods, honours, and prizes, for instance, that can only exist on condition that this *is* the criterion—and desert is a differentiating rather than an equalizing notion. Attempts to mount a general defence of equal distribution by appeal to desert are bound to collapse.[9]

The virtue of Walzer's notion of complex equality is that, rather than reducing distributive justice to some simple principle of egalitarian form, he openly acknowledges the plurality of principles of justice and seeks to make this very pluralism the basis of equality. An egalitarian society must be one which recognizes a number of distinct goods—money, power, office, education, and so on—and which ensures that each of these is distributed according to its own proper criterion. The enemy of equality is *dominance*, which occurs when holders of one good are able to capitalize on their position in order to obtain other goods for which they do not fulfil the relevant criteria. In each particular sphere of distribution, some people will succeed in getting more goods than others, but so long as they cannot convert this sphere-specific advantage into general advantage by means of illicit conversions, their overall relationship will still be one of equality.[10]

The precise sense in which this ideal can legitimately claim to be an ideal of *equality* is considered in the following section. What Walzer's view promises, however, is a free-standing concept of equality that is empirically linked with, but not conceptually reducible to, the idea of distributive justice. Needless to say this gain comes at a price: if the empirical link fails, then we may be forced to sacrifice equality for the sake of justice, or vice versa. But if we think social equality has a value that is independent of justice, while still holding on to distributive justice as a value in its own right, the view I am sketching must seem an enticing one.

There are of course many who would deny that equality has any independent value. They would claim that such currency as the ideal of equality has in our society arises from a confusion between justice and equality. Once that confusion is sorted out, equality evaporates as an ideal.[11] The following case may serve as a test of

---

[9] I have explored this point more fully in 'Arguments for Equality', in P. A. French, T. E. Uehling, and H. K. Wettstein (eds.), *Midwest Studies in Philosophy*, vii (Minneapolis: Univ. of Minn. Press, 1982).

[10] See Walzer's formulation of this point as cited on pp. 2–3 of my Introduction.

[11] Vigorous arguments to this effect can be found: e.g. in A. Flew, *The Politics of Procrustes* (London: Temple Smith, 1981) and W. Letwin (ed.), *Against Equality*

intuitions about this claim. Suppose that in a school there is one boy who is outstanding in all directions. He gets top marks in the examinations, he wins the victor ludorum in the school sports, he plays the leading role in the annual play, etc. There is no question that he has fairly achieved these rewards; each child, let us suppose, was given an equal chance to develop and display his or her talents. Nor is there any question of the avenues of achievement being tailored to his capacities—these are the activities, let us suppose, that any school should sponsor and recognize performance in. So justice has been done when this boy gathers all the honours. One may still, none the less, feel some regret that this is how things have worked out. One may believe that it would be better for relationships within the school, and for the self-estimation of both this boy and the other children, if honours were more widely distributed. Anyone who does believe this sees a value in social equality which is independent of justice (since *ex hypothesi* justice has been fully realized in the case as described). It is not necessary in order to have this belief to have some concrete proposal for achieving greater equality. In the case in question it may be that there is no way to enhance equality without trespassing on justice, and we may think that justice should take precedence.[12] So I want to focus attention on the bare belief that a state of affairs in which one person wins in all of the spheres of distribution is less desirable than one in which goods are distributed in more varied fashion. Holding this belief is the litmus test for a commitment to social equality.

EQUALITY OF STATUS

Having set out the general grounds for favouring a complex notion of equality to a simple notion, I want now to say something about the sense in which complex equality is indeed a notion of equality. For it is by no means obvious why pluralism in the distribution of social goods should give rise to anything we could recognize as

(London: Macmillan, 1983). I have argued elsewhere that egalitarianism is integral to social relations in modern market societies, so that wholesale rejection of the ideal of equality makes no sense: this still leaves it open, of course, which kind or kinds of equality we should pursue. See Miller, 'Equality'.

[12] Of course, if this were universally the case, social equality would cease to function as a political ideal capable of guiding policy. I return to consider this point in the final section of the chapter.

social equality. This aspect of his position is left undeveloped by Walzer, whose attention is mainly focused on demonstrating the plurality of spheres of justice in contemporary societies. His failure to specify the precise character of the argument connecting pluralism to equality leaves him open to the charge that his egalitarianism is vanishingly weak.[13]

I have argued elsewhere that there are different ways of reading Walzer's claim that, where each social good is distributed according to its appropriate criterion, the outcome is a complex form of equality.[14] One reading would make this claim into a claim about compensation: being relatively disadvantaged in one sphere (money and commodities, say) is compensated for by being relatively advantaged in another sphere (public office, say) so that, summing up advantages across all spheres, each citizen achieves roughly the same total. But although Walzer sometimes uses language which suggests this reading, it does not seem consistent with his underlying contention that the goods in question are fundamentally different in kind. For the latter implies incommensurability: if money and political power, say, represent two radically different currencies, no conversion between them will be possible. And equally it will not make sense to think of person A being *compensated* for his low standing in the sphere of money by his advantaged position in the sphere of public office.

A second reading of Walzer's claim would make it a claim about equality of power. Where the separation of spheres of justice is maintained, no one is able to use his privileged position in one sphere to obtain goods in other spheres to which he is not entitled by the criteria applying there. Thus complex equality stands opposed to tyranny—the dominance of one particular good and its holders. But although equality of power in this broad sense is undoubtedly part of what Walzer has in mind, it does not appear to me to exhaust his understanding of complex equality. A society which respected the separation of the spheres could in principle also be one in which there were a few very wealthy people, a few with great political power, and so forth, but in which the vast majority registered low scores on all these dimensions. This does not seem to match Walzer's underlying idea that complex equality

---

[13] See e.g. R. Arneson in Ch. 10. [14] Miller, 'Equality', s. iii.

gives us a society in which men and women are fundamentally one another's equals.

As I have indicated, I believe we should read Walzer's claim as a claim about status. In a society which realizes complex equality, people enjoy a basic equality of status which overrides their unequal standing in particular spheres of justice such as money and power. Now we need to be clear here about what 'status' means when the claim is made. There is a sense of 'status' which brings it close to 'prestige'—for instance, sociologists will talk about 'occupational status' when referring to the different levels of prestige enjoyed by different jobs. 'Status' here is a differentiating notion and refers to a person's position on some ladder of achievement. In this sense, clearly, people will not enjoy equality of status under complex equality, since they will typically rise to different levels in the various spheres of justice. In another sense, however, status can refer to a person's basic standing within a society, as manifested by the way in which he or she is regarded by the public institutions and by other individuals. Some societies draw a line between those of their inhabitants who enjoy full rights of citizenship and those who are excluded: here a person either has the status of citizen or the status of non-citizen and there are no gradations within those categories. Thus we would naturally describe all citizens as enjoying an equal status *qua* citizens.

It is status in this latter sense which is intended in the claim that complex equality is best understood as equality of status. The argument for this claim can be put as follows. Where a society recognizes many separate spheres of distribution, individuals will characteristically rank very differently in the several spheres. Some will be successful at making money, others will achieve recognition as artists or scientists, others will gain prominence in political circles. Because the goods they enjoy are incommensurable with one another—there is no common currency in terms of which money, recognition, and power can be valued against one another—it is not possible from a social point of view to rank individuals against one another overall.[15] One cannot say that Smith, a successful businessman, stands higher than Jones, a well-regarded scientist, in general, although Smith of course will rank higher than Jones in

---

[15] It is of course possible for anyone to impose his or her own ranking by assigning weights to the different goods. But this would be a matter of individual judgement, and would not translate into social inequality of status.

the sphere of money just as Jones will rank higher than Smith in the sphere of recognition. Where overall ranking is impossible, the status of individuals depends only on their common position as members of a particular society. Provided they are defined as equals by the public institutions of their society, this status must be an equal one.[16]

A society of complex equality is contrasted with a ranked society in which there is consensus about where people stand in a more or less sharply defined system of social classes. People think of themselves as belonging to one or other of these classes, and interact with other individuals on the basis of norms and expectations governing inter- and intra-class relations. Typically there will be titles, special forms of address, conventional modes of displaying deference, and so forth. Social ranking is clearly a matter of degree, and one should regard complex equality as standing at the end of a spectrum, the other end of which is occupied by a caste system in which inequalities of rank are fixed, pervasive, and publicly affirmed.

The appeal of an egalitarian society, the reason why social equality is widely valued, is that it aspires to be a society in which people deal with one another simply as individuals, taking account only of personal capacities, needs, achievements, etc., without the blocking effect of status differences.[17] This is by no means an incontestable ideal. There is nothing incomprehensible about aristocratic disdain for the easy familiarity between people implied by it. Nevertheless it seems to be an ideal that is widely endorsed in societies that are already individualistic, but have not yet achieved

[16] As I have argued in 'Equality', this implies that equal rights of citizenship are a necessary (though not sufficient) condition of complex equality, since they define the equal formal status of all members of society. I take these rights for granted in the discussion that follows, and concentrate on what other conditions are necessary for complex equality to obtain.

[17] This demonstrates a convergence between my own characterization of social equality as involving equality of status, and Runciman's approach, which involves distinguishing between inequalities of praise and inequalities of respect, and then summarizing the ideal of social equality in the maxim: free inequality of praise, no inequality of respect: W. G. Runciman, ' "Social" Equality', *Sociology in its Place* (Cambridge: Cambridge Univ. Press, 1970). I believe, in fact, that these two characterizations are simply two sides of the same coin. However, I resist the suggestion that one can understand equality of status *in terms of* equality of respect, because the latter notion is fraught with ambiguities and can be developed in different ways (Runciman anchors it somewhat by defining it in contrast to praise). One might say that equality of status corresponds to *one conception* of equality of respect.

a full measure of complex equality. The values at stake here can perhaps best be suggested by the responses invoked in a survey sample by the question 'What sort of changes in social class in America would you like to see in the future, and why those?' Among those who favoured moving towards a classless society, the following reactions were typical:

Social class as a way of treating others should be eradicated. People should be treated equally.

I think everyone should be judged as a person, not by his job or how much money he has. Judging that way is the main thing wrong now.

I hope the time will come when everyone will get along as one class without regard for race, creed, and colour, and all these extraneous things like income and material well-being.[18]

Each of these reactions appears to pick up a different aspect of the ideal of an egalitarian society in which people's behaviour towards one another is not conditioned by differences of rank, in which specific inequalities—in income, say—do not crystallize into judgements of overall personal worth, and in which barriers of class do not stand in the way of mutual understanding and sympathy. This, I am suggesting, is the meaning that equality has for us when it is a free-standing value, not merely a corollary of a notion of distributive justice which in particular circumstances has egalitarian implications.[19]

Let me conclude this section by clarifying the formal status of the complex equality argument. The argument holds that distributive pluralism plus equal citizenship leads to equality of status. These conditions should not be seen as strictly necessary for equality of status to obtain. We might envisage a very simple society with few goods which achieved equality of status by practising simple equality with respect to those goods. As I understand the complex equality argument, it holds that simple equality of this kind is precluded by well-known features of modern societies. But it tries to turn one such feature—the plurality of spheres of justice—to

[18] Quoted in R. P. Coleman and L. Rainwater, *Social Standing in America* (London: Routledge & Kegan Paul, 1979), 299–300.

[19] After writing this chapter I found a rather similar interpretation of equality crisply presented in M. Kaus, *The End of Equality* (New York: Basic Books, 1992). Like me, Kaus argues for a link between distributive pluralism and social equality as understood here. Kaus goes on to argue, however, that reducing inequalities in income and wealth is essentially irrelevant to the pursuit of social equality, and here I part company with him, for reasons to be given later.

positive advantage by connecting it to social equality. On the other hand, distributive pluralism plus equal citizenship are not strictly sufficient for equality of status: the linking mechanism may fail to operate, for reasons that will be explored in the next section. So the argument should be understood roughly as follows: if you care about social equality and are concerned to achieve it in modern social conditions, the best prospect is via distributive pluralism and equal citizenship together. Complete success is not guaranteed, but there is no other feasible route to follow.

CHALLENGES TO COMPLEX EQUALITY

Having identified the sense of equality that underlies complex equality and sketched the argument that links pluralism with equality, I now want to examine that argument more carefully and critically. Let us accept for the moment the basic Walzerian assumption that social goods are irreducibly plural and that each has its own proper criterion of distribution. Why might a society embodying these principles fail to achieve the condition we have identified as complex equality?

One possibility is simply that the same individuals might win out in all the spheres of distribution. This possibility is considered by Walzer and his reaction to it is that such an outcome is highly unlikely to occur (since the qualities needed to succeed in the various spheres are quite different), but that if it did this would 'suggest in the strongest way that a society of equals was not a lively possibility' (*Spheres*, 20). To take this further, we need to look more closely at what it means for one set of individuals to outstrip others across the spheres. Let us say that A outranks B when A scores more highly than B in every distributive sphere that engages our sense of justice (is wealthier than B, more highly educated, has greater political influence, etc.).[20] If we apply this criterion to a multi-member society, there are three relevant possibilities.

[20] In the case of at least two of Walzer's spheres ('Security and welfare' and 'Hard work') this notion of scoring more highly does not make sense if applied literally. In the case of hard work, one needs to run the argument in the other direction (as Walzer says, it is a negative good): A outscores B if he does less (degrading) hard work than B. I am not sure that the other sphere referred to, covering medical and other needs, can be fitted into the present part of the argument; it seems better to treat it as an adjunct of citizenship.

1. No individual outranks any other individual.

2. Some individuals outrank other individuals, but it is not possible to partition society into two subsets such that all the members of one outrank all the members of the other.

3. Some individuals outrank others, and it is possible to partition society as in (2).

It might seem at first glance that, for a society to embody equality of status, (1) must obtain. But in fact this is far too stringent a criterion, as can be seen from the following thought experiment. Suppose we begin with a situation in which (1) does indeed obtain, and suppose that A comes to score more highly on some dimension on which she was previously inferior to B and thereby comes to outrank B (but there are no other changes). Does this upset equality of status? Surely not, for A still ranks equally with everyone bar B and B still ranks equally with everyone bar A. Reiterating this example, we can see that a society meeting condition (2) can still embody equality of status even in the face of a large number of individual outrankings. For status judgements are made not by considering how particular individuals rank against other particular individuals, but by considering individuals, or sets of individuals, against society as a whole. So A may on the whole be a successful individual in the sense that she outstrips many people across the board, but because her ranking *vis-à-vis* many *other* people is indeterminate, there is no reason to regard her as occupying a superior station.

On the other hand, if condition (3) is realized, then we do have the basis for a systematic inequality of status and complex equality is undermined. So much will depend on whether it is reasonable to expect individual outrankings to lead to (2) or to (3). In general they will lead to (2). In contemporary Western societies, we might expect to find many individual instances of outranking, but very few cases in which sets of individuals outranked the remainder. This is in contrast to hierarchical societies of the feudal or caste types, where the same small group of people typically possess superior shares of power, wealth, prestige, etc. To the extent that modern Western societies incorporate an underclass, in the familiar sense of a category of people suffering from poor educational levels, unemployment, low income, social marginality etc., we may find sufficient systematic outranking to defeat equality of status. One of the tasks of the complex egalitarian is then to show that a regime of complex equality can prevent the emergence of such an under-class.[21] This is no easy task, but my point is that there are specific features in this case which point towards a social division along the lines of condition (3). If we look at the rankings of people above the underclass, then what we find is captured by (2) rather than (3).

It might be argued here that condition (3) is too strong when considered as a necessary condition for inequality of status. I have said that A outranks B when A scores more highly than B across all relevant spheres; but suppose we weaken this to say that A is ahead of B in most (but not necessarily all) spheres. Saying this requires us to make some rough judgements about how spheres are to be counted when establishing a person's overall standing, but it may be that we can make such judgements even if we hold on to the idea that the goods distributed in the different spheres are strictly speaking incommensurable. We might then have a state of affairs in which those belonging to set H collectively outranked those belonging to L, in the sense that some individual members of H strictly outranked individual members of L, while rather more individuals in H loosely outranked (as explained above) individuals in L; whereas within both H and L outranking in either sense was uncommon. This may represent the present position of the upper class in Western societies: the members of this group score highly enough in most spheres for us to judge that they do indeed form a separate and superior class, notwithstanding dramatic downward dives in particular cases (princesses with no formal educational qualifications, the domestic unhappiness of many of the very rich, etc.).

The complex egalitarian does not need, or indeed want, to say that contemporary societies already fulfil the conditions for complex equality. On the other hand, if the conditions are made too stringent, the ideal becomes utopian. Insisting on (1)—the complete absence of individual outrankings—is utopian in this sense. Condition (2) is more feasible and appears to be fulfilled in the case

[21] Walzer has addressed this question in 'Exclusion, Injustice, and the Democratic State', *Dissent*, 40 (1993), 55–64. His argument is that members of the underclass are indeed excluded from equal citizenship, but that this reflects not merely a failure of complex equality, but of distributive justice. In various subtle, perhaps unrecognized, ways, the dispossessed group are given less than their fair share in spheres such as those of work, education, and welfare. So on Walzer's view the problem is not just one of systematic outranking, but of the distributive mechanisms that lie beneath the outranking. Kaus also addresses the underclass question in *The End of Equality*, and makes some robust proposals for solving it.

of roughly the middle 70 per cent of the advanced Western societies. So the task facing the complex egalitarian is to find the means whereby those who now constitute the underclass and the upper class can come to share in the basic equality of standing which this middle 70 per cent now enjoy.

The first challenge to complex equality arose from the possibility of individuals systematically outranking one another across the spheres. The second challenge that I want to consider holds that one sphere of distribution may become so pre-eminent that people can be ranked socially simply on the basis of how they perform in that sphere. Because overwhelming importance is attached to people's performance in sphere W, the fact that their relative ranking in that sphere is not mirrored in spheres X, Y, Z, does not prevent confident social judgements of relative standing. In our social context, this is most likely to take the form of the pre-eminence of money. What matters most in judging people's standing is their wealth or income. This may swamp other factors, it is alleged, to the extent that class distinctions may exist merely on account of large monetary differences.

Before assessing this challenge, let me make it clear that I am treating it as a claim about the *pre-eminence* of money, not a claim about the *dominance* of money in Walzer's sense. To claim that money is a dominant good is to claim that possession of money allows people to achieve pre-eminence in other spheres to which they are not entitled by their performance in those spheres (e.g. to buy political office or recognition). I shall return to the issue of dominance later. Here I am contemplating the possibility that, although money is not allowed to trespass beyond its proper sphere, a person's standing in that sphere none the less exercises a controlling influence on his or her social standing generally, undermining the argument for equality of status that I sketched above.

There is evidence that suggests that the pre-eminence claim holds true in contemporary societies. People generally perceive their society as embodying class distinctions, and when asked what it is that determines an individual's class position, the main factor cited is level of income. In one study, an attempt was made to quantify the respective weights that Americans gave to income, job, and education level in arriving at judgements of social standing: the conclusion reached was 'that variations in income status account for almost two-thirds of the variation in general social standing, and that schooling status and job status split the remainder about evenly. Income is of overwhelming importance in how Americans think about social standing'.[22] Moreover 'this is especially true of people's intuitive weighing and dividing when incomes are extreme. Very low incomes are almost invariably a source of very low ratings of general standing. Very high incomes are not quite so invariably translated into equally high general status, but at least they always seem to place their recipient far above the common man.'[23]

To consider the significance of this evidence, we should note that the weightings were arrived at by presenting survey subjects with descriptions of hypothetical people characterized in terms of income, job, and education (e.g. 'What standing would you assign to a truck driver with five years of secondary education and an income of $7,500?'). Thus other factors bearing on standing that might weigh with people in concrete cases were automatically excluded. Under these circumstances, it is possible that people attach a great deal of weight to income not because they regard it as of overwhelming intrinsic importance in determining status, but because they regard it also as a proxy for other factors which also weigh heavily as determinants of status (but which the survey excludes). Why might this be? One possibility is that people themselves regard income as a dominant good, in the sense that they think of possessing a high income as the key to attaining other goods such as power or recognition. Alternatively, they might think of income as a sign that its holder possessed a range of abilities that would tend to ensure success in other spheres too. In either case, they would be acting on the rule of thumb: if you have to guess a person's social standing on the basis of limited information about them, the best indicator of performance across the spheres of distribution is the person's income. If that *were* the case, then confident income-based judgements about standing in hypothetical cases might be replaced by much more uncertainty if people had to estimate the relative standing of actual persons, given full evidence about performance in different spheres of distribution.

[22] Coleman and Rainwater, *Social Standing*, 220.   [23] Ibid. 218.

However, although for the reason just given we need to treat with some caution the discovery that people seem ready to make judgements of general social standing based primarily on income levels—a discovery which appears to threaten the claim of complex equality—I do not want to exclude the possibility that the scale of income inequality in contemporary societies constitutes an independent obstacle to complex equality. It may be that where income differences are very large they are sufficient by themselves to give rise to perceived class divisions, even when they are offset by other distributive spheres. In that case, the complex egalitarian will no longer be able to confine his attentions to the control of dominance: maintaining the separation of the spheres of justice may not be sufficient to achieve equality of status. In addition there may need to be some bounding of inequality in whatever sphere threatens to become pre-eminent—the sphere of money in contemporary market societies, perhaps the sphere of political power in societies of other types.[24]

I want now to move on to the third, and final, challenge to the idea of complex equality that I shall consider here. This holds that there is a virtually irresistible tendency for people's rankings in the various spheres of distribution to converge, so the notion that equality of status can emerge from disparate rankings lacks an empirical basis. This is because the spheres of distribution are interlinked in such a way that high ranking in one sphere tends to translate into high ranking in each of the others. Walzer is of course well aware of this possibility—it is what motivates his whole argument for blocking exchanges between the spheres—but the challenge I want to consider maintains that the process of transference is unstoppable, for sociological reasons.

There are in fact two rather different versions of this challenge. The first can be crudely expressed as follows.[25] The supposedly autonomous spheres of distribution all allocate advantages or desired resources. But these advantages, although no doubt valued

[24] Here, then, I am departing in principle from the position laid out in *Spheres*, although in practice the measures that Walzer describes to contain the dominance of money would very likely destroy its pre-eminence too. The difference comes out when Walzer remarks 'If we succeeded absolutely in barring the conversion of money into political power, then we might not limit its accumulation or alienation at all' (p. 127)—although he then concedes that in practice conversion can only be prevented by setting limits through redistributive taxation.

[25] The case is argued with a great deal more subtlety by Adam Swift in Ch. 11.

for their own sake, are also power bases, in the sense that they provide their holders with the means to move the world in the direction that they favour, including the acquisition of advantages of other kinds. Thus, to take some obvious cases, money can buy access to the holders of political power; reputation can be traded upon to influence the behaviour of others; education provides a means of entry into favoured occupations; and so on. The various currencies are inherently convertible, and so we should normally expect people who achieve a high ranking in one sphere to use at least a part of their relative advantage to boost their rankings in other spheres. Dominance, therefore—the capacity of the holders of one kind of good to use it to obtain goods of other kinds—is not an aberration which we can guard against, but a virtual inevitability. But even if individuals will almost unavoidably be tempted to convert the goods they possess across the spheres, it is also true that social systems vary considerably in the extent to which they permit or block such conversions. Consider, for instance, the following claim about Polish socialism in the mid-1960s:

Under capitalism the convertibility of values is generally based upon the enormous significance of income and the universal role of money. Income can be translated into political influence, education or prestige. . . . Many key correlations between values are lessened in socialism. First and foremost, the role of income as a universal source of supply of other values is diminished. One cannot acquire political influence with money. Education and health services are increasingly less dependent upon financial resources. Prestige no longer depends to such an extent upon wealth, and the convertibility of power into prestige has declined.[26]

There seems no reason to doubt the general truth of this claim, which Wesolowski backs up with empirical data, particularly with respect to the disseverance of occupational prestige from income. To say this is not to hold up Polish socialism as a paradigm of complex equality. It seems likely that the distributional mechanisms employed in Poland were in other respects worse than those employed under capitalism. We also need to ask whether the way the goods in question were distributed corresponded to what the Polish people themselves thought was fair (there is evidence, for

[26] W. Wesolowski, *Classes, Strata and Power* (London: Routledge & Kegan Paul, 1979), 127.

instance, that Poles believed that educational achievement should be rewarded by better paid jobs, a link that was often broken at the time Wesolowski was writing).[27] I use the example only to make the point that the extent of convertibility between spheres of distribution depends upon a society's institutional arrangements. There is nothing inevitable about the dominance of money, for example. In so far as the ideal of complex equality requires us to search for those arrangements that best contain dominance, we have no reason yet to think that such a search is futile. What we should concede, though, is that establishing institutions that block the illicit conversion of goods may have its costs in terms of other values. If we believe, for instance, that on grounds of liberty and/or efficiency the market should play a central role in economic life, then it is going to be difficult entirely to prevent the conversion of money into other goods. (We can establish the best system of state schools that the budget will bear; but we cannot prevent people from, say, buying extra tuition for their children, unless we are prepared to impose drastic restrictions on personal liberty.) So the quest for complex equality must be limited by our regard for these other values.

Challenge three, version one, claims that rankings in separate spheres of distribution will tend to correlate because goods are unavoidably convertible. We have seen there is no reason to accept this challenge in its strong form. Version two points to a quite different mechanism. It claims that people generally prefer to see correlated rankings; that is, if someone is rich, say, people expect him also to be powerful, prestigious, well-educated etc., and are uneasy if they are confronted with contrary evidence. Faced with disparities, they may do one of two things: change the distributions themselves, or change the way they think about the situation (by, for instance, raising their estimate of the person's social standing). So

---

[27] Wesolowski himself has explored Polish attitudes to distributive justice, based on a survey in 1979, in 'Stratification and Meritocratic Justice', in D. J. Treiman and R. V. Robinson (eds.), *Research in Social Stratification and Mobility*, i (Greenwich, Conn.: JAI Press, 1981). Note, however, that attitudes appear to have shifted quite markedly since the late 1950s, broadly speaking from an egalitarian to a meritocratic conception of justice: see the evidence in J. Koralewicz-Zebik, 'The Perception of Inequality in Poland', *Sociology*, 18 (1984), 225–38. It is beyond the scope of this chapter to consider how changing conceptions of justice were related to institutional change in Poland. What is abundantly clear is that by the early 1980s the distribution of goods in Poland fell foul of any reasonable conception of justice, whether egalitarian or meritocratic.

the claim here is that complex equality is unstable because it contravenes basic tenets of social psychology.

The best-known piece of theory supporting this claim is probably George Homans's work on status congruence.[28] Homans ties the idea of status congruence closely to that of justice, as can be seen from the following summary definition:

Fair exchange, or distributive justice in the relations among men, is realized when the profit, or reward less cost, of each man is directly proportional to his investments: such things as age, sex, seniority or acquired skill. As a practical matter, distributive justice is realized when each of the various features of his investments and his activities, put into rank-order in comparison with those of other men, fall in the same place in all the different rank orders.[29]

Homans ties distributive justice to rank equivalence by adopting an open-ended notion of 'investments', which are simply whatever personal traits the relevant group happens to value in such a way as to influence each member's general standing within it. As his examples show, a feature such as sex can count as an investment. He has been rightly criticized for ignoring questions about the relevance of different 'investments' in his account of distributive justice.[30] Even if we confine ourselves to the standards of justice used by the group we are studying and refrain from external criticism, it seems likely that there will be a distinction between features regarded as relevant to the fairness of a particular distribution and other valued features that are not. Thus a work group may attach a higher status to being male than being female without thinking that, if a man and a woman hold positions of equal responsibility, the man should get higher pay.

But although Homans's attempt to tie justice and status congruence closely together fails for this reason, the latter idea may still point to a factor of relevance to our inquiry that is quite distinct from justice. People may prefer it if there is congruence between various rank orderings, even where there is no reason of justice why the person who is ahead in order X should also be ahead in order Y. The reason Homans gives is social certainty:

[28] G. C. Homans, *Social Behaviour: Its Elementary Forms* (London: Routledge & Kegan Paul, 1961), esp. ch. 12.
[29] Ibid. 264.
[30] See W. G. Runciman, 'Justice, Congruence and Professor Homans', *European Journal of Sociology*, 8 (1967), 115–28.

faced with a person with incongruent rankings, we are not sure how to behave towards them. For instance

if one woman holds more responsibility than another but gets the same pay, a third party seeing them both may be tempted by the equality in pay to treat them as social equals and not to accord to the first woman the higher respect that her responsibility would otherwise deserve. The incongruence throws her status in doubt in the eyes of her companions.[31]

What should we make of this argument? It effectively turns the case for complex equality on its head. The complex equality argument says: if you want to achieve overall equality of status, ensure that there is enough incongruence between rankings in different spheres that no overall ranking is possible. The status congruence argument says: we want to achieve a clear overall ranking, so we will try to eliminate incongruence between different spheres. The mechanism invoked is the same, but the second argument postulates in addition a desire for social certainty which is met by having an unequivocal status hierarchy.

Is the postulate valid? Let us note first of all the difference between the desire to maintain overall ranking *where it already exists* and the desire to introduce it where it does not. If we belong to a highly stratified society (such as a caste system) in which the way we interact with people is strongly affected by their place in the hierarchy, then we may be disoriented by someone who breaks the crystallized rank order by, for instance, taking on a type of work usually reserved to another caste and valued accordingly. But it does not follow that people in general prefer ranking to equality, or that they have difficulty coping with a state of affairs in which overall social equality prevails and in which one's behaviour towards others is governed by their position in particular spheres of distribution. Next, it is worth noting that Homans's evidence is drawn from small groups and organizations within which it is plausible to suppose a relatively clear status hierarchy exists, even though this is not the predominant character of the wider (American) society to which they belong. Thus one example is drawn from a street gang and concerns the position of a particular member who had low status within the gang as a whole, because of his failure to conform to gang norms, but who was particularly skilled at bowling. The research documents how the other

---

[31] Homans, *Social Behaviour*, 250.

gang members disrupted his bowling to prevent him obtaining high rank in bowling competitions.[32] A street gang seems to me a paradigm case of a small well-structured group with a clear status hierarchy. Other evidence comes from work organizations and concerns the relative pay of groups of workers with different amounts of responsibility.[33] This evidence can, I think, be explained simply by reference to norms of distributive justice, without bringing in the additional idea of status congruence, but in any case work organizations are well-known for embodying a status hierarchy in line with the structure of authority and embodied in symbolic ways such as the quality of office furniture one is allowed at different levels of seniority. My point is that these cases cannot be generalized to demonstrate a preference for status congruence in society as a whole.[34]

There is also some evidence that people resist excessive degrees of status congruence. One of Homans's claims is that work teams are more efficient when their members achieve status congruence so that, for instance, they operate best when led by older, more highly qualified, better paid males. But even he has to concede that, in one of the cases he cites (a study of the effectiveness of bomber crews),

the relationship between congruence and effectiveness was curvilinear. . . . a bomber whose crew had very low congruence was apt to be a rather ineffective one. From then on an increase in congruence was associated with an increase in effectiveness until *medium* congruence was reached: . . . but after that any further increase in congruence meant a sharp falling-off in effectiveness, until at the other end of the distribution a very congruent bomber was apt to be a very ineffective one.[35]

[32] Ibid. 234. The research was originally reported in W. F. Whyte, *Street Corner Society* (Chicago: Univ. of Chicago Press, 1943).

[33] See Homans's discussion of the Eastern Utilities Co., *Social Behaviour*, 237–47.

[34] This conclusion seems to emerge from the substantial empirical research on the status congruence hypothesis, subsequent to Homans and its other pioneers. The main upshots are (a) that although status incongruence *is* generally a source of dissatisfaction, the effect is quite weak once incongruence is disentangled from other factors (such as the bare fact of having a low status on some dimension); (b) that the desire for status congruence is essentially a micro-level phenomenon and loses its explanatory power at social level. See e.g. E. Zimmerman, 'Almost All You Wanted to Know About Status Inconsistency But Never Dared to Measure', in H. Strasser and R. W. Hodge (eds.), *Status Inconsistency in Modern Societies* (Duisburg: Verlag der Sozialwissenschaftlichen Kooperative, 1986).

[35] Homans, *Social Behaviour*, 263.

An independent piece of research, designed to test the status congruence hypothesis, points in the same direction.[36] This was an experimental study of three-person groups in which three variables were manipulated: members' personal standing, the difficulty of the task they were allocated, and the degree of responsibility they were given for representing the group (in each case the rank assigned could be high, medium, or low). Using these variables, a series of groups was composed in which relationships between the rank orders ranged from complete congruence (where the most senior member was given the most difficult task and was also made group representative, and so on for the other two members) to complete incongruence (where, say, the senior member had the least difficult task and no position of responsibility, and so on). The groups were then set to work and after a period members were asked to say how congenial they found relationships within the group and how much incentive they felt to work well. The status congruence hypothesis would suggest that the most preferred arrangement would be one of maximum congruence, but this turned out not to be the case. Although subjects disliked extreme status incongruence, they preferred moderate congruence to complete congruence: specifically, they liked the most senior member to be group representative, but having 'rewarded' seniority with responsibility, they then preferred to balance this by giving the most difficult job to someone else.[37] They were, it seems, Walzerians *avant la lettre*: they recognized different criteria for distributing different goods, and they preferred a state of complex equality to one of complete consistency of rank.

Other sociologists have pointed out that incongruence between rankings within a group or organization can be a source of strength, since it means that no member is exposed to the degradation involved in constantly occupying the lowest position. Simmel, who referred to this condition as one of 'reciprocal supersubordination', gave the example of Cromwell's army:

The same soldier who, in military matters, blindly obeyed his superior, in the hour of prayer often made himself into his moral preacher. A corpo-

[36] A. C. Brandon, 'Status Congruence and Expectations', *Sociometry*, 28 (1965), 272–88.
[37] They also wanted the congruence to be relevantly based; so they disliked an arrangement in which the most difficult task and the leadership position were combined but then given to a junior member of the group, even though the degree of incongruence in a mathematical sense would here be the same as in the most preferred arrangement.

ral could preside over the worship in which his captain participated in the same way as all privates. The army which unconditionally followed its leader once a political goal was accepted, beforehand made political decisions to which the leaders themselves had to bow. As long as it lasted, the Puritan army derived an extraordinary firmness from this reciprocity of superordination and subordination.[38]

I suggest, therefore, that we do not find a general desire to achieve overall status congruence, or rank consistency, in social life. Very often what appears as a desire for status congruence is better seen as an effort to achieve distributive justice: someone's high score on one dimension is taken to be a relevant reason for her to achieve a high outcome on another (via a principle of desert, for instance). Where status congruence is not simply justice under another name, it reflects the dynamics of a particular kind of social group and, as we have seen, it may be neither the outcome that the members prefer nor the outcome that is 'functional' from the point of view of the group's objectives.

I have spent most time on status congruence theory as a potential critique of complex equality because it seems to me to challenge the latter ideal most directly. The other objections we considered all concerned social processes that might undermine complex equality without anyone intending this outcome: for instance, individual self-interest might bring about conversions between goods in different spheres even though people in principle favoured retaining the boundaries. (Thus I may believe in a public system of education but, if I can afford to, send my children to private schools, all the while thinking that the system which permits this to happen is unjust.) Status congruence theory might seem to suggest that complex equality is not merely difficult to maintain, but unnatural, in the sense that it conflicts with deep-rooted psychological propensities. It is important, therefore, that no such conclusion can be drawn.

COMPLEX EQUALITY AS A POLITICAL IDEAL

Having defended the idea of complex equality against what I take to be the main empirical challenges it faces, I would like to end

[38] K. H. Wolff (ed.), *The Sociology of George Simmel* (Glencoe, Ill.: The Free Press, 1950), 288.

with a few remarks about its relevance as a political ideal. It would be understandable for someone presented with the idea to react as follows. It may be an interesting fact about modern societies that they differentiate between spheres of distribution in such a way that, if all goods are distributed by their own appropriate criteria, a state of complex equality obtains; but complex equality is here at best a welcome bonus, a spin-off from achieving justice across the spheres. It has no independent practical force. We cannot modify our institutions with the aim of bringing about a greater equality of status, other than by doing what we already have sufficient reason to do, namely ensuring that each social good is allocated by its own criterion of justice.

This reaction would be reinforced if we accepted Walzer's claim that the criterion of justice is provided by the social meaning of the good. 'If we understand what it is, what it means to those for whom it is a good, we understand how, by whom, and for what reasons it ought to be distributed' (*Spheres*, 9). For this seems to remove the possibility of arguing about how some particular good ought to be distributed. We can choose to have it or not to have it, but once that decision is made there is no further question to be settled. And this seems to remove the possibility of appealing to complex equality in cases of dispute. That is to say, we are not in the position of having to decide whether good X ought to be allocated by criterion A or criterion B, in which case we might argue that, from the point of view of preserving complex equality, B would be more helpful. If Walzer's claim is accepted there is no room for such a decision.

As indicated in the Introduction, I do not think we need to accept Walzer's claim in its strongest form in order to defend the spheres of justice argument. That argument requires that it should be possible to establish a separate criterion of distribution for each good, but it does not require that the criterion should be directly determined by the good's social meaning. The claim itself seems to hold in the case of goods like love and public honours, but not in the case of goods like money, power, or office. Although very bizarre proposals for distributing these latter goods might be knocked out by Walzer's test, over a smaller range our reaction to a proposal with which we disagree is likely to be 'If you think that, you don't understand what justice is', rather than 'You don't understand what money (power, office) is'. But although for this reason I am doubtful about Walzer's claim in general, I do not want to defend the relevance of complex equality by suggesting that the distributive criteria for particular goods may be in dispute. Let us simply take it that for one reason or another these criteria are fixed. What practical role can the idea of equality of status still play?

To begin with, it helps support the principle of equal citizenship. This principle is now so firmly established that it might not seem to need additional support, but it is worth recalling that for centuries the mainstream of the liberal tradition favoured a two-tier model of citizenship in which only those citizens who met certain requirements (independence, property-ownership, etc.) were admitted to full or 'active' status. In this context it is relevant to point out that citizenship is important not only because of the instrumental effects of distributing political power in this way rather than that, but because by defining who is a (full) citizen, we also define who has equal standing in the society in question. The fight for women's suffrage provides a good example. Women wanted the vote partly because they thought they could use it to influence policy, but also because they wanted the public institutions of their society to define them as men's equals. Nor do these issues belong only in the past.[39] Guest workers and welfare recipients in quite different ways both raise difficulties for the claim that equal citizenship is fully established in contemporary liberal societies.

What now of the specific spheres of distribution? It is worth noticing that, in general, the more spheres a society contains, the better from the point of view of complex equality. This is true first of all because multiplication of spheres lessens the likelihood of outranking (where A stands higher than B in all relevant arenas of distribution), and secondly because it lessens the likelihood of one good becoming pre-eminent. The more social goods there are, the less likely it is that individuals can be ranked socially on the basis of their performance in one sphere alone. It would be absurd, however, to recommend increasing the number of spheres for this reason. Whether or not we accept Walzer's claim that the social meaning of a good fixes its criterion of distribution, it makes no sense to invent new goods on the grounds that this will then lead to greater pluralism in social distribution generally.

[39] Indeed the quest for equal citizenship between men and women is still far from over in most liberal democracies, as Susan Moller Okin argues in Ch. 6.

What the complex egalitarian can do, however, is provide reasons for not collapsing existing spheres into one another. Suppose there is currently disagreement as to whether medical care should be regarded as a commodity like any other commodity, or whether it is a distinct good with its own criterion of distribution. The debate will primarily be about the nature of medical care itself, about whether it has special properties that decisively differentiate it from other goods and services. But suppose this debate is inconclusive, as it is liable to be. It is then relevant to point out that the first position would imply the loss of a distributive sphere, and a probable falling away from complex equality. If medical care is treated as a commodity and provided through market mechanisms, then by and large the quality of care people get will depend upon their incomes. Rather than money inequality being left behind at the hospital door, we would have a position where people's unequal standing in the sphere of commodities was publicly displayed in the treatment they received. Although no single change of this sort would of itself demolish equality of overall status, it would remove one of the supporting pillars.

The idea of complex equality not only counsels us to preserve distributive spheres that are under threat of assimilation; it may encourage us to amplify spheres that are in danger of being drowned out. I mean here that the institutions through which particular distributions occur may have a more or less prominent place in public consciousness, and this will be open to alteration. The clearest example is perhaps the system of public honours. Under complex equality there will be various forms of public recognition of achievements that stand alongside, and can serve to offset, achievements in spheres such as those of money and power. Honours are distributed to people who have performed acts of public service, to artists and scientists, and so forth. This distribution can be more or less extensive, it can be done in a low-key or high-key way, and so forth. The underlying distributive principle is not up for negotiation, but its institutional expression is (within limits). So in a society in which money threatens to become a pre-eminent good, complex equality can be fortified by boosting the sphere of recognition, especially by making sure that the avenues of recognition are open to those who do not stand high in the other spheres. (If honours are given for charitable activity, they should go to those who are active in community service, say, not to those

who are simply willing to write large cheques.) In a similar way, as
Walzer himself has pointed out,[40] the extent of the spheres of education and welfare reflects political choices. The distributive criteria for these goods are determined internally to each sphere, but
the size and shape of the budget, which establishes how much of
the good there is to distribute in the first place, is decided by the
state. If expanding the provision of these goods helps to restore
equal citizenship, the complex egalitarian will favour it.

Complex equality is not an ideal that translates in a simple,
mechanical way into public policy. As I have presented it in this
chapter, its *modus operandi* is through specific spheres of justice,
and it would have no purchase in a society governed by a single
monolithic principle of distribution. Given the degree of pluralism
already present in modern liberal democracies, however, the complex egalitarian's claim, that social equality may be achieved
through justice being done in a multiplicity of autonomous distributive spheres, is a plausible one. Moreover, as I have tried to
show in this final section, the ideal is far from being practically
toothless in such a context.

[40] Walzer, 'Exclusion, Injustice', 63–4.

10

Against 'Complex' Equality

RICHARD J. ARNESON

The norm of distributive equality prescribes that the goods of the world should be divided equally (in some respect) among persons. Is such equality a worthy moral ideal? Conceptions of equality have taken a beating in recent years at the hands of political theorists, and some non-conservative theorists have joined in the assault.[1] An interesting but largely ignored feature of Michael Walzer's *Spheres of Justice* is his attempt to refurbish the ideal of equality by redefining it.[2] Walzer's strategy of response to conservative critics of equality is to shift the ground of debate. He rejects the 'simple equality' that he claims philosophers are wont to favour and defends his own version of what he calls 'complex equality'. I will show that complex equality is a very weak brew, in which any element of anything that could plausibly be identified with egalitarianism is so diluted as to be virtually undetectable. The rhetoric of *Spheres* is at odds with its substance: Walzer seems not to notice how little equality remains in his 'complex equality', and propounds this notion in a spirit that suggests his conviction that he is defending the liberal egalitarian tradition rather than retreating from it.[3] Since Walzer is an intelligent and sensitive cultural critic,

---

This is an expanded version of a paper which first appeared under the same title in *Public Affairs Quarterly*, 4 (1990), 99–110.

[1] See e.g. Antony Flew, *The Politics of Procrustes* (Buffalo, NY: Prometheus Books, 1981); Robert Nozick, *Anarchy, State, and Utopia* (New York: Basic Books, 1974); Jan Narveson, 'Equality vs. Liberty: Advantage, Liberty', *Social Philosophy and Policy*, 2 (1984), 33–60; Peter Westen, 'The Empty Idea of Equality', *Harvard Law Review*, 95 (1982), 537–96; Harry Frankfurt, 'Equality as a Moral Ideal', *Ethics*, 98 (1987), 21–43; and Joseph Raz, *The Morality of Freedom* (Oxford: Oxford Univ. Press, 1986), ch. 9.

[2] (New York: Basic Books, 1983). See also his *Radical Principles: Reflections of an Unreconstructed Democrat* (New York: Basic Books, 1980), and 'Liberalism and the Art of Separation', *Political Theory*, 12 (1984), 315–30.

[3] Perhaps a fairer judgement is that in *Spheres*, chs. 2–12, Walzer sensibly pursues

it will be worth analysing his argument to see what is driving it, and whether the dissatisfaction he evidently feels with notions of equality less sophisticated than his own is well-founded. At the end of this chapter I examine an interpretation of complex equality as equality of status advanced in recent essays by David Miller.

SIMPLE EQUALITY AND LITERAL EQUALITY

By stipulation *simple equality* is the condition in which everyone in society has the same amount of money, the same income and wealth. It is not immediately clear what sort of property right is envisaged when people are imagined to own money subject to the constraint that anybody's holding of money must equal everyone else's. Suppose the regime of simple equality is in place in a three-person society, so initially each has the same, but one person then spends all his cash on cotton candy (so he has less and the seller of the candy has more), must redistribution then take place to re-establish equality of cash holdings? It seems that the ideal would be better formulated as equality of purchasing power among citizens over the course of their lives.[4] Ignore differences in people's life spans and assume there is a population in which everyone happens to live for fifty years and each person has exactly $1,000 to spend over the course of her life. This is the condition of simple equality as Walzer conceives of it.

The ideal of simple equality so far described might seem indeterminate, pending a specification of what people may do with their equal allotments of cash. People's equal cash gives them equal power to purchase whatever is for sale on the market. At least, this is so if discrimination in trading is prohibited. (If it were not, a customary bias against trading with those of a disliked racial background might bring it about that a person of that race could make no purchases at all, despite the fact that her cash holding exceeds

a democratic egalitarian agenda that is not conceptually well integrated with the framing theoretical discussions in the Preface and the first and last chapter, which develop his complex equality conception.

[4] For improving modifications in the ideal of equal purchasing power, reformulated as equality of resources, see Ronald Dworkin, 'What is Equality? Part 2: Equality of Resources', *Philosophy and Public Affairs*, 10 (1981), 185–246. See also Dworkin, 'What is Equality? Part 3: The Place of Liberty', *Iowa Law Review*, 73 (1987), 1–54.

the ostensible purchase price of many commodities.) Over their lifetime, persons with equal amounts of cash face a possibly changing array of goods, for sale at possibly fluctuating prices. Presumably there must be some moral constraints on the operation of the mechanism that determines what goods will be offered for sale at what prices at any given time, if simple equality is to be represented as a worthy ideal. Evidently, equality of money needs to be supplemented by a principle that stipulates what is to count as a fair economic mechanism determining the opportunities for purchase that the market provides.

Walzer does not trouble to fill in the details or sketch a context, to enable us to see better what equality of money amounts to, or might amount to if thought through systematically and coupled to kindred moral principles. Simple equality is a foil. This becomes apparent once one notes that Walzer's full stipulation of 'the regime of simple equality' identifies a society 'in which everything is up for sale and every citizen has as much money as any other' (*Spheres*, 14). This sounds like a Brechtian vision of hell. Simple equality turns out to be a compound of the norm of equal market purchasing power and a gratuitous expansion of the common-sense scope of permissible market activity to include votes in the democratic process, places in schools and universities, sexual services of any kind that consumers (however degraded) might desire, verdicts of juries in criminal trials, and so on, as legitimate goods to be traded on the market. But not everything should be for sale: some potential exchanges that individuals might want to make should be blocked by law or social custom.[5] So let us set aside the 'everything is for sale' component of simple equality.

Walzer's initial objection to equality of money is that the movement to achieve it inevitably leads to state tyranny. His formulations recall Robert Nozick's famous 'Wilt Chamberlain' argument against enforcement of patterned principles of justice.[6] Left unrestricted, individuals initially placed in a regime of equality of money would act to further their own purposes in ways that would generate, as a by-product, the subversion of this regime.

[5] Walzer himself provides reasons backing this judgement in a perceptive chapter that approvingly describes deeply entrenched moral judgements concerning the limits of permissible market activity in contemporary democratic culture. See *Spheres*, 99–108.

[6] Nozick, *Anarchy, State, Utopia*, 160–4.

Individuals vary in such qualities as talent, foresight, luck, and determination to get rich, and through free exchange these qualities would over time produce increasing inequalities in wealth and income. Nothing in the operation of free exchange would trigger any countertendency back towards equality of monetary possession once initial equality was perturbed. Nozick stresses that continuous maintenance of equality (or any pattern of distribution) would require continuous and (from his natural rights perspective) unjustifiable interference with individual liberty.

In company with Nozick, Walzer stresses the danger of statism. In order to maintain equality of money against the eroding tendency of market exchange, we would have to monitor exchange outcomes and frequently redistribute resources so as to offset the tendency to inequality.[7] To accomplish these tasks we would need a powerful state, which would then become an irresistible target for those who seek a monopoly of political power. At this point Walzer's argument appears to be that thinking through the predictable effects of any serious attempts to attain equality must impress on us the lesson that it is an elusive goal and that a serious effort to achieve one form of equality, monetary equality, will just render other forms of inequality more salient and onerous and will exacerbate the social processes that generate these other newly salient inequalities.

Against the claim that equality of money matters, one observation suggested by Walzer's remarks is that several kinds of equality matter. Accepting this observation for the sake of the argument, I deny that it follows that equality of money does not matter or is not worth promoting. The point would rather be that what is needed is to articulate a comprehensive ideal of equality, in which all morally considerable equalities would have their place, so that the relative importance of equality of money (and whether its importance is instrumental or intrinsic) would be ascertained.

Walzer appears to be confident that his objection against simple equality generalizes to all varieties of literal equality—that is to say, to all principles of distribution that prescribe that everybody

---

[7] Nozick emphasizes the violations of libertarian individual rights that would be required to sustain equality of condition. Walzer stresses the self-defeating character of egalitarianism literally construed. The attempt to achieve one sort of literal equality begets (or exacerbates) other literal inequalities that are just as bad or worse.

should get the same quantity and quality of goods according to some standard specified by the principle. 'Equality literally understood is an ideal ripe for betrayal', he writes (*Spheres*, p. xi). It is a sucker's game, which sophisticated egalitarians should eschew. From this standpoint, the attempt to elaborate a comprehensive ideal of literal equality would be misguided, naïve. But why think this is so? One might believe that the various worthwhile equalities are incommensurable; hence, no comprehensive ideal of equality could be formulated. But Walzer gives no argument on this point, so I am going to ignore this.

It might be that Walzer's objection against any variety of literal equality is really an objection against an extreme doctrine of equality which holds that it is of overriding moral importance that the distribution of socially valued goods must be exactly equal in some crucial respect. No deviation from equality is tolerated, and the pursuit of equality trumps (takes lexical priority over) all other values. The extreme doctrine of equality is implausible on its face. But its implausibility does not gainsay the possibility of elaborating a moderate doctrine that holds that (*a*) small deviations from equality, below a threshold, do not matter morally, (*b*) above the threshold, inequalities should be reduced, *ceteris paribus*, but (*c*) equality does not trump all other moral concerns and must be balanced sensibly against competing values. So the lack of appeal of extreme egalitarianism would not plausibly support a sweeping rejection of equality literally construed. (Notice that the more a doctrine of equality tends towards moderation, the less severe will be the conflict between maintenance of an acceptable degree of equality and preservation of desirable individual freedom.)

The Nozickian argument that maintenance of equality (or any other pattern) would require excessive and morally unjustifiable interference with individual liberty has attracted a counterargument that helps elucidate Walzer's thinking. The rejoinder to Nozick is that if people care about equality, conceived as a public good supplied by the state or other collective agency, they will not mind the restrictions on their liberty that are necessary in order to preserve a valued egalitarian condition.[8] The gain might be worth the cost to all citizens, or to the overwhelming majority of the

---

[8] See G. A. Cohen, 'Robert Nozick and Wilt Chamberlain: How Patterns Preserve Liberty', in John Arthur and William H. Shaw (eds.), *Justice and Economic Distribution* (Englewood Cliffs, NJ: Prentice-Hall, 1978), 246–62.

citizens. Alternatively, if there is a consensus in society that equality is morally valuable, reasonable restrictions on citizens' freedom in order to preserve equality will not be experienced as onerous. Egalitarians do not propose to institute a regime of equality in a society where people both care nothing for equality and judge it to be of little moral value. Walzer's further thought on this theme is that the distribution of social goods in modern society is pluralistic. There are distinct social goods, each one associated with distinct social practices and conventional understandings of the nature of the good and the proper criteria for its distribution. The goods that are the concern of distributive justice are created and parcelled out in separate spheres. Any viable ideal of equality for modern society must be sensitive to this variety and pluralism. If some abstract principle of literal equality is imposed across the board, it is bound to provoke resistance from individuals who rightly will be loyal to the ideal of distributing goods according to the specific social meanings that are distinctive for each distributive sphere. Walzer does not accept Nozick's libertarian doctrine of inviolable individual rights. Instead, he holds that the legitimate interventions of a liberal state must conform to communal understandings of the goods embodied in the various spheres. An abstract principle of equality that became a steamroller flattening out all separate spheres would be an engine of tyranny and any pattern of distribution achieved in this way would be purchased at too great a cost in human freedom—the freedom to live one's life in conformity with shared understandings of the goods of the world.

This objection takes us to Walzer's ideal of complex equality, which is complex in virtue of registering the moral import of the fact of distributive spheres. Before discussing complex equality I want to consider a further doubt that Walzer insinuates regarding the moral significance of simple and literal equalities.

Walzer offers the conjecture that when people have banded together to struggle under the banner of equality, in movements that have proved to be historically significant, their real motivations have been quite different from the egalitarianism they professed. Not the striving for any sort of equality of condition but the hatred of domination has been the spur to protest and revolt. Walzer encapsulates the point in this sentence: 'The experience of subordination—of personal subordination, above all—lies behind the vision of equality' (*Spheres*, p. xiii). It is not the mere fact of difference between rich and poor, aristocrat and commoner, that rankles, but the additional fact that the haves lord it over the have-nots, command deferential behaviour, rule paternalistically, display their privileges ostentatiously, insist on controlling the lives of those who lack the badges of privilege. The rich 'grind the faces of the poor' (ibid.). So the experience of personal subjection gives rise to the call for equality. Walzer implies that the true motivations of rebels and protestors should alert us to a more important moral demand than the demand for a literal equality of condition that the rhetoric of egalitarianism has suggested to philosophers. In Walzer's words, 'The aim of political egalitarianism is a society free from domination' (ibid.). It is not important that some people have more and other people less of whatever socially valued goods are currently prominent. What is important is that none should dominate over others.

I mean to leave aside Walzer's conjecture about the motivational wellsprings of egalitarian protest throughout history. What concerns me is an inference that Walzer seems to draw from this conjecture: that literal equality or equality of condition does not matter morally, or matters hardly at all in comparison to the goal of eliminating domination. No significant personal relations, and *a fortiori* no personal relations of domination, obtain between persons who live in geographically distant regions of the earth. Consider then the great inequalities in income and wealth, and the inequalities in opportunities for lifetime welfare that these monetary inequalities generate, as between the best-off people in the richest nations of the earth and the poorest inhabitants of the poorest nations. These vast inequalities are not tainted even slightly by coexisting relations of domination. Here we seem to have a fairly pure case of vast inequality of condition, or literal inequality, that is not accompanied by even a slight degree of domination. I have no argument to show that this pure inequality is morally consequential to anybody whose intuitions incline him to deny it. I merely point out that anyone who is prepared to admit that inequality of condition, or literal inequality of this sort, is morally troublesome in this pure case, will not find in Walzer any arguments that would tend to show that in mixed cases, where both literal inequality and domination are present, only the domination matters from the standpoint of egalitarianism rightly understood.

COMPLEX EQUALITY

The type of equality that Walzer asserts is worth seeking is a non-literal equality that he terms 'complex'. According to Walzer, the distribution of social goods takes place in distinct spheres, or sets of social practices, with associated customary beliefs, values, and expectations. The criteria of proper distribution of a good are part of its social meaning.[9] As Walzer defines the term, *complex equality* obtains when the distribution in all spheres is autonomous, and distribution is autonomous when goods are distributed according to their social meanings.

It is compatible with the definition of *autonomous distribution* that the distribution of goods in a society is fully autonomous, so that complex equality fully obtains, yet the same individuals always fall at the top end and bottom end of the distributional profile in every single sphere. Complex equality is also compatible with the supposition that the spread between the top and bottom of the distributional profile in every sphere is enormous. Winners win big, and losers get small crumbs, in each autonomous distribution, and furthermore the same individuals can be the winners and losers in every separate sphere. Complex equality is only equality in a Pickwickian sense.

Walzer has two responses to this objection. One response is to characterize a society in which complex equality obtains: 'Though there will be many small inequalities, inequality will not be multiplied through the conversion process. Nor will it be summed across different goods, because the autonomy of distributions will tend to produce a variety of local monopolies, held by different groups of men and women' (*Spheres*, 17). It is arbitrary to assume that inequalities in each sphere will be 'small'. No theoretical support is provided for this hope. In the case of one of the spheres that Walzer identifies, the sphere of money and commodities, the market economy, there is good reason to expect that autonomous market distribution will generate what anyone would regard as large

---

[9] E.g. according to the common understanding of love and romance in modern Western societies, these goods are appropriately bestowed by individuals on each other either in reciprocal exchange or by freely chosen marriage contract. For sensible doubts about whether the social meanings of goods do generally determine the appropriate criteria for their distribution, see Brian Barry, 'Intimations of Justice', *Columbia Law Review*, 84 (1984), 806–15 and Ch. 3 above.

inequalities. Leaving this aside, we must also consider the possibility that inequalities will be 'summed' across different goods, because the autonomous criteria of distribution will tend to favour the same individuals in each sphere. Mulling over this possibility, Walzer has a second response: 'This would certainly make for an inegalitarian society, but it would also suggest in the strongest way that a society of equals was not a lively possibility' (*Spheres*, 20).

This second response gives the game away. Since it is stipulated that the situation Walzer is pondering exhibits complex equality, Walzer's references to 'inegalitarian society' and 'society of equals' must invoke the supposedly discarded notion of literal equality.[10] Complex equality cannot be recommended as a genuine egalitarian ideal in its own right, but at most as an institutional means to realize some literal, old-fashioned ideal of equality that has not yet been specified. 'Complex equality' is only contingently egalitarian and, for all that Walzer has claimed, the contingencies look to be quite remote.

In broad terms, the contingency issue is whether the possession of traits that lead to success (or failure) in one distributive sphere is statistically independent of the possession of traits that lead to success (failure) in other spheres. Or is possession of the wherewithal for educational success correlated with possession of traits that make for high income and wealth, the ability to attract desirable romantic and marital partners, stable good health and avoidance of disability, a gratifying career, attainment of positions of influence and authority, and other elements of the good life? The answer to this question will surely differ to some extent for different societies, which value different goods and embrace divergent standards for their distribution. Walzer needs to distinguish two questions: (1) In contemporary democratic societies, are the social meanings of goods such that autonomous distribution would lead to egalitarian outcomes (by a norm of literal equality)? (2) Could we imagine a society in which the social meanings of goods are

---

[10] On David Miller's reading of Walzer, complex equality, rather than being *defined* as autonomous distribution, is said to be what autonomous distribution is likely to produce. Complex equality itself on this construal is identified with equality of status. But here literal equality is being invoked, for if equality of status prevails in a society, there is something, namely status or social prestige, of which all members have the same. Since Walzer does not mention equality of status, I treat this proposal as a possible revision of Walzer's view, and consider it later in this chapter.

such that autonomous distribution would lead to egalitarian outcomes (by a norm of literal equality)? Most of Walzer's book wavers between questions (1) and (2), but actually answers (2) alone.[11] Walzer imagines that answering (2) affirmatively shows a deep affinity between complex equality and an unspecified literal equality ideal that hovers in the background, so that promoting complex equality in contemporary societies is promoting equality in some genuine, substantive sense. Nothing could be further from the truth—just as showing that we can imagine a dictatorship in which the dictator generously enforces wide respect for important individual freedoms does not show that there is a deep affinity between dictatorship and freedom.

Promotion of complex equality in some (likely) circumstances can obstruct the pursuit of desirable literal equality. Consider the example of affirmative action in contemporary American society. Affirmative action policies are various, but the general idea is that in response to the history of American racial discrimination, places in universities and posts of responsibility in government and in private firms should go to underrepresented minorities over other applicants who would be judged better qualified but for the consideration of applicants' race. Given the poverty of the groups favoured by affirmative action, successful execution of this policy would promote equality of wealth and income. But in so far as we can usefully speak of distinct distributive spheres of market exchange and educational provision, the social meaning of the goods of superior positions in the labour market and superior places in higher education tends towards a meritocratic norm of distribution: better positions should go to those most qualified for them. In these crucial spheres, current social meanings are anti-egalitarian.

Another contemporary example in which complex equality and literal equality conflict is provided by contemporary Chinese industrial culture, as analysed by Andrew G. Walder.[12] He finds Chinese industry organized around neo-traditional patronage relations. In a Communist society with thin markets in consumer goods, the distribution of a wide range of important consumer goods occurs at

[11] On this point, see Joshua Cohen, 'Review of *Spheres of Justice*', *Journal of Philosophy*, 83 (1986), 457–68.
[12] *Communist Neo-Traditionalism: Work and Authority in Chinese Industry* (Berkeley, Calif.: Univ. of Calif. Press, 1986).

the workplace, under the auspices of Communist Party cadres who dispense material benefits to loyal workers who support the political line of the party in the factory setting. These patronage relations are not generally viewed by employees to be illegitimate, according to Walder's informants. Chinese factory culture affirms these client-patron ties; they are an accepted part of the social meaning of industrial work in that society. But equality would be better served if this system of patronage were broken, firms organized by a distribution system that rewarded excellent job performance rather than loyalty to political superiors, and the efficiency gains used to better the lot of the worse-off rural sector of the population.

DOMINANCE AND DOMINATION

Recall that Walzer has yet another arrow in his quiver, to be brandished in support of the complex equality ideal. He believes that what lies behind egalitarian sentiment is resentment against domination and that the society of complex equality is above all one from which domination has disappeared. Then perhaps it may not matter so much whether complex equality achieves much equality, if a more important goal is reached. Walzer asserts a tight connection between complex equality and non-domination:

The critique of dominance and domination points toward an open-ended distributive principle. *No social good X should be distributed to men and women who possess some other good y merely because they possess X and without regard to the meaning of Y* (*Spheres*, 20).

... the disregard of these principles [of autonomous distribution] is tyranny.... In political life—but more widely, too—the dominance of goods makes for the domination of people.... The regime of complex equality is the opposite of tyranny. It establishes a set of relationships such that domination is impossible (*Spheres*, 19).

But in fact the connection between complex equality and non-domination which Walzer insists on is spurious. Let us call the principle quoted in italics above the principle of non-dominance.[13]

---

[13] Satisfaction of the principle of non-dominance does not guarantee that distribution in a given sphere is autonomous, because a good might be distributed in ways that violate its social meanings, yet this does not happen just because the beneficiaries of these non-conforming distributions possess some other social good.

Note also Walzer's stipulation that distribution within a sphere is *autonomous* when the goods within the sphere are distributed according to criteria that conform to their social meaning. Non-dominance and autonomy in these senses are closely related but not exactly the same. Satisfaction of the principle of non-dominance does not guarantee that distribution in a given sphere is autonomous, because goods might be distributed in ways that violate their social meanings, yet not just because the beneficiaries of these non-conforming distributions possess some other good. Finally, note that complex equality obtains when distribution is autonomous in every sphere.

One person *dominates* another when the first exercises a great deal of control over the life of the second, the second does not have reciprocal control over the life of the first, and the first exercises control in ways that are with good reason experienced by the second as onerous, galling, or degrading. This definition corresponds to what Walzer seems to have in mind when he uses the term.

How closely then is domination related to dominance and to autonomous distribution and complex equality? Not very, in my judgement. First, the social meaning of some goods may render domination legitimate within their spheres. For example, the distribution of honour and status under feudalism was such that certain modes of domination of serfs and other vassals by lords were culturally approved. In these cases autonomous distribution fits hand in glove with domination. Nothing in the definition of 'complex equality' prevents a society of complex equality from being heavily laced with domination. Feminists would note that the sphere of contemporary family life countenances domination of wives by their husbands (albeit in somewhat subtler forms and with less moral assurance than in the past). Many modern societies contain a sphere of markets and commodities marked by hierarchical firms and a culturally endorsed expectation that the employer and his managerial agents will exercise a tight authority over subordinate employees. No doubt a society in which distribution occurs piecemeal in several distinct spheres places limits on domination practices. The authority of the boss is supposed to stop at the factory gate. The preacher, who may be a tyrant to his flock, has no special writ of authority beyond his church. But the limited and piecemeal character of authority that is a feature of societies divided into separate spheres does not *per se* tend to block domination within the separate spheres. In short, a society could be characterized by no dominance and fully autonomous distribution, yet also be marred by deplorable excesses of domination. Walzer has identified no mechanism or inner tendency within autonomous distribution that would produce non-domination. So far as I can see, there is no such mechanism to be identified. On this score the most that can be said is that, if distribution accords with prevalent social meanings, then whatever degree of domination is bound up with that distribution will probably not be experienced as morally improper by those who accept these social meanings.

I do not mean to deny that Walzer is inspired by a compelling vision of a society of complex equality that is free of domination and characterized in each of its spheres by practices that reflect a consensus on liberal tolerance and respect for individual dignity and autonomy. My claim is that this vision hangs very loosely on the conceptual apparatus around which Walzer builds his analysis. No rigorous analysis connects the vision to the structure of concepts in terms of which Walzer develops extravagant claims for the ideal of complex equality.

FREEDOM AND COMPLEX EQUALITY

Walzer's concerns about statism and individual freedom, though interesting, do not support the complex equality ideal as he supposes. His hunch is that, whereas pursuit of literal equality requires the creation of a strong state that would then be captured by a new élite, creating new dominant inequalities, complex equality is much closer to self-enforcing. Under a regime of complex equality, he writes, 'the resistance to convertibility would be maintained, in large degree, by ordinary men and women within their own spheres of competence and control, without large-scale state action' (*Spheres*, 17).

But no theory or analysis is developed to bolster this hunch. The jurisdictions of distributive spheres can overlap. Health care, for example, is both a commodity distributed by the market and a human need that might be met by society's collective arrangements for meeting basic needs. As administered by medical doctors, health care is not a good at all according to certain religions, notably Christian Science. Overlapping jurisdictional claims give rise to conflicts that require state decision and state enforcement. Also, the boundaries of distinct distributive spheres are susceptible to breach. To preserve whatever degree of integrity of the separate spheres is deemed desirable, state action is required. Finally, despite the metaphor of 'separate spheres', the social meanings of goods are continually disputed, contested, and renegotiated. Protagonists in these disputes regularly call on the modern state to enter the fray on their side. State action is always on the agenda even where the state currently adopts a *laissez-faire* posture. In these circumstances one hopes that institutions and associations of civil society will carry forward traditions and allegiances that will be a counterweight against the danger of tyranny that is inherent in the power of the modern state. Notice, however, that this salutary hope is pertinent whether the society is committed to complex equality or not, and whether or not it is committed to literal equality. The extent to which the private life of civil society protects against wrongful incursions on individual liberty depends entirely on the character of that private life. The question is not whether distribution accords with social meanings, rather what the social meanings are.

At the level of abstraction at which Walzer's analysis is pitched, there is no way to predict whether pursuit of literal or of complex equality would require dependence on a state that is likelier to turn repressive of individual freedom.

WHAT'S IN A NAME?

It might be objected that I am vehemently challenging only the name that Walzer attaches to his distributive ideal, and not the ideal itself. But why quibble about a name? My objection is that 'complex equality' permits any degree whatsoever of inequality and that it stands in a much more tenuous relation to satisfaction of the non-domination ideal than Walzer asserts. I do not mean to deny that, other things being equal, goods should be distributed according to their social meanings. This is so for two reasons: (*a*) it is desirable that institutions should conform to the moral beliefs of those people affected by them and (*b*) it is desirable that institutional rules should conform to the preferences of those who live under the institutions, as to what the rules should be. (In my view these two considerations are very weak, when the beliefs and preferences in question are unreasonable or based on ignorance.) This 'distribute according to social meanings' norm is an empty vessel, the content of which could be anything.

Is there a version of distributive egalitarianism that is worth promoting even at significant cost to other moral values? What is the most perspicuous way to formulate a norm of equality? What sorts of trade-offs between equality and other moral values are reasonable? I take these to be important questions. Walzer's complex equality doctrine appears to offer guidance on these questions, but this appearance, under examination, proves false. Walzer advances complex equality as a rival to literal equality, as though they were competing interpretations of the concept of equality, but this presentation of the issue is confused. I think it is fair to conclude that Walzer has provided no good arguments against the egalitarianism that he rejects and no good arguments in support of the 'complex equality' that he favours, and which as we have seen is misdescribed as any sort of equality.

This exploration of Walzer's doubts regarding egalitarianism has turned up two positive points that should be retained as constraints on any acceptable principles of distributive equality. One constraint, already noted, is that distributive equality is at most one moral value among others and does not generally take priority over the others, singly or together. Distributive equality competes with other social values and should sometimes gracefully lose the competition. A second constraint, implicit in some of Walzer's expressed doubts about simple and literal equality, is that an acceptable principle of equality must leave room for individuals, by their free and voluntary choices, to act in ways that shift outcomes away from an initial distribution in which everyone has 'the same' by an appropriate measure. In this sense an acceptable principle of distributive equality will require equality of opportunity, not equality of outcomes. Walzer lays stress on the practical undesirability of attempting to enforce an egalitarian norm that requires continuous coercive redistribution by the state of people's property holdings. One could as well appeal to the moral authority that free and voluntary choice confers on a given outcome: certainly, when you and I start equal and I then freely and voluntarily give you my share, no norm of equality that should matter to us is violated—

though, there may perhaps be an adverse shift in position suffered by non-consenting third parties to the transaction. But following through this insight to specify an appropriate equality of opportunity principle is a topic for other occasions.[14]

WALZER REVISED

In two recent essays David Miller offers a sympathetic interpretation and reconstruction of Walzer's position on complex equality. The criticisms I have raised so far do not cut deep if it should turn out that they inflict no damage on a revision of Walzer that is close to the spirit of his doctrine and otherwise plausible, so it will be worthwhile to examine Miller's Walzer carefully.

Miller suggests that in a modern society marked by separate spheres of distribution, if the ideal of autonomous distribution is achieved, so that the goods within each sphere of distribution are distributed according to their social meanings (that is, the criteria of distribution that are internal to that sphere), then it is empirically likely that complex equality will obtain among the members of society. Complex equality emerges as a by-product of autonomous distribution in a society of separate spheres. By 'complex equality' is meant equality of status. Miller initially characterizes this notion as follows: 'Let us say provisionally that equality of status obtains when each member of society regards himself as fundamentally the equal of all the others, and is regarded by the others as fundamentally their equal.'[15]

Before going any further, I should register a provisional doubt. In a feudal society that was also a Christian commonwealth, in which all the members regarded themselves as children of God and so fundamentally equal in God's eyes, equality of status as construed by Walzer could obtain even if the society was also marked by a feudal hierarchy with the inequalities of lord and serf viewed as divinely ordered. As good Christians, in this idealized feudal society all members would regard themselves as of equal status

---

[14] For further discussion, see my 'Equality and Equal Opportunity for Welfare', *Philosophical Studies*, 56 (1989), 77–93; 'Liberalism, Distributive Subjectivism, and Equal Opportunity for Welfare', *Philosophy and Public Affairs*, 19 (1990), 158–94; and 'Primary Goods Reconsidered', *Nous*, 24 (1990), 429–54.

[15] David Miller, in Ch. 9 and 'Equality', in G. Hunt (ed.), *Philosophy and Politics* (Cambridge: Cambridge Univ. Press, 1990).

along the fundamental religious dimension, while they would accept great inequalities in non-fundamental matters of secular standing. The fact that one can so readily imagine a society that satisfies Miller's version of the complex equality ideal but is grossly inegalitarian by any common-sense standard fuels the suspicion that the egalitarianism in Miller-style 'complex equality' is very attenuated.

Miller further elucidates the idea of equality of status or social standing. He observes that, within individual distributive spheres, there may well be inequalities of rank or status. Those who do better according to the standards that determine the appropriate distribution of the goods of a particular sphere will likely have higher standing within that sphere. The ideal of equality of status applies rather to the society as a whole. We are concerned with status as referring 'to a person's basic standing within a society, as manifested by the way in which he is regarded by the public institutions and by other individuals'. In what appears to be a canonical formulation, equality of status is said to obtain in a society 'in which people's behaviour towards one another is not conditioned by differences of rank, in which specific inequalities—in income, say—do not crystallize into judgements of overall worth, and in which barriers of class do not stand in the way of mutual understanding and sympathy'.[16]

Of course, in a society in which the distribution of important goods takes place within distinct and autonomous spheres, people's behaviour towards each other within any given sphere will likely be conditioned by their ranking within that sphere. What would defeat the equality of status ideal would be the development of a status ranking of individuals on a society-wide basis, across all of the spheres, that was a matter of consensus among the members of society. A salient and consensual status hierarchy within each separate sphere would be consistent with equality of status, as would an overall society-wide status ranking of all individuals by each individual, provided that the various individual rankings were not in agreement.[17]

[16] Miller, Ch. 9, 206–8. The quotation just above in the text is from 208.

[17] This point bears stressing. Equality of status can obtain in a society because there is a consensual society-wide prestige ranking, and everyone's score is the same. Equality of status can also obtain if there are several dimensions of status or spheres in which status rankings occur but no society-wide consensual prestige ranking weighting the scores in separate spheres, so that, except when some score higher

Miller's discussion tends to run together two distinct possible social ideals. One is equality of status as construed above. As Miller puts it, the society with equality of status prevailing 'is contrasted with a ranked society in which there is a consensus about where people stand in a more or less sharply defined system of social classes'. A second and quite distinct ideal is absence of status consciousness—as we might put it, a status-free society. A society approaches this latter ideal to the extent that status rankings are not salient in social life: individual members of society are not particularly concerned about their position in the status hierarchies that form in the various sectors of the society and these status rankings do not much influence people's behaviour towards one another, either within individual spheres or in the society as a whole.

Let us say that a society is *status-free* to the degree that no member's behaviour towards any other member is significantly influenced by status rankings in the society as a whole, or in its distributive spheres, and sympathy and mutual understanding are not blocked by perceptions of status. Let us say that *equality of status* prevails in a society to the extent that society-wide rankings of the members' overall status do not become an object of consensus dividing the society into distinct social classes. Evidently a society can enjoy equality of status without being status-free. We can imagine a society in which (*a*) within each distributive sphere, status hierarchies rigidly determine the appropriate behaviour of individuals to one another, and concern for one's position in the hierarchy is of paramount concern for all members of society, and (*b*) across the society as a whole, people are obsessed with status and each person's own status ranking greatly influences his behaviour towards others, but there is no society-wide consensus on overall status rankings. But for all that has been said so far, this imagined society could be one in which equality of status prevails. Miller tends to assume that a society marked by equality of status will also at least to a considerable degree manifest freedom from status. My first comment, then, about Walzerian complex equality in Miller's revised interpretation of it, is that complex equality understood as equality of status might be embraced either as an

than others in every sphere, no one's overall prestige ranking is determinately higher or lower than anyone else's.

intrinsically desirable social ideal or as a means to another goal, freedom from status.

The question arises to what extent either equality of status or freedom from status is a desirable, worthy ideal. Another question that needs to be addressed is whether or not autonomy of the spheres as understood by Walzer would be empirically likely to produce complex equality understood as equality of status. On this latter question, Miller's position is open-ended. Miller thinks it is a plausible empirical conjecture that in modern societies autonomous distribution plus equality of citizenship (one person, one vote; no politically defined caste status for any member of society; equal rights and duties of citizenship for all members of society) would suffice to bring about a condition of complex equality as equality of status. But the derivation is not watertight. The issue is open for empirical investigation, and Miller discusses plausible reasons for thinking that autonomous distribution plus equal citizenship would not in fact generate equality of status if distribution of goods and status was too lopsided in various ways. I share Miller's sense that the empirical connection between autonomous distribution and equality of status is likely to be loose, but my discussion leaves this empirical question to the side and concentrates on the normative issue.

I do not think there is a general answer to the questions (1) whether or not equality of status is desirable and (2) whether or not freedom from status is desirable. We have to ask, freedom from status or equality of status of what sort, with respect to which people, under what circumstances? Social life is full of examples of debilitating status competition. Society upholds an unworthy standard, such as getting one's income by unearned rather than earned income, and people waste their lives trying to do better than other people as measured by the false standard. But these depressing examples do not show the badness of status competition, just the badness of status competition organized around an unworthy standard. Even if the standard that determines relative status is worthy, one might worry that focusing people's attention on their relative standing with respect to this standard, rather than on their absolute level of performance or satisfaction of the standard, is bad. But why? Why is it inappropriate to wish to be the best, or better than most, and appropriate to wish to be good or excellent? For many activities in which humans engage, the standards of good performance are essentially comparative, so there is no saying what is good performance without having an idea of how people on the average tend to perform. And even if one's conception of good in some sphere is not parasitic on one's notion of better, still, what's wrong with wanting to be better?

Another thought that suggests the undesirability of status hierarchy is that it may induce wasteful or unprofitable competition. But surely some competition for status along a dimension of worth is socially useful. The desire for high status might be derogated as essentially competitive, necessarily producing losers as well as winners. If all want to be best, all but one (except in the case of ties) must be frustrated. But of course since most desired goods are in scarce supply, even when goods are not essentially competitive in character, it is contingently the case that often your desire for a good can only be satisfied if other people's desire for the same good is frustrated. It may simply be a fact about values, humans, and the world we inhabit that many goods well worth having are either essentially or contingently the object of competitive striving. Moreover, even if many want to be best and only one can win, perhaps the nature of the competition is such that the gains of the winner overbalance the losses of the losers (who do not much care about losing). Again, we often find status competition invidious when the competition generates negative aggregate utility, the losses of the losers outweighing the gains of the gainers (here I assume cardinal interpersonal utility comparisons can be made). But only some status competitions generate aggregate utility losses. By 'utility' or 'welfare' here I just mean to name whatever it is that makes a person's life good for that person herself, or in other words, whatever a person seeks for its own sake when she is being rationally prudent. Different accounts of human good— perfectionism, hedonism, rational preference satisfaction, and so on— give rival interpretations of utility.

My suggestion then is that equality of status and freedom from status are neither intrinsically good nor intrinsically bad. They are good or bad depending on their effects on people's welfare. Consider a simple example in which equality of status and freedom from status are in conflict with human well-being. Suppose that in some society it is politically feasible to introduce higher tax rates for upper-income persons and to redistribute the extra tax proceeds to worse-off members of society, but only if these higher taxes are accompanied by a multiplication of honorific titles (such as 'Doctor' for educated medical specialists) to be distributed among better-off members of society. If this reform package is implemented, there will be greater inequality of status and more status consciousness in the society, larger resource shares for the worse off, greater welfare for all, and a greater gain in welfare for the worse off than for better off sectors of the population. The explanation might be that the multiplication of titles for the notables represents a significant utility gain for them (more than offsetting the higher taxes) but is a matter of unconcern for the worse off members of society, who have little social contact with the notables anyway. In this example we must choose between fulfilling the norms of equality of status and freedom from status to a greater extent, and increasing people's welfare and more closely approximating equality of welfare. My own inclination is to give no weight at all to the status values when they conflict with welfare values. We might ask why the status values should matter more to society than they matter to the worse off individuals who are supposedly the victims of status ranking but who in fact are indifferent to this ranking and are not unreasonable to be so indifferent. That is, in the example we are imagining, the indifference to status ranking among the worse off individuals is not caused by ideological manipulation or ignorance or any other cognitive defects. They might care, but they do not, and their not caring is not irrational. In these circumstances I submit that status values should not be included among the values that a decent society is morally obligated to fulfil. But I have no argument for the view that the status values matter only in so far as they affect welfare values. I am simply posing an example to clarify what is at stake and to elicit the reader's moral judgement.

A comparison of a different sort might throw further light on the suggestion that equality of status and freedom from status adequately represent the moral concerns that have motivated and should motivate egalitarians. Like Miller, Walzer offers the conjecture that the 'experience of subordination—of personal subordination, above all—lies behind the vision of equality' (*Spheres*, p. xiii). But consider the example of global disparities of wealth and life prospects mentioned previously in this chapter. The poorest people in the poorest countries do not occupy the lowest rung on a status hierarchy that includes the wealthiest members of the wealthiest nations at the very top. At least, many of the world's poorest inhabitants live in culturally isolated settings and affirm parochial ideals of social standing that generate no common rankings of wealthy aliens in comparison to themselves. If the inequality that really matters for purposes of normative political theory is status inequality, then these global inequalities in wealth and income and life prospects are not morally significant. In contrast, my own sense is that the inequality of life prospects between someone born into a family of poor peasants in Asia or Africa and someone born into a family of wealthy notables in Europe or North America is the pure case of a type of inequality that is morally disturbing and that the liberal egalitarian theories that Walzer criticizes have rightly placed at the centre of their concern.[18]

A status hierarchy need not hold sway across an entire society to be invidious. Imagine a society divided into local communities. Within each community, the major spheres of distribution generate a prestige hierarchy, and those at the top of the community social pyramid contrive to 'grind the faces of the poor' in Walzer's words and generally to make life miserable for the rest of us. This society of local snobbery could be a constitutional democracy. Moreover, nothing in the description so far rules it out that in each sphere goods are distributed according to their social meanings. Recall that Walzer's norm of autonomous distribution does not prohibit possession of the goods in one sphere from influencing one's prospects of gaining a high ranking in other spheres, provided such interlocking of spheres accords with the social meanings in each sphere. Miller and I would agree that, even though distribution is autonomous in the society of local snobbery, something in it is untoward, which he would describe as inequality of status and I would describe as inequality of status of a sort that is unjustifiably injurious to the welfare of the worse off. But to the extent that status hierarchies do not make people's lives worse, I would not be troubled by them.

What is wrong with feudalism then, on my view? It depends on the alternatives. In a feudal social order local military chiefs

---

[18] For representative liberal egalitarian theories, see the essays by Ronald Dworkin cited in n. 4; also John Rawls, *A Theory of Justice* (Cambridge, Mass.: Harvard Univ. Press, 1971) and *Political Liberalism* (New York: Columbia Univ. Press, 1993); and Amartya Sen, *Inequality Reconsidered* (Cambridge: Harvard Univ. Press, 1992).

provide minimal goods of public safety. From the peasants' point of view, it is better than anarchy and social banditry. If a social code that exalts the non-bandit warriors of the chief is the price of ending anarchy, so be it. From any of a variety of egalitarian welfarist standpoints, a feudal order is radically defective once a more democratic and less hierarchical society is feasible.

Miller attempts to elicit the reader's agreement that equality of status is a morally considerable ideal by imagining a school in which one boy wins all the school prizes. Justice has been done— the contests have been fairly conducted and they test the skills that schools ought to instil. None the less Miller thinks that it is unfortunate that one boy wins in every sphere of competition and that one's sense of regret in the face of the boy's grand sweep registers an egalitarian sentiment that the ideal of equality of status captures. But suppose that there are 100 schoolchildren and ten contests. Is it really a victory for any attractive ideal of equality if there are ten separate winners? Would it be ideally better from the standpoint of equality if all the children scored the same on all contests? One source of suspicion of Miller's reading of the situation is that a measure of equality should be responsive to other features of the situation. Suppose the grand winner is a tortured genius who, even after winning the prizes has far lower prospects of utility over the course of his life than the average child. The status superiority does not compensate fully for other deficits. Moreover, if the grand winner is a fortunate child blessed with unusually high life prospects just in virtue of a fortunate natural endowment of talent, one might prefer that the boy be asked to lend his talents to the less fortunate in some way rather than that his talents should fail to develop or be kept under wraps.

Miller argues that complex equality construed as equality of status is a more worthy social ideal than any form of simple equality. According to Miller, a simple egalitarian holds there is some X such that everyone in society should have the same amount of X. Miller asserts that there is no suitable notion that can play the role of X in the simple egalitarian formula, but even if there were, the problem arises that in order to maintain equal X for all it may be necessary sometimes to reduce everyone's holding of X (or to reduce some people's holding) without securing an increase in anyone's holding of X. But if X is valuable for people, why prefer a situation in which everyone enjoys a certain level of X to an alternative situation in which someone's level is increased and no one else's level is decreased? One might suppose that, for any X, implementing a norm of equal distribution will require wastage of X in circumstances where one can get more of X for some people but not all from a starting-point of equal distribution of X. But consider a good like status that is strictly competitive in the sense that, however it is measured, if one person gets a unit more of status, at least one other person must suffer a one unit loss. Then the maintenance of equality of status cannot lead to 'wastage' of status, because more of this good for some always results in less for others.

However, even if the above claims are accepted, the objection that underlies the complaints against simple equality applies to equality of status as well. If equal distribution of some good X competes with an alternative arrangement in which shares of X are unequal but everyone has more X, we would not care if equality gives everyone less X unless it was also the case that people preferred more X for themselves to a condition of equality. The objection against equality is that, in some circumstances, insistence on equality makes people's lives go worse. But insistence on equality of status can make people's lives go worse in the same sense: from a *status quo* of equality of status, in some circumstances an alternative arrangement involving inequality of status would make someone better off on the whole without making anyone else worse off on the whole. Insistence on equality of status can conflict with the Pareto norm, itself a requirement of fairness, and the question arises which norm should trump: equality or Pareto.[19]

There are reasons to doubt that equality of status should be interpreted as a norm of complex as opposed to simple equality. Recall that my complaint against Walzer's preference for his notion of complex equality over simple or literal equality is that complex equality as defined by Walzer does not seem to contain any substantive ideal of equality at all. Miller reinterprets complex equality as equality of status. There is no question but that equality of status involves a substantive idea of equality in an unproblematic sense: according to Miller we are to define a measure of status as fundamental social standing, and when equality of status obtains among the members of a society then everyone's status score is the same. But why is it helpful to speak of complex rather

---

[19] See the Appendix at the end of this chapter.

than simple equality here? Miller identifies an idea of equality as 'simple' when it 'holds that equality requires the equal possession or enjoyment of some characteristic X'.[20] Equality of status seems to fit within this notion of simple equality. Miller adds that simple equality is about distribution to individuals whereas complex equality is a characteristic of social relationships. According to Miller, a norm of simple equality prescribes that to obtain equality of some X either X is directly distributed by institutional arrangements or something else (Y) is distributed so as to yield equality of X. Thus one might distribute health care so as to get equality of health among persons, and one might distribute resources so as indirectly to get equal utility or welfare among persons. But Miller asserts there is no Y that will in this way generate equality of status, because, for any Y, whether or not a certain distribution of Y contributes to equality of status depends on shared social understandings. But this point holds equally of the idea of equality of utility or welfare which Miller does want to count as a form of simple equality. For example, whether a given distribution of resources contributes to equality of welfare depends on the social meanings of these resources—if receipt of income maintenance from the state attracts an invidious social stigma in the eyes of most citizens, then my welfare may drop when I get an income maintenance assistance cheque from the state, even though I could certainly use the extra cash. My conclusion is that the distinction between simple (what Walzer calls 'literal') and complex equality is not clarifying, because either the notion of equality you espouse really does entail equality along some significant dimension or it does not. If it does, then some notion of simple or literal equality is being advanced and you may as well acknowledge it. If it does not, then some non-egalitarian ideal is being advanced, and I see no motivation for calling this new non-egalitarian ideal 'complex equality'.

AN ECUMENICAL PROPOSAL

My objection against Walzer and Miller is that their analyses of equality throw out the baby with the bath water. The question

---

[20] Miller, Ch. 9.

arises how to give a perspicuous characterization of the baby whose careless disposal I am lamenting. This is a large topic. I make no claim that this chapter points the way towards its resolution. My suggestion is that to qualify as genuinely egalitarian, a political theory or set of principles must be able to explain and justify the 'generic egalitarian intuition', which goes as follows: other things being equal, if a good is being distributed, it is intrinsically (non-instrumentally) morally better that the good should go to a worse off rather than to a better off person, even if supplying the good to the already better off person would produce more utility overall than would supplying the good to the worse off person. In this sense egalitarian distribution tilts in favour of the worse off. This generic egalitarian intuition could be explained by a preference for equality *per se* or by many other principles.[21] Perhaps generic egalitarianism is wrong; nothing asserted in this chapter amounts to a defence of it. But it does not serve clarity to propound Walzerian complex equality as a genuinely egalitarian notion.[22]

APPENDIX

Pareto efficiency is often supposed to be opposed to distributive fairness, so the claim that the Pareto norm itself is a requirement of fairness needs some elaboration. The Pareto norm states that if the *status quo* can be altered by making someone better off without making anyone worse off, then the *status quo* should either be altered in this way or in another way such that the resultant *status quo* cannot be altered by making someone better off without making someone worse off. This is a mouthful, but the idea is simple. A necessary though not sufficient condition of fair distribution is that the outcome it precipitates should not be alterable by making someone better off without making anyone worse off. Call the person whose position could be improved when the Pareto norm is not met the *victim*. The victim has a valid complaint against the *status quo*. The complaint is that society should not gratuitously leave her worse off than she might be made at no cost to others. Tolerating a *status quo* that violates the Pareto norm shows too little concern for the welfare of the victim. The

[21] For some suggestions, see my 'Equality', in Robert E. Goodin and Philip Pettit (eds.), *A Companion to Contemporary Political Philosophy* (Oxford: Basil Blackwell, 1993), 489–507.
[22] I thank David Miller for helpful comments on a draft of this chapter.

victim does not have an entitlement to be made better off: rather she has the right either that she be accorded the benefit that costs others nothing or that another outcome be implemented from which no one can make a victim's complaint. When the Pareto norm is violated, society—all of us together—manifest a dog-in-the-manger attitude with respect to the victim, and this is unfair.

Objection: suppose that Smith and Jones are being paid a fair wage for doing the same work, and the employer arbitrarily favours Smith by giving her a 50% wage increase. Smith is better off and no one is worse off, but the change is hardly fair. The objection shows a misunderstanding of the Pareto norm. In the example as described, one supposes that if Smith's salary is increased, others must suffer losses. Let us stipulate that this does not occur. Smith's gain causes no one's position to worsen. But an obvious alternative to giving Smith a 50% raise is to give both Smith and Jones a 25% raise. *Ex hypothesi*, they seem equally deserving, so this solution would be more fair. The Pareto norm does not distinguish these two alternatives. In picking among Pareto-optimal outcomes, other norms such as deservingness have a role to play. Suppose the example is specified in this way: the only feasible alternatives are that Smith and Jones get salary X or that Jones gets X and Smith gets 1.5X. In this case, the Pareto norm may conflict with other fairness norms such as equality or distribution according to desert. A strong Pareto norm would hold that Pareto should win all such contests; a weak Pareto norm would hold that other things equal, the Pareto norm should be upheld, and leave the weight of the norm undecided when it comes into conflict with other principles.

11

The Sociology of Complex Equality

ADAM SWIFT

Hitherto, sociology has most obviously informed normative debate on social justice through its investigation of social mobility, reflecting sociologists' preoccupation with the value of equality of opportunity. The idea of an 'open' society in which merit alone determines an individual's place in the distribution of social advantage is a key component of conventional liberal conceptions of social justice, and much stratification research has taken as its specific focus of inquiry the measurement of the extent to which, and the investigation of the reasons why, given societies depart from this ideal of 'openness' or 'fluidity'.[1]

Recently, political theory has turned its attention to the question rather of how we should conceive what G. A. Cohen has nicely called 'the currency of egalitarian justice', where the force of 'egalitarian' here is such that the issues involved concern not just (in)equality of opportunity as conventionally understood but (in)equality of condition as well.[2] This raises the question of

I am grateful to G. A. Cohen, David Miller, John Torrance, and Albert Weale for their helpful comments on various of my previous attempts to make something coherent out of this material.

[1] This preoccupation characterizes both the dominant approaches to stratification research: the status attainment and the class structure approach. See D. L. Featherman and R. M. Hauser, *Opportunity and Change* (New York: Academic Press, 1978) and R. Erikson and J. H. Goldthorpe, *The Constant Flux* (Oxford: Oxford Univ. Press, 1992). For examples of stratification research informing political theory, see J. S. Coleman, 'Inequality, Sociology and Moral Philosophy', in his *Individual Interests and Collective Action* (Cambridge: Cambridge Univ. Press, 1986); J. S. Fishkin, *Justice, Equal Opportunity and the Family* (New Haven, Conn.: Yale Univ. Press, 1982); and S. J. D. Green, 'Is Equality of Opportunity a False Ideal For Society?', *British Journal of Sociology*, 39 (1988), 1–27.

[2] G. A. Cohen, 'The Currency of Egalitarian Justice', *Ethics*, 99 (1989), 906–44. The reader should beware a possible ambiguity in 'opportunities'. It is natural to characterize social positions in terms of the 'opportunities' they yield to their possessors where these are not opportunities to climb the social ladder but constituents

whether, and in what ways, stratification research can increase our understanding of the latter as it has that of the former. How, to borrow Frank Parkin's distinction, can sociology inform the egalitarian critique of existing inequalities as it has the meritocratic critique?[3] The tactic employed in this chapter is to confront Walzer's political-theoretical conception of justice—which provides an answer to the 'currency' question 'how should we think about the goods for which it is the task of a theory of a justice to provide distributive principles?'—with sociological work that formulates its conceptualization of social stratification, and approach to questions of equality, in apparently similar ways.

To attempt a summary of the former would be redundant, partly because the reader will already be familiar with Walzer's general position, partly because I will shortly discuss various possible interpretations that might be put upon it. Compare, instead, his talk of 'spheres' and 'complex (rather than "simple") equality' with the following suggestion put forward by two Polish sociologists, Wesolowski and Slomczynski, who, having claimed that some inequality is necessary to the proper functioning of the division of labour given the stage of development reached by the productive forces, went on to consider whether to accept this is to rule out all further reduction in social inequalities.

In trying to answer this question, we shall first introduce the concept of the general status of a group or individual . . . The status of a particular unit of observation will be treated as the weighted average of the positions it occupies in *various spheres of social differentiation*. As such elements of general status one can, for example, regard the following: education, professional skills, responsibility, complexity of work, income, standard of living, consumption of cultural goods, prestige and so on. Each of these elements can of course have a different meaning for status as a whole, which can be expressed by the appropriate weights. However, having weighted the particular positions, one can speak of levelling of social inequalities in the sense that the averages of the positions in the population, that is general statuses, do not have large differences among them-

---

of the individual rungs. If I, because of my lengthy academic vacations, have greater opportunity to go on holiday than you with your job in the civil service, this does not mean that I have greater opportunity to be upwardly mobile. The opportunities that mobility researchers are interested in measuring and explaining are opportunities to move *between* social positions.

　　[3] F. Parkin, *Class Inequality and Political Order* (London: McGibbon & Key, 1971), 13.

selves. It is possible to attain such a state of affairs *not only through simple reduction of inequalities* in the particular spheres of social differentiation, but also by combining high positions with low positions. This type of situation, where the units of observation have even closer global statuses, at the same time maintaining differences in particular positions, we shall term *complex reduction of social inequalities*.[4]

Empirically, Wesolowski and Slomczynski claimed that correlations between dimensions such as education, income, prestige, and cultural consumption were lower in Poland than in the capitalist West: while inequality within spheres remained, goods did not convert between spheres to the same extent and people were, overall, more equal.

Just as Walzer rejects theories of distributive justice that fail to acknowledge the 'multiplicity of goods' and corresponding 'multiplicity of distributive agents, procedures and criteria',[5] so this sociological perspective denies that social inequality can be understood as consisting in a single hierarchy of advantage. As Landecker puts it: 'In any stratified population one finds that its members are unequal to one another not just in one respect but in various ways. A stratification system must be viewed, therefore, as a composite of several, qualitatively different, kinds of inequality'. And having defined the concept of class crystallization as 'the degree to which equivalent ranks of different rank systems overlap in their membership', he continues:

A society with a great deal of class crystallisation is a society in which inequality is highly generalised. Strong class crystallisation is synonymous with wholesale inequality. The lower the degree of class crystallisation, on the other hand, the less often social inequality carries over from one rank system to another . . . Weak class crystallisation does not eliminate or even reduce inequality within one rank system, but to the extent that it approaches a condition in which everybody holds high status in one respect and low status in another, it approaches equality in the distribution of unequal positions. Hence, weak class crystallisation diverges less from egalitarian values than does strong class crystallisation.[6]

[4] W. Wesolowski and K. Slomczynski, 'Reduction of Inequalities and Status Inconsistency', *Angewandte Sozialforschung*, 11 (1983), 185–94, at 186, emphases added. This paper was first presented in 1974, and the data on which it relies were collected in the two periods 1964–7 and 1971.

[5] M. Walzer, *Spheres of Justice* (New York: Basic Books, 1983), 3.

[6] W. Landecker, *Class Crystallisation* (New Brunswick, NJ: Rutgers Univ. Press, 1981), 18, 48, 50–1.

My purpose is to consider Walzer's normative ideal in the light of sociological literature that formulates its ideas in strikingly similar ways.

INTERPRETATIONS OF COMPLEX EQUALITY

This assimilation of Walzer to the sociological perspective just outlined is not unproblematic, as may be seen by noting that there are various different senses in which complex equality might be equality. His open-ended distributive principle—'No social good x should be distributed to men and women who possess some other good y merely because they possess y and without regard to the meaning of x' (*Spheres*, 20)—has no obviously egalitarian content and, although Walzer provides various clues as to what might justify giving his theory of justice this label, these are not developed systematically. The sociological passages quoted above indicate the kind of egalitarian content to be attributed to the theory here, but it would be foolish to deny that my approach picks up on some of Walzer's remarks whilst neglecting or ignoring others.

On one reading it is the methodological aspect of complex equality that makes it egalitarian. Walzer's most thorough defence of the injunction that justice consists in conformity to 'social meanings' runs as follows:

By virtue of what characteristics are we one another's equals? One characteristic above all is central to my argument. We are (all of us) culture-producing creatures; we make and inhabit meaningful worlds. Since there is no way to rank and order these worlds with respect to their understandings of social goods, we do justice to actual men and women by respecting their particular creations. (*Spheres*, 314)

In his preface, Walzer claims that the entire book is an answer of a complicated sort to the question 'In what respects are we one another's equals?' (*Spheres*, p. xii), and although he there distinguishes this from the question asked and answered in the passage just quoted, it is not easy to see where exactly the difference lies. Taking seriously the claim that this characteristic is 'central', one might think that complex equality gets its egalitarian credentials because it is implied by a notion of equal respect for the capacity of all human beings to create culture.

An alternative reading would appeal to Walzer's prefatory observations on what motivates egalitarian politics. In his view, what is at stake in all struggles for equality is the ability of a group of people to dominate their fellows—it is the experience of subordination that lies behind the vision of equality. 'The aim of political egalitarianism is a society free from domination.' The link to the open-ended criterion of complex equality is then achieved by the claim that it is through the possession of particular goods—different in different societies, and ranging from blood or birth to capital and divine grace—that some dominate others. For Walzer, 'men and women are one another's equals (for all important moral and political purposes) when no one possesses or controls the means of domination' (*Spheres*, p. xiii).

What really matters about equality, on this account—and it is unclear whether this is an empirical political-sociological claim about the motivation underlying appeal to the rhetoric of equality or a normative claim about all there really is of substantive value in such rhetoric—is the absence of domination. According to Walzer, 'domination is ruled out only if social goods are distributed for distinct and "internal" reasons' (*Spheres*, p. xv)—a claim about the means by which some dominate others—and this implies the complex egalitarian formula cited above. Equality is equated with the absence of domination and domination is effected through the possession and monopolization of 'dominant' goods. The way to prevent domination, and hence to achieve all the equality that is morally and politically important, is to prevent goods from converting illegitimately across spheres, where their social meanings indicate that they should be distributed autonomously, for different reasons.

One could sensibly deny both that all important equality consists in non-domination and that domination is achieved solely, or even primarily, through the possession of 'dominant' goods. Perhaps more interesting is that Walzer himself seems to hanker after more equality than he officially permits himself. At one point he writes:

But what if dominance were eliminated, the autonomy of the spheres established—and the same people were successful in one sphere after another, triumphant in every company, piling up goods without the need for illegitimate conversions? This would certainly make for an inegalitarian society, but it would also suggest in the strongest way that a society of equals was not a lively possibility. (*Spheres*, 20)

Walzer imagines here a society that satisfies the demand of complex equality—no goods are dominant and, on his own assumptions, nobody is dominating anybody else—but that is neither 'egalitarian' nor even 'a society of equals'. He clearly has in mind here a notion of equality, and presumably one of moral and political importance, that differs from the absence of domination.

A third kind of equality his theory might be thought to embody is that discussed by David Miller in his contribution to this volume. On this view, complex equality is best understood as equality of status. Miller's suggestion is that all members of modern societies can only enjoy equal status if distributive mechanisms are radically pluralistic and incommensurable, so that although individuals can rank themselves against one another in terms of particular spheres of distribution there is no basis for judgements as to overall social standing. 'Where overall ranking is impossible, the status of individuals depends only on their common position as members of a particular society. Provided they are defined as equals by the public institutions of their society, this status must be an equal one.'[7]

It is crucial to this third view that the plurality of goods belonging to the different distributive spheres are incommensurable, in the sense that there is no socially agreed upon way of combining people's standing in the different spheres into an overall judgement. It is this claim about incommensurability that most clearly contrasts with the kind of equality I have in mind, for my fourth sense in which complex equality might be regarded as egalitarian requires precisely that one be able to make aggregative judgements as to individuals' overall positions: one must at least say that people are more equal if those who score high with respect to some goods score low with respect to others than if the same people score high (and low) on all. This is to take complex equality to be egalitarian in a fairly conventional sense—it is a version of equality of condition, that holds that people are (more or less) equal when they have, or have access to, bundles of goods that are, overall, (more or less) equally good.

Further caveats are in order. The extent to which Walzer's theory of justice—formulated in terms of individual goods being distributed autonomously and for 'internal' reasons—is egalitarian in

---

[7] Ch. 9, 207.

this sense is obviously contingent. We have already noted Walzer envisaging the possibility that a complex egalitarian society will be 'inegalitarian' just because the same people score high in all spheres without illegitimate conversion of advantage, and this, though also suggesting that he has something like my conception of 'equality' at work somewhere in his thinking, is sufficient to make the contingency clear. How much overall equality in the distribution of goods is implied by Walzer's open-ended distributive principle is a doubly empirical issue. It depends upon the content of the social meanings in the society in question. We should not forget that Walzer admits the possibility of societies in which social meanings, because integrated and hierarchical, 'will come to the aid of inequality' (*Spheres*, 313—another usage indicating that he thinks there is more to equality than complex equality as he defines it). And, given the social meanings of any particular society, it depends upon the abilities and characteristics of its members.

Granting that Walzer has correctly identified the meanings in contemporary America of, let us say, health care, education, money, and political power, my own view is that a society in which these goods are distributed autonomously would be more equal, in my fourth sense, than one in which people are able, as they are to a significant extent at present, to use their advantage in one sphere to procure it in others. Of course it would not be strictly equal; it may even contain important, and perhaps even unjust, inequalities. But people would have, or have access to, more equal amounts of these good things, considered as a whole, than they would in a society that allowed people's ability to make money the determinant of their access to these other goods.

It is this avowedly contingent aspect of complex equality that I intend to discuss. A society in which conversions between goods belonging to different spheres were prevented would, let us suppose, result in lower correlations between such goods, and hence be more equal, than would a society where such conversions are permitted. Complex equality, on this account, is equality achieved by the disaggregation of components of advantage that would otherwise go together—it is 'complex' simply in virtue of recognizing that people can be unequal to one another with respect to their possession of, or access to, a multiplicity of different goods, and that one way to achieve greater overall equality is to reduce correlations between those goods.

There are traces of this thought in Walzer's own writings. Consider the following passage

Imagine now a society in which different social goods are monopolistically held—as they are in fact and as they always will be, barring continual state intervention—but in which no particular good is generally convertible . . . This is a complex egalitarian society. Though there will be many small inequalities, inequality will not be multiplied through the conversion process. Nor will it be summed across different goods, because the autonomy of distributions will tend to produce a variety of local monopolies, held by different groups of men and women. (*Spheres*, 17)

It is a feature of a complex egalitarian society that 'inequality will not be multiplied through the conversion process'. Most telling of all, the reason why inequality will not be summed across different goods is not that such summation is impossible, as it would be if the goods were incommensurable, but because, according to Walzer, different people will tend to monopolize different goods. Goods will not be 'summed' in the sense that they will not tend to accrue to the same people, rather than in the sense, required by Miller, that there will be no socially agreed judgements as to people's overall positions with respect to a composite index of advantage.

This equality-via-multiplicity strand appears also on the last page of *Spheres*. Comparing his own vision with Aristotle's claim that justice in a democracy requires the citizens to rule and be ruled in turn, Walzer writes:

But politics is only one (though it is probably the most important) among many spheres of social activity. What a larger conception of justice requires is not that citizens rule and are ruled in turn, but that they rule in one sphere and are ruled in another—where 'rule' means not that they exercise power but that they enjoy a greater share than other people of whatever good is being distributed. The citizens cannot be guaranteed a 'turn' everywhere. I suppose, in fact, they cannot be guaranteed a 'turn' anywhere. But the autonomy of spheres will make for a greater sharing of social goods than will any other conceivable arrangement. (*Spheres*, 321)

What matters ultimately, it seems, is the greatest conceivable sharing of social goods, which can only be read as a version of the kind of equality of condition to be investigated here.

I do not want to claim that this fourth sense in which the theory of justice as complex equality is egalitarian is that truest to the position put forward in *Spheres* overall. My reasons for thinking it worthy of investigation would survive my being persuaded, for example, that the incommensurability of the spheres was central to Walzer's position, and to what, if anything, makes it a theory of equality. It is not my primary aim to be true to Walzer, but rather to cast a sociologically informed eye over a conception of, or strategy for, equality with which his theory at least overlaps. Walzer's emphasis on the differentiated nature of the goods with which a theory of justice has to deal opens the way to a potentially fruitful interaction between sociology and political theory. It also invites consideration of the possibility of a form of equality of condition that has not received sufficient attention generally: equality-via-disaggregation.

SOCIAL STRATIFICATION AND THE CONVERSION OF ADVANTAGE

In this and the following section, I use the stratification literature to consider two issues raised by complex equality. There is nothing exhaustive or even systematic about my discussion—here simply are two places where what sociologists have had to say seems most relevant to an inquiry into the prospects for complex equality. (I will, in my conclusion, attempt to tie the two issues together, but hope that each taken separately is of sufficient interest to make this something of an optional extra). First, and quite generally, does not a proper understanding of the 'stuff' of which the various dimensions are dimensions suggest that there is a natural tendency towards conversion and equilibration, as if advantage were somehow inherently convertible? Second, and more specifically, is there anything in the idea that social status might be disaggregated, to complex egalitarian ends, from the goods with which it tends to be associated?

The first worry, then, is that the stuff of stratification is inherently convertible, in such a way as to make a strategy of blocking exchanges impossible, or achievable only at excessive cost. As has already been made clear, I am taking complex equality in a sense that requires that it be possible to regard the different goods or dimensions that are to be disaggregated as, in some sense, components of the same stuff. How else might advantage with respect to one good compensate for, or in any way offset, disadvantage with respect to another? But if convertibility is in the very nature of the stuff whose conversion the complex egalitarian seeks to prevent, then it would seem that her task is hopeless from the start.

It is notable, then, that the idea that conversions are normal—that other things being equal we should expect strong correlations between dimensions—is a point conceded even by sociologists concerned to insist that stratification must be regarded as multidimensional. It is regularly stressed that manifestations of non-coincidence are exceptions to the rule, and perhaps especially worthy of study for that very reason. Thus, for example, Benoit-Smullyan's classic paper, which was in large part responsible for the introduction of the multidimensional framework into American sociology, talks about 'status conversion processes which are normally at work in every society' and which result in 'a real tendency for different types of status to reach a common level', a tendency he terms 'status equilibration'.[8]

Some have been brave enough to attempt to provide a general definition of the stuff of stratification, which has then been taken in the same direction. Goldthorpe and Bevan claim that the study of stratification is concerned with 'phenomena of unequal power and advantage arising out of institutional arrangements' and go on to assert that,

insofar as power and advantage are in their very nature 'convertible' from one mode or form to another, it is to be expected . . . that, other things being equal, the positions of individuals and groups in respect of different types of inequality will exhibit a strain towards consistency. . . . Thus, what we would take as chiefly problematic is the extent of inconsistency . . . that may be empirically established . . .

The link between advantage and power, together with a definition of power as 'the capacity to mobilise resources in order to bring about a desired state of affairs' combine, on this account, to convey a necessary connection between advantage and convertibility. If my advantage yields me power to do or get what I want, then one of the things it yields me is the power to convert that advantage into other 'modes or forms'.[9]

---

[8] E. Benoit-Smullyan, 'Status Types and Status Interrelations', *American Sociological Review*, 9 (1944), 151–61, p. 160.

[9] J. H. Goldthorpe and P. Bevan, 'The Study of Social Stratification in Great Britain: 1946–76', *Social Science Information*, 16 (1977), 279–334, pp. 280, 283–4.

This kind of claim is at such a high level of abstraction that it is hard to know how to assess it. Two thoughts point in opposite directions. One way to voice suspicion is to observe simply that the possibility of conversion between dimensions or goods depends on the availability of conversion processes. As Runciman nicely puts it, 'it is true that to a holder of power of one kind there will inevitably accrue power of another to the extent that the institutions of the society do provide for convertibility between them'.[10] We should not think that there is anything more in this inherent convertibility claim than the contention that there are mechanisms by which people are able to convert advantage with respect to one good into advantage with respect to others, and it is perfectly possible for a society to decide that particular mechanisms should cease to be available. The complex egalitarian may be well aware that conversion processes exist: she is arguing precisely that they should be abolished.

On the other hand, it would be naïve not to acknowledge that conversion processes are many and myriad, and that while we might try to prevent particular transmission mechanisms there seem always to be others that will act as functional equivalents. However we may try to block exchanges between goods or dimensions of advantage, however successful we may be in blocking particular channels, there will always and inevitably be modes of conversion that we cannot prevent. If advantage is Protean, then the task of fettering it is Sisyphean.

To see this, consider, as Goldthorpe and Bevan suggest, the analogy with intergenerational social mobility and the processes that enable parents to transmit advantage to their children. These too can be thought of as processes of conversion—across time and generations rather than across dimensions of stratification. Just as, given the institution of the family, intergenerational stability in social position is only to be expected, so we should not be surprised if individual units exhibit consistency among different types of inequality.

But when we think about *why* it is that we should expect intergenerational continuity of units' location in the stratification system we find ourselves pointing simply to well-known and commonsensical explanations in terms of family strategies and the

[10] W. G. Runciman, *A Treatise on Social Theory*, ii (Cambridge: Cambridge Univ. Press, 1989), 16.

various means—some institutional and consciously intended (inheritance laws, private education), some neither (Bourdieu's 'cultural capital', Bernstein's linguistic 'codes')[11]—of their realization. There is no magical (or scientific) understanding of the essence of the 'stuff' of stratification as 'inherently convertible'; there is just the fact of certain obvious mechanisms of intertemporal and interpersonal conversion of advantage. The claim that the stuff of stratification is 'in its very nature' convertible across time and persons points simply to familiar sociological processes, some of which could realistically be imagined otherwise.

The counter-claim, that the conversion of advantage across generations will survive our attempts to prevent it, points to the variety of, and inaccessibility of some of, those processes of transmission. If we were to prevent direct transfer of wealth, children of the advantaged would still have the benefits of a superior education and superior health care. Abolish private education and health care and they would still be better off than children of the disadvantaged: they would be healthier through having lived in bigger houses and eaten better food and gone on longer and sunnier holidays; they would be better placed in the competition for education because of their nursery toys and books. Abolish, *per absurdum*, their superiority in houses, food, holidays, toys, and books, and their subcultural *savoir-faire* or their personal contacts will serve them in good stead.[12] And so on. When we assert the sociological generalization that it is 'normal' for advantage to be transmitted across generations, we are pointing to conversion processes of this sort. And the point that will be made in favour of the inherent convertibility claim is that, while some of these processes can be prevented, there seem always to be others on hand.

None of this impugns appropriately modest and realistic

---

[11] P. Bourdieu, 'Cultural Reproduction and Social Reproduction', in J. Karabel and A. H. Halsey (eds.), *Power and Ideology in Education* (New York: Oxford Univ. Press, 1977); B. Bernstein, *Class, Codes and Control*, iv. *The Structuring of Pedagogic Discourse* (London: Routledge, 1990).

[12] See G. Marshall and A. Swift, 'Social Class and Social Justice', *British Journal of Sociology*, 44 (1992), 187–211, the finding that not all the intergenerational transmission of class position passes via education. Even if one grants the (implausible) claim that the differential distribution of educational achievement by class is just because members of different classes differ in those abilities appropriately rewarded by the education system, and the (less implausible) claim that educational achievement is appropriately rewarded in class terms, still one cannot defend existing mobility patterns as just.

attempts to reduce the extent of conversion and equilibration. Against those insisting on the inherent convertibility of the stuff of stratification, the complex egalitarian can sensibly and cogently point to the reduction in correlations between dimensions or goods that can be achieved by blocking those exchanges that can be blocked. While it would be utopian to assume that all conversions are preventable, there remains every reason to prevent those that are so.[13]

The complex egalitarian's major institutional move will be to decommodify, and distribute in accordance with criteria other than the ability to pay, components of advantage that are currently for sale in the market. But part of the case of those who emphasize the links between advantage and power, in order to maintain a version of the inherent convertibility claim, is to insist that we acknowledge the significance of all those conversions that are effected by other means. There is a deal of evidence to suggest that what happened in decommodified Eastern Europe was the substitution of influence or contacts for money as the means of procuring desired goods, and research into the distributional effects of the welfare state in Western societies suggests that the middle classes are able to exploit their non-pecuniary advantages (articulacy, ability to work the system) to benefit disproportionately with respect to goods that are provided on a non-market basis.[14]

To this the complex egalitarian might respond that the important question is not whether those goods are distributed perfectly equally (or in accordance with their autonomous principles of distribution) but whether non-market modes of distribution produce outcomes that are more (complexly) egalitarian than those that would result from the free play of the market. The crucial questions for the complex egalitarian envisaging decommodification are

[13] A recent comparative study of social mobility in industrial societies finds evidence that social democratic Sweden has been more socially fluid than the other non-social democratic countries investigated, which suggests that mobility processes at least are not completely impervious to political action taken to promote equality of opportunity. See Robert Erikson, 'Politics and Class Mobility—Does Politics Influence Rates of Social Mobility?', in I. Persson (ed.), *Generating Equality in the Welfare State* (Oslo: Norwegian Univ. Press, 1990).

[14] On Eastern Europe, see P. Kende and Z. Strmiska (eds.), *Equality and Inequality in Eastern Europe* (Leamington Spa: Berg, 1987). On Western welfare states see J. Le Grand, *The Strategy of Equality* (London: Allen & Unwin, 1983), and R. Goodin and J. Le Grand, *Not Only the Poor: The Middle Classes and the Welfare State* (London: Allen & Unwin, 1987).

twofold. First, are conversions that operate other than via the cash nexus as efficient as those that do? If they are not, then at least decommodification will have some (complexly) egalitarian impact. Second, what factors determine the distribution of the good or goods that are likely to act as functional equivalents to money, to be (in Walzer's sense) 'dominant'? In the pure market case, money will be distributed in accordance with the ability to satisfy, and get paid for satisfying, other people's preferences. Alternative currencies might be distributed in a variety of ways.

A final thought on this question of inherent convertibility supports the claim that conversions are normal or natural, at least in the sense now to be outlined. While the complex egalitarian can indeed point to the contingency of conversion processes and their significant dependence on the status of goods as commodities, it would be foolish not to acknowledge the relation between conversion and individual freedom. If the exchange of my CD player for your performing a knee operation on my son is mutually agreeable, then both our freedoms are restricted if that transaction is forbidden. Money facilitates the process of free exchange, for as Simmel noted, money's divisibility and 'unlimited convertibility' makes it possible for every exchange to become, at least in principle, equally advantageous to both parties. Whatever else one may think of a culture that reduces (nearly) all distinctions of quality to differences of quantity, whatever there is of value that one suspects might be lost by such a reduction—and Simmel was clear that much is lost—it remains the case that individual freedom is curtailed by the prevention of those exchanges that people would willingly undertake and that are facilitated by money and commodification of the goods which they might want to buy with it.[15]

This view does not presuppose that the kinds of property claims we are accustomed to make are valid—my freedom to swap the CD player for the operation is restricted even if I cannot justify my claim to the CD player in the first place (though of course that restriction is rather more likely to be justified). And it certainly does not imply that a system of private property and free exchange maximizes individual freedom.[16] But in any case, it is as a social-

[15] G. Simmel, *The Philosophy of Money*, 2nd edn., ed. D. Frisby, tr. T. Bottomore and D. Frisby (London: Routledge, 1990), 292–3.
[16] W. Kymlicka, *Contemporary Political Philosophy* (Oxford: Oxford Univ. Press, 1990), 132–52, presents an excellent short (but extensively referenced)

scientific rather than a normative political-theoretical point that this relation between convertibility and freedom is most relevant. What matters in the current context is whether there is a sense in which the stuff of stratification is inherently convertible, where this is formulated as a social-scientific issue, and the connections between the market and widespread notions of individual freedom and well-being strongly suggest that there is such a sense. Where conversions between goods are officially prohibited, either unofficial (or 'black') markets tend to arise (consider the market in back-street abortion before its legalization) or those wishing to exchange look to places where that exchange is permitted (an important argument against the abolition of private education in Britain is that private schools, and the children they educate, will simply move abroad). These examples, which are grounded in as commonsensical a sociology as one could imagine, not only testify to the normalness of convertibility but also suggest that, if we do want to counteract the market, we will need a strong centralized authority to do it. Conversion is normal at least in the sense that state power is required to prevent it, to police the boundaries between dimensions or goods that free individuals will want to exchange one for another.

OCCUPATION, INCOME, AND STATUS

The second objection to the viability of complex equality turns our attention not to the ways in which people are able to convert advantage with respect to one dimension into advantage with respect to others, but to the claim that one particular dimension of the stratification system is causally explained by others. Here again the emphasis is on the interconnectedness of the various components of advantage that the complex egalitarian might seek to disaggregate, but the suggestion now is that where the distribution of some goods follows the distribution of some others, and as a result of causal processes operating at sufficient depth, then attempts to separate them will look misguided. The specific suggestion is that social status might be such a dependent good.

The good of 'prestige' or 'status' is sometimes put forward as

discussion that is sharply and persuasively critical of libertarian claims that the free market provides more freedom than would any other distributive mechanism.

something that might be disaggregated from the other goods with which it is usually associated. Consider the policy implication that Hirsch draws from his influential analysis of the positional economy. For him, 'top jobs' in advanced societies 'currently exert a double magnetism. They offer both relatively high pay and relatively large nonfinancial benefits—work-satisfaction deriving either from the nature of the job or the status it carries in the community or both . . . As long as the nonfinancial attractions of positional jobs are strong, the salaries attached to them can be regarded as incidental benefits.' The suggestion here is that both 'status' and 'work-satisfaction' can and should be regarded as dimensions of reward distinct from the monetary gains attaching to particular jobs. Barry, rejecting Rawls's purported concentration on wealth and power and neglect of status, makes a similar move, suggesting that 'people might be paid in the coinage of status as an alternative (perhaps a partial alternative) to being given wealth or power'. If, however, status is something that you get for earning a lot of money, then it makes little sense to pursue a policy of disaggregation between the two. In this it may differ from 'work-satisfaction' that is the other alternative form of reward that Hirsch proposes.[17]

There are hints of this line of thought, and of these doubts also, in Walzer's own writing. Acknowledging that, in contemporary societies, a person's 'status' is primarily a function of her standing in the Hobbesian race, he suggests that 'free appraisal would require the disaggregation of social goods, the relative autonomy of honor'. As well as leading to a more decentralized system of recognitions, as different people honoured different others for different qualities, he conjectures, it would not be difficult to imagine valuations very different from those that currently prevail: 'a new respect for socially useful work . . . or for physical effort, or for helpfulness in office rather than mere office holding' (*Spheres*, 256–7). What follows may be thought of as an attempt to fill out some of these ideas by looking at what sociologists have had to say about 'status' and to investigate its potential role in a complex egalitarian strategy.

The concept of status has undergone a double dilution since its classic treatment by Weber, for whom 'class', 'status', and 'party'

---

[17] F. Hirsch, *Social Limits to Growth* (Cambridge, Mass.: Harvard Univ. Press, 1976), 183. B. Barry, *The Liberal Theory of Justice* (Oxford: Oxford Univ. Press, 1973), 47.

are 'phenomena of the distribution of power within a community'.[18] In the first place, it has been taken to refer to any 'dimension' of stratification, and not only to the subjective dimension or that relating to the distribution of 'social honour'. When the Hungarian Kolosi talks about 'division of labour status' or 'financial status' he is clearly using the term in a sense very different from, indeed antithetical to, Weber's, for the term 'status' has come to be used to refer to any gradational variable—it means no more than 'standing in some hierarchy'—and the reference to the specifically subjective in the original concept has disappeared.[19] Weber's claim that status was something distinct from class was conflated with the quite distinct, but also anti-class, claim about the gradational nature of stratification, to yield the conclusion that status referred by definition to that about stratification which was gradational. In some contexts, as Lockwood says, 'the term "status" means nothing more than position in a potentially status-relevant rank dimension'.[20]

The second way in which Weber's concept of status has been cheapened is more substantial: even when taken in its original sense as something distinct from the objective or material aspects of stratification, the concept has been rendered an implausible contender for the role of autonomous component of advantage that the complex egalitarian might look to it to play. For Weber, status can certainly offset class, but this is because it refers to 'social honour', which stands by its very nature opposed to the principle of the market and the realm of the economic: 'The market and its processes "knows no personal distinctions": functional interests dominate it. It knows nothing of "honour". The status order means precisely the reverse, viz.: stratification in terms of "honour" and styles of life peculiar to status groups as such'. According to Weber, social honour 'normally stands in sharp opposition to the

[18] M. Weber, *From Max Weber*, tr. and ed. H. H. Gerth and C. W. Mills (London: Routledge & Kegan Paul, 1948), 181.
[19] T. Kolosi, 'Status and Stratification', in R. Andorka and T. Kolosi (eds.), *Stratification and Inequality* (Budapest: Institute for Social Sciences, 1984). Cf. P. Blau's stipulation: '*Status* refers to all attributes of people that exhibit gradations, not only those associated with prestige or power. For example, age is a status, as the term has been defined'. *Inequality and Heterogeneity: A Primitive Theory of Social Structure* (New York: Free Press, 1977), 8.
[20] D. Lockwood, *Solidarity and Schism* (Oxford: Oxford Univ. Press, 1992), 119.

pretensions of sheer property' and '"Status groups" hinder the strict carrying through of the sheer market principle'.[21]

In contemporary sociology, when sociologists avoid the first trivialization and use status to refer specifically to the subjective aspect of stratification, they tend to regard it as denoting occupational status—the social standing of different occupations. Scales are derived by getting people to rank the titles of occupations according to their 'prestige', 'social standing', 'social status', and so on, but the problem here is that such scales do not identify the distinctively symbolic aspect of stratification. While it is conceptually possible that the occupational order should form the basis of a symbolic hierarchy, autonomous of the material rewards attaching to it, there is a deal of empirical evidence to suggest that prestige scales pick up little other than social perceptions of the material or objective rewards attaching to occupations. According to Hope and Goldthorpe, when asked about the relative 'social standing' of various occupations, most respondents do not adopt a distinctively 'prestige' frame of reference but rather 'assess the occupations presented to them on the basis of what they know, or think they know, about a *variety* of more "objective" occupational attributes—most often, perhaps, job rewards or requirements—which they see as relevant to the ordering of occupations simply in terms of *some rather unspecific better-worse dimension*' (emphasis in original). Scales of occupational status represent people's synthetic judgements about the 'general desirability' of occupations.[22]

More specifically, the ranking of occupations in terms of the one dimension of 'social standing' is very close (correlation of .98) to the simple average of the rankings performed with respect to the four attributes of standard of living, power and influence over other people, level of qualifications, and value to society. Three of these are objective or material attributes. In similar fashion,

---

[21] Weber, *From Max Weber*, 192, 187, 185. While Weber stresses the opposition between class and status, he is well aware of the causal relations between them, so that even though status honour normally stands in sharp opposition to the pretensions of sheer property it is also the case that, in the long run, 'and with extraordinary regularity' (p. 187) property is recognized as a status qualification. And, while propertied and propertyless people can, and frequently do, belong to the same status group 'this "equality" of social esteem may . . . in the long run become quite precarious' (ibid.). For Weber, 'the social order is of course conditioned by the economic order to a high degree, and in its turn reacts upon it' (p. 181).

[22] J. H. Goldthorpe and K. Hope, *The Social Grading of Occupations* (Oxford: Oxford Univ. Press, 1974), 11–12.

Featherman and his colleagues argue that ' "prestige" scores for occupations are fallible estimates of the socio-economic statuses of occupation' and Townsend maintains that 'the hierarchy of occupational prestige cannot be treated as an independent dimension of stratification. The prestige of people depends primarily on the material and political privileges they hold by virtue of their occupational class . . .'. Here is widespread agreement that occupational prestige is not autonomous of the distribution of material resources in society. And if it is not, then it makes little sense to think in terms of the one offsetting or compensating for the other.[23]

How might the complex egalitarian seek to rescue the subjective aspect of stratification in such a way as to enable it plausibly to be regarded as a separable component of overall distributional position? Two strategies seem to be worth exploring, each ascribing a different role to a person's occupation as determinant of her place in the distribution of advantage. First, keeping the centrality of occupation to modern stratification systems, she might seek to distinguish *within* occupation between those aspects that are rewarded materially and those that are, or could be, rewarded in more symbolic fashion, and to build a complex egalitarian strategy around that distinction. Second, reducing the extent to which occupation is associated with other goods, she might aim rather to develop a concept of status that can stand against occupation as an alternative source or component of advantage. The latter, in attempting to dethrone occupation from its currently dominant role, is the more radical move and I will turn to it briefly in my conclusion. The issue there will be whether it might make sense to concede that 'prestige' or 'social standing' are likely to follow the distribution of material rewards that result from the workings of the labour market, but to seek to reconstruct some stronger notion of status that is quite separate from, and can stand against, occupation.

The more modest proposal grants that the occupational structure will continue to be the crucial determinant of the distribution of advantage in society, but asks whether those aspects of occupation that are rewarded with prestige can be separated from those that receive more material returns. A hint of this idea has already

[23] D. L. Featherman *et al.*, 'Assumptions of Social Mobility Research in the US: The Case of Occupational Status', *Social Science Research*, 4 (1975) 329–60, at 329; P. Townsend, *Poverty in the United Kingdom* (Harmondsworth: Penguin, 1979), 399.

appeared, when it was noted that one of the dimensions of occupation apparently underlying people's status judgements was its 'value to society'. If, other things being equal, people do regard more highly those occupations that they consider more valuable to society, could we perhaps build on this and attempt in some way to lay greater emphasis on this aspect of people's jobs? Are there perhaps other facets of occupation that might warrant a similar strategy?

The sociology of the Eastern Bloc under Communist or state-socialist regimes is the natural place to turn for relevant theory and evidence, for this idea figures in the literature there in a number of guises. At the theoretical level, Wesolowski attaches some importance to this disentangling of status or prestige from the material rewards attaching to occupation. Having cited such examples as doctors 'who enjoy high prestige but receive only moderate salaries' and nursing 'for which a low income is received and moderate prestige accorded', he claims that 'prestige is now associated not so much with such matters as income but rather with sentiments of esteem or respect for the type of job done . . . Examples of incongruences between income and prestige point to the autonomisation of prestige with respect to income and also in relation to the principle "to each according to his work"'.

This last clause seems odd—surely it is 'work' that is rewarded with prestige, albeit aspects of work that material rewards may ignore—but Wesolowski continues more promisingly by identifying 'three possible variants of "psychological" reward in the form of prestige' that can be observed in socialist society:

First, it can be treated as a form of recompense for depressed (in relation to qualification) income . . . On the subject of remuneration for teachers in Poland just such a view of the compensatory role of social prestige can be detected. Second, prestige may constitute a reward for past highly skilled work which the individual is no longer able to contribute to society . . . Finally, prestige could be an 'off-setting reward' for work which, while not requiring especially high qualifications, is nevertheless dangerous (pilot), or unhealthy (miner), or requires a high degree of vocational and emotional involvement (teachers for handicapped children, geriatric nurses, etc.).[24]

    [24] W. Wesolowski, *Classes, Strata and Power*, tr. G. Kolankiewicz (London: Routledge & Kegan Paul, 1979), 139–40. This book first appeared in Polish in 1966.

On the empirical side, the evidence is mixed, and it is in any case hard without properly comparative or even comparable data either to interpret the significance of the correlations between income and prestige that Polish sociologists claimed to be unusually low, or to know whether prestige was more closely associated with aspects of occupation other than income in the East than in the West. Even if the income–prestige association was low, this may be because, where the role of the market is constrained and goods scarce, income may not be a very good measure of people's actual material rewards. And if income was a less significant component of material advantage in the East than in the West, then perhaps low correlations between income and prestige indicated rather a lack of association between income and material advantage than between that advantage and prestige.[25]

These mixed findings and various complications make it very difficult to draw any clear conclusions from the East European literature as to the viability of the complex egalitarian strategy of rewarding some jobs, or aspects of jobs, with prestige rather than income. What is undeniable is that, even in the West, certain specific occupations enjoy a high regard that cannot be explained by their large material rewards, and may even be explained by their lack of them: nurses, when in uniform, are doubtless treated better in daily life (by bus conductors, by shopkeepers) than are others who earn a good deal more; the same used to be true of teachers and perhaps remains so to some extent, at least in certain kinds of community. While scepticism about the general viability of such a strategy is justified, and while any claim of this sort must be weak and heavily qualified, we need not go so far as to dismiss the autonomy of social honour from material advantage altogether, for these examples suggest that there may be scope for at least a limited complex egalitarian strategy along the lines suggested here.

A third line of thought might also be pursued. This is more concessionary even than the modest proposal just discussed, for it accepts not only the centrality of occupation to the stratification system but also the inseparability of prestige from the material rewards attaching to occupations. If in this sense it is hostile to the claim that the subjective can be detached from the objective, what brings it properly under the complex egalitarian umbrella, what

[25] Kende, 'Introduction', to Kende and Strmiska (eds.), *Equality and Inequality*, 23.

justifies regarding it as an attempt to achieve greater overall equality by disaggregating components of advantage that currently cumulate, is the fact that it seeks to reward—with (*ex hypothesi* inseparable) objective *and* subjective goods—dimensions of occupation that warrant compensation but tend not to get it. And this relates to the issue of the autonomy of the subjective because the claim here is that the subjective can be the cause or independent variable, material rewards the effect or dependent.

I have in mind the ideological glorification of manual work that is, or was, perhaps the most distinctive feature of stratification systems in Eastern Europe.[26] Marxist theory, as filtered through into the official ideology of societies needing rapidly to industrialize, led manual work to be considered especially important, and non-manual work second-rate. This glorification manifested itself in the prestige system of these societies, when compared with those of the West: all research converges on the finding that the prestige judgements in the East with respect to the manual and non-manual division were out of line with the rest of the world. Miners, cleaning women, unskilled construction labourers all scored substantially above the standard international metric; government ministers, accountants, office clerks, and lawyers all scored substantially below.[27]

Does this establish the autonomy of the subjective? The sense in which it does not is that insisted upon by Treiman, who recognizes that there is a pronounced tendency in the East for clerical occupations to be downgraded (and for manual occupations to be upgraded) in prestige relative to the world as a whole, but none the less denies that this tells against his general thesis that 'the division of labour creates inherent differences in the power associated with various occupational roles wherever they are found, and these differences, in turn, create differences in privilege, and power and privilege beget prestige'. There is no separation of material and subjective here, for Treiman, because the manual/clerical pay ratio

[26] I am not aware of any studies undertaken since the demise of state socialism that reveal how people in these societies think about occupations now. It will be very interesting to see if the glorification of manual work survives the death of the ideology that generated it.

[27] M. Alestalo *et al.*, 'Patterns of Social Stratification', in E. Allardt and W. Wesolowski (eds.), *Social Structure and Change: Finland and Poland: Comparative Perspective* (Warsaw: Polish Scientific Publishers, 1980), 136–43.

was much higher, and manual workers had better access to other non-financial rewards, in the East than in the West.[28]

But while Treiman's claim, that prestige follows privilege and power, may be right, and not contradicted by the East European case, he is surely acknowledging that there is a second and alternative sense in which the material follows the subjective. For the prime mover here is the ideological evaluation of different occupations: the reason why manual workers earn more than non-manual ones is because of the status accorded to them by official ideology. Even if we grant that prestige depends on material position, in the sense that popular judgements reflect the privilege and power attaching to occupations, it is also and crucially the case that material position can itself depend upon 'subjective', or ideological, judgements about the importance or value of occupations. Even for Treiman, the status of occupations can be changed in accordance with 'ideology'. What cannot be done is to change the way they are evaluated by the society as a whole without also changing their material rewards.

This, then, is a third strategy available to the complex egalitarian. The case of Eastern Europe suggests that a society can decide which aspects or dimensions of occupations are rewarded both materially and symbolically, and this counts as complex egalitarian in so far as it involves the idea that we can compensate people in these dimensions for aspects of their work that warrant compensation. If we want to reward those who engage in particularly dangerous (or dirty or noisy or boring or emotionally demanding) work, this can be thought of as offsetting within occupation, but in this version it is the negative aspects of people's jobs that are compensated with both money and prestige—there is no attempt here either to reduce the importance of occupation as determinant of life-chances or to disentangle the financial and symbolic rewards that attach to occupation.

CITIZENSHIP

The imposition of an official ideology by a political élite is, of course, a far cry from anything implied by Walzer's concern to

---

[28] D. Treiman, *Occupational Prestige in Comparative Perspective* (New York: Academic Press, 1977), 2, 144–6.

respect social meanings. Even those suspicious of Walzer's methodology and interested in complex equality for other reasons may
have felt a certain unease about the extent to which my discussion
has drawn upon theory and evidence from East European societies
which might be thought to have earned their (complex) egalitarian
credentials, if at all, only at unacceptable moral cost. It is a particular merit of the thought to be pursued in this final section—the
possibility of a status that can stand against occupation as an alternative source or component of advantage—that the status I have
in mind is central to the self-understanding of liberal democracies,
and can plausibly be regarded as a 'social meaning' that is indeed
shared by their members.

That status is citizenship. Citizenship is something enjoyed by
people irrespective of their position in the occupational structure
and there are familiar lines of argument claiming that the proper
recognition of citizenship requires that certain goods be distributed
on non-market bases.[29] To the extent that citizens' common standing is recognized or made good by the distribution of the goods
that people need *qua* citizen, then life-chances are being distributed
in accordance not with occupation but with a dimension of the
stratification system that can be regarded as fundamentally symbolic or subjective—a function of the way in which the members
of society regard one another. As Lockwood puts it, 'the ways in
which the ideal of full citizenship seeks expression are manifold,
but all of them entail the replacement of class-determined by
status-determined life chances'.[30]

My claim is that citizenship is a status that stands as something
distinct from, and is strong enough to be capable of offsetting, the
distribution of resources resulting from the occupational structure.
Let me be clear about what I do not mean by this. I am not using
'status' in the Weberian sense outlined above: I do not envisage a

[29] The *locus classicus* here is T. H. Marshall, *Citizenship and Social Class*
(London: Pluto, 1992). See the helpful discussion by D. King and J. Waldron,
'Citizenship, Social Citizenship and the Defence of Welfare Provision', *British
Journal of Political Science*, 18 (1988), 415–43, who rightly view Rawls as offering
a version of this argument. Rawls can be regarded, in true Walzerian fashion albeit
for non-Walzerian reasons, as interpreting the social meaning of citizenship in constitutional democracies. This suggestion is discussed at greater length in S. Mulhall
and A. Swift, *Liberals and Communitarians* (Oxford: Blackwell, 1992), 179–80.

[30] D. Lockwood, 'On the Incongruity of Power and Status in Industrial Society',
in H. Strasser and R. W. Hodge (eds.), *Status Inconsistency in Modern Societies*
(Duisburg: Sozialwissenschaftlichen Kooperative, 1986), 20.

society in which all, in virtue of their equal citizenship, share the same 'style of life', or in which there are no observable 'status groups' constituted by patterns of association, endogamy, commensality, and so on. People can enjoy an equality of status as citizens that can stand alongside, and serve to offset, not only inequalities of reward from the labour market but also those inequalities in the estimation of social honour to which Weber referred.

Expanding on this last point may help to explain how the suggestion arrived at here, through discussion of complex equality as equality-via-disaggregation, differs from the (in many respects similar) reading of complex equality as a theory of equality of status offered by David Miller and outlined very briefly above. On Miller's account, it matters that distributive mechanisms be incommensurable because otherwise members of a society will be able to form judgements of overall social standing: equality of status requires that no such judgements be possible, or at least that there not be social agreement in such judgements. The fact that Miller then spells out equal status in terms of citizenship should not be allowed to obscure the difference between his proposal and mine. I think that the idea that we could avoid overall socially agreed judgements of social standing is unrealistic, and I offer citizenship as an alternative basis for the distribution of at least some material resources (and hence access to life-chances). This is complexly egalitarian in so far as it seeks greater overall equality of condition than would result in a society in which all goods were distributed in accordance with people's ability to make the money to pay for them.[31]

I have in mind, then, a notion of status as something other than 'social standing' as conventionally understood. On my account, members of a society can regard one anther as equals—recognize their status as citizens and acknowledge the justice of their claims to particular goods (those essential to their fulfilling the role of citizen)—whilst simultaneously agreeing in their judgements that person X stands higher socially than, perhaps should be deferred to by, and perhaps even should not be expected to marry, person Y. At least I hope so, since I think that equal citizenship matters but

---

[31] One way to see this is to note that Miller spells out citizenship in terms of formal political rights whereas it is central to my view that citizenship generates rights to citizenship goods that go beyond these.

am very doubtful that a society in which all have equal social
standing is a real possibility. In that sense, I agree with Walzer that
the idea of equality of recognition is 'a bad joke' (*Spheres*, 255),
and think this remains true even if pursued not simply, in the version that Walzer derides, but in the complex and interesting way
Miller proposes.

Full discussion of exactly what goods people might have claims
to *qua* citizens is matter for another paper. Here let me conclude
by discussing only the aspect of the question that is necessary to
forge a connection between the two issues outlined in this chapter.
The reader will recall that the claim that the stuff of stratification
is inherently convertible was most charitably read as pointing to
the relation between exchange and individual freedom, and the
necessity of coercive state action to counter the tendency for
advantage in one sphere to procure advantage in others. If we want
to block exchanges, then it looks as if we need the state to do it
and citizenship, by explicitly conceiving the individual in terms of
her relation to the state of which she is a member, is the identity
appropriate to legitimize that action. The two points would coincide neatly if there were reason to think that the only exchanges
that the state is justified in preventing are those that are implied by
its commitment to guaranteeing citizenship goods to all of its
citizens.

There are reasons to think this. It seems to me that a great deal
of the intuitive appeal in the idea that goods should be distributed
autonomously and for sphere-specific reasons derives from the
view that people have justifiable claims to certain goods that the
state should be obliged to satisfy irrespective of their ability to pay
for them, and this can helpfully be articulated in terms of their status, and needs, as citizens.[32] And while Walzer is clearly committed to the purity of the spheres even at levels of provision beyond
those relating to citizenship (and is interested in the distribution of
goods—love, divine grace—that, on any account, have nothing to
do with that role or status), it is arguable that the only conversions

---

[32] As Amy Gutmann has argued, the usefulness of the claim that goods should
be distributed in accordance only with relevant reasons, of which Walzer's position
is a variant, will depend upon 'how closely the language of relevant reasons reflects
the universal needs of citizens within the society one is addressing': *Liberal Equality*
(Cambridge: Cambridge Univ. Press, 1980), 103.

that the state is justified in preventing are those that would infringe the citizenship-claims of others.[33]

Clearly which exchanges the state will be justified in preventing depends on what goods are regarded as citizenship goods and, in particular, on whether they raise any issue of relativities: does someone using her market power to procure more of a good mean that others are being denied that to which they are entitled as citizens? Even if one espouses a basic minimum or threshold conception of citizenship, one might care about inequalities in (and hence conversions of market advantage into) particular goods if they have effects on the absolute level of citizenship goods enjoyed by some.

I cannot explore this issue in any depth, and a single example will have to suffice to illustrate the kind of considerations that arise at this point. Suppose, for example, that equality of opportunity is something that people should have *qua* citizens. In that case, one might object to non-autonomous inequalities in the distribution of education because of the relation between education and opportunity. Consider the contrast with health care. It is plausible to hold that a basic minimum commitment to guaranteeing all citizens equality of opportunity is itself enough to tell against inequality in the distribution of education, and hence against the conversion of market power into educational advantage, but not in itself enough to tell against inequality or conversion in the case of health care. This is because in the case of the former but not the latter there is a concern with relativity built into the good as it relates to citizenship. Because of the positional aspect of education, the fact that it is the relative amount of education one has that affects one's opportunities in life, equality of opportunity as bare citizenship good rules out the conversion of money into education. Health care is different because other people getting more health care than me does not in itself affect the characteristics or the value to me of the health care that I get. I can get all the health care that I need

---

[33] In an unpublished MS, Simon Thompson interprets Walzer as a citizenship theorist, only really concerned that goods be distributed in accordance with their internal criteria up to the level required by (and, where there are two or more rival criteria for the same good, deciding between them on the basis of their relation to) citizenship. Walzer's real master principle of distributive justice requires all social goods to be distributed so as to achieve effective democratic citizenship. This reading seems to me overcharitable.

as a citizen even if others are getting more than me.[34] The same is not true of education.[35]

I think that one can hold on to a great deal of what is normatively appealing about Walzer's vision of a society in which goods are distributed autonomously by restricting his quite general claim about the injustice of conversions to cases where to permit them would be to deny the equality of people as citizens. If a couple of the sociological lessons that are relevant to an assessment of complex equality, understood in the way it has been taken here, are indeed those outlined above—that the state will be needed to prevent conversions and that notions of status weaker than citizenship are less plausible constituents of a complex egalitarian strategy—then it looks as if we might have, and I do not want to put it more strongly, a happy coincidence of normative and sociological plausibility.

[34] I assume here that supply is not restricted. If it is, then of course some using their superior market power to buy health care will reduce the amount available to others, quite possibly to an extent that takes that amount below the level needed by people *qua* citizens.

[35] Exchanges might also be prevented on citizenship grounds if a system of provision in which some are able to buy their care in the market while others get it free from the state would, over time, reduce the level of care available to the latter below the level required by them as citizens. If forcing the better off to participate in the public system of health care is the only way to ensure that citizenship needs are properly met, the opting out could be prevented on these grounds.

Response

MICHAEL WALZER

———=+◊+=———

It is not easy to figure out how best to respond to the chapters in this book. I don't want just to answer the various criticisms that they offer one by one, but rather to rethink central aspects of 'complex equality'—prodded by the critics but not entirely directed by them. Some of these essays usefully respond to one another. Richard Arneson denies the egalitarianism of complex equality, arguing in good philosophical style, and then Adam Swift comes along, as if joining a conversation, and provides the more appropriate sociological frame for the argument. David Miller, so it seems to me, carries the argument forward, and Arneson, at the end of his chapter, disputes the advance. Jeremy Waldron seems to claim not only that I have offered no coherent account of 'blocked exchanges' (a point I won't argue), but that no coherent account is possible; Judith Andre provides an account that bears all the marks of coherence and is also sociologically illuminating, perhaps even politically useful. Brian Barry's broad indictment of the entire project is answered at many points, implicitly and explicitly, by all the writers here who take the project seriously, refine and revise its categories, and further its purposes.

I will deal with seven issues: the meaning and possibility of complex equality; the centrality of democratic citizenship; the danger of complex inequality; the injustice of current international distributions; the role of ordinary morality in distributive justice; the importance of efficiency; and the need for a historical account of social differentiation and distributive complexity. These are disparate subjects, but I hope that I can move naturally from one to the next—the ease of the transitions demonstrating that the argument for complex equality has at least a loose theoretical structure.

THE MEANING AND POSSIBILITY OF COMPLEX
EQUALITY

What is complex equality? It has to do with the autonomy of the spheres of justice, but the story is complicated. 'Spheres' is a metaphor; I can't provide a diagram nor decide upon a definitive number (my own list was never meant to be exhaustive). There isn't one social good to each sphere, or one sphere for each good. Efforts to construct a systematic account along these lines quickly produce nonsense—so quickly that even minimally generous critics ought to notice that I neither offer nor endorse any such account. Consider the easy example of food, which answers, as it were, to very different descriptions (from which different distributions follow) in a time of extreme scarcity and in time of plenty, or at one and the same time for very poor people and for affluent people. Hence soup kitchens and food stamps on the one hand and the grocery store on the other: needs communally provided and commodities available on the market. Defenders of complex equality have no difficulty recognizing both, and it requires a very peculiar single-mindedness to insist that we should have difficulty.

As I argue in *Spheres of Justice*, the case is the same for education, which obviously has no singular meaning.[1] Education for citizenship and basic social competence and education for the professions require different distributive principles. Similarly, again, for work or employment which, as Judith Shklar argued in her book on American citizenship, is a critical mark of inclusion in this (though probably not in every) society.[2] It follows that full employment is a morally desirable policy, whether or not it is economically desirable. The American political community has, Shklar writes, 'a comprehensive commitment . . . to provide opportunities for work to earn a living wage for all who need and demand it'. Work of some basic sort is 'a right derived from the requirements of local citizenship, not a primary human right'. But no one has a right to a particular job for which it is necessary to qualify in some way: 'jobs', differently conceived, must be both provided and merited.

[1] (New York: Basic Books, 1983), ch. 8.
[2] Judith N. Shklar, *American Citizenship: The Quest for Inclusion* (Cambridge, Mass.: Harvard Univ. Press, 1991). The quotations below appear on pp. 100 and 101.

I don't believe that there is, as Amy Gutmann suggests (p. 104), a third conception of jobs that underlies the practice of affirmative action. As in any plausible moral argument, the claim that distributions follow meanings is not absolute; it allows for reasonable exceptions. And the argument for complex equality, applied, let us say, to the American case, can account for affirmative action only as an exception to its principles. But that is exactly how the supporters of affirmative action describe it—as a necessary remedy for past injustice, a violation of the equal opportunity principle to make up for past violations, temporary in its operation. It is to be replaced as soon as possible by meritocratic or qualifying procedures. The recent American argument has taken place, with only a few deviant examples, entirely within the framework of our shared understandings of social goods like education, work, and office. (Susan Okin's argument for electoral quotas has exactly the same form.)

Now, complex equality will be the product of autonomous distributions—when all the necessary remedies for past injustice are in place (and working effectively). This is a prediction, not a definition, and it can be empirically falsified, though I continue to believe that it won't be. How will we know? What is the standard against which evidence might be measured? Arneson argues that I am appealing here (without acknowledging the appeal) to a notion of 'literal' or simple equality (p. 234). In a sense, of course, this is true (and acknowledged): complex equality is a version of equality; the adjective qualifies the noun, it doesn't replace it. So the prediction will 'come true' only if people are in fact more equal, on some measure, than they are now. The distribution of different goods for different reasons by different agents must produce a distribution of different goods *to different people* before we can talk about complex equality. Dominance, I now see, is not produced only by the multiple conversions of a single good (though that is how it is commonly produced today) but also, more simply, by the possession of all the most valued goods, however they come to be possessed. Complex equality is the opposite of both these conditions, its egalitarianism manifest in a radical decline in the dominance of some people over others.

I am inclined to think that the everyday experience of men and women living within such a distributive system will give rise to something like what David Miller means by 'equality of status'. This is not an objective condition (hence the role of experience in generating it), though we might try to objectify it through an inquiry into the sensibility of the participants in the system: how do they feel about themselves and the others? Or we might look for patterns of conduct expressive of egalitarian and inegalitarian sensibilities. My own preference is for a negative account along both these lines, such that complex equality brings with it a decline in arrogance and class conceit on the one side, humility and fearfulness on the other—and also in peremptory command and instant deference. I see no reason to think that this transformation is incompatible with significant inequalities in particular distributive spheres. Think of the difference in the relation of rulers and ruled when the ruler is a democratically elected president or prime minister and when he is an hereditary monarch or a landed or moneyed oligarch—and yet the power inequalities among these individuals may not be different at all.

Complex equality is not best measured, as Adam Swift suggests, by some kind of 'weighted averaging' (of the relative standing of individuals *vis-à-vis* the different social goods: see p. 254). I find it as difficult as he does to imagine non-tyrannical political arrangements that would meet the requirement this procedure suggests: that all the pluses and minuses of all the distributions to all individuals add up to, or even come close to, a literal equality on some overall scale—possession of this good compensating for deprivation of that one. There will certainly be compensating effects in a system of complex equality, though these will probably be realized most clearly in self-appraisals. My job, say, doesn't pay very well, but the work is important (or prestigious or exciting), or it leaves me with additional leisure time, or it makes possible a bid for leadership in the local union, and so on. I don't want to argue, as David Miller does, for the radical incommensurability of goods like money, prestige, excitement, leisure, and leadership, though the necessary weighing, once we turn from self- to social appraisal, will certainly make for fierce disagreements. Perhaps the disagreements themselves will have an egalitarian effect: if two people dispute the relative value of money and leisure, say, then it doesn't matter if each of them produces an overall ranking, for there won't be any *commonly recognized* overall ranking.[3] The greater the

---

[3] Such rankings clearly exist today and are much studied: see e.g. Richard Coleman and Lee Rainwater, *Social Standing in America: New Dimensions of Class* (New York: Basic Books, 1978).

autonomy of the spheres, the greater the likelihood of this result. But it may also be a result of complexity that people just won't bother with this sort of social arithmetic.

Once again, my argument is negative in character: so long as no good, and then no single group of men and women, is dominant, so long as all value doesn't flow in one direction, we won't be counting and measuring all the time. Actual inequalities in this or that sphere will matter less than they do now; we will measure ourselves locally but won't need to fix our place in some larger and more general hierarchy. Or, more likely, some people will still need to do that and will look for some way of doing it, but enough of the rest of us will think this activity slightly ridiculous or beside the point. This might be a useful test of complex equality: that people are inclined to mock those of their fellows who make a fetish of relative social standing.

Is this negative achievement possible? Something like it may well be exemplified in certain sorts of youth societies, like that of American undergraduates, say, once the dominance of wealth over education has been defeated. There are so many available goods (academic, intellectual, artistic, athletic, sexual, and political); the time for acquisition, enjoyment, and use is relatively brief and the goods can't be passed on; the same people don't win in all the 'spheres'; and the (male) student who tries to be a BMOC (big man on campus) is likely to be ridiculed. Even if we leave aside professors and administrators, colleges are not literally egalitarian societies, but they are more egalitarian than the world the students have come from and will return to, and the reason lies in their complexity, the many-sidedness of the life they allow.

A more historical (and adult) example: I grew up in a steel town where the mill owners and managers once literally ran the town, autocratic in their own company, on the factory floor, and in the city itself, the mayor and council members virtual hirelings. New Deal politics and the rise of the CIO led to a separation of economy and polity: the imprisonment of the mayor and several councillors (for taking bribes) and the partial democratization of the factory floor (a strong union, shop stewards, grievance procedures).[4] The effect was a radical change in the 'feel' of social relations—and the reality too. The workers were now also citizens;

---

[4] For a brief account, see Irving Bernstein, *Turbulent Years: A History of the American Worker, 1933–1941* (Boston, Mass.: Houghton Mifflin, 1970), 490–4.

their children were closer to being equals in the educational system (though differences within the new 'consolidated' schools were still marked out more or less along class lines); their churches played a larger role in the social and philanthropic life of the city; fearfulness and deference were far less visible in everyday life. The small decline in income differentials brought about by collective bargaining cannot account for the extent of this transformation. Workers and managers were still highly unequal in earning power and accumulated wealth. The point that I want to make (against Arneson) is that this particular inequality really did mean less when some of the things that money once bought were decisively cut off.

The arguments for these changes were of exactly the sort that the theory of complex equality incorporates and elaborates: they had to do with the integrity of democratic politics; the need for relative equality and uncoerced consent in the labour market; the illegitimate tyranny of foreman on the factory floor. Further changes along these lines, carried beyond what was achieved in Johnstown, Pennsylvania, in the 1940s, would bring us closer to complex equality. I see no reason to believe that advances of this sort would make only for a weak egalitarianism.

THE CENTRALITY OF DEMOCRATIC CITIZENSHIP

This last example suggests the centrality of democratic citizenship—in this case, as both means and end. New Deal politics would have been impossible without an enfranchised, mobilized working class which, though it never seized state power on the Marxist model, did use the state to alter the pattern of social relations across several of the spheres of justice. And in the new pattern, established by citizen power, citizenship itself was an enhanced, more widely distributed, and more visible political role. Democratic participation is a vehicle of social change, and it also gives to the agents of change a strong sense of their own and each other's agency—a crucial condition of Miller's equality of status.

We might think of citizens as agents of last resort in all the spheres. I did not grasp the significance of this extended role when I was writing *Spheres*; I was focused on the agents of first resort, the makers, distributors, and recipients of the goods in question.

My idea was that these people should work out among themselves the meaning of the goods and the appropriate mechanisms of distribution—and that they should defend the integrity of the sphere against external, tyrannical interventions. Imagine priests in the medieval church opposing nepotism and simony, or professors in a modern university resisting the automatic admission of children of wealthy alumni, or the Johnstown workers striking against the autocracy of foremen and managers. But this is only part of the story, for these internal agents disagree among themselves or fail to win the results they seek, and then some of them appeal to the state, and so to their fellow citizens, to intervene and adjudicate the dispute or help one of the sides. A number of critics have pointed out the frequency of such appeals, about which I had nothing to say.

I would suggest now that we distinguish two different sorts of intervention. The first is simply an act of political domination—as when universities, say, are required to admit only party members or teachers are required to inculcate some ideological orthodoxy. The second attends to the goods in question, honestly attempts to resolve the disagreement about their meaning, and then, having reached a (temporary) resolution, leaves the sphere to its 'inhabitants'. The same intervention, obviously, will be differently described by different parties, and so this is one more thing that we will have to argue about—much as we argue about whether intervention in another country violates or enhances its political independence and cultural integrity (and the rights of its members). Citizens are people who cannot justly be excluded from these arguments, not only about the boundaries of the spheres but also about the meaning of the goods distributed within them: hence citizenship takes on heightened instrumental and also symbolic value. Indeed, this value may itself be critical, as both Miller and Swift suggest, in adjudicating the internal disputes. Education, for example, must be so defined as to serve the interests of democratic citizens, that is, to make them competent performers of their political responsibilities. I would only add that this is already a feature of our common understanding of the good that public (state) schools, at least, try to distribute.

But the argument thus far assumes the existence of a modern state, where politics is taken to be an autonomous activity. That sort of state is the focus of my own and my critics' interest. But I am reluctant to say that the theory of justice has nothing to do with states of any other sort—or that it brings to them nothing more than the peremptory demand that they become states of *this* sort. Where politics is not recognized as an autonomous activity (or where other of our 'spheres' are not yet separated out), complex equality, as I said in *Spheres*, has less scope; I would add now that justice itself is less well served. The historical record suggests that in societies with fewer boundaries, the boundaries that exist are less effectively guarded: powerful men roam more freely across political, social, and economic space.[5] None the less, even here the theory of justice can mark out just and unjust distributions—as the members of such societies, and especially the social critics among them, commonly do.

So let me respond to Joseph Carens's question about democracy (see p. 65) by considering the case of a religious republic like contemporary Iran, where there is no separation of mosque and state and no effective citizenship for non-Muslim minorities.[6] Religious identity replaces citizenship, and while this identity has its own inclusiveness (it rules out considerations of race, ethnicity, and class), the borders it establishes are different from those of the state. So the requirement of justice in an Islamic republic might be the full autonomy of all the other religious communities. Democratic citizenship is not available where there is no secular state (and no coherent *demos*), so it makes moral sense to let membership be determined by the communities that actually exist and that are capable of regulating the life of their members. There are two provisos: that everyone be a member somewhere and that membership be a genuine good (autonomy must be real and extensive).

Where does this requirement (with its two provisos) come from? I suppose that it comes all the way from Carens's outermost circle, which is to say, on his account, that it is external to Muslim culture; it is also minimalist and universal, though it represents only 'our' understanding of universalism. But this seems to me an inadequate account of what is at stake here. What I mean to require, most generally, is reciprocity, and some version of this has been

---

[5] I take this 'freedom' to have been characteristic e.g. of feudal societies in Europe.

[6] I cannot respond here to the hard questions that Carens poses with regard to gendered social practices. I have attempted to treat some of the problems involved in an essay on 'Objectivity and Social Meaning', in Martha Nussbaum and Amartya Sen (eds.), *The Quality of Life* (Oxford: Clarendon Press, 1993), 165–77.

accepted in Muslim states in the past—witness the autonomous
Jewish communities of medieval Islam and the millet system of the
Ottoman empire. Reciprocity is not wholly an external idea, even
if some Muslim militants, who may from time to time seize power,
reject it. Nor do I think that it is wholly external to any other culture, however often it is rejected. In any case, a principle of this
sort requires only a reiteration of local self-understandings (first for
us, then for them), not a radically new self-understanding. Insisting
that Iranian Muslims recognize 'the normative force of the democratic ideal' is obviously a further step, and one that I would hesitate to call a requirement of justice (though the democratic ideal
is my own ideal, as it is Carens's).[7]

I don't mean to dismiss the many problems that autonomy
poses, especially with regard to non-believers, who are forced to
take on religion as a kind of ethnic affiliation. (I suspect that most
religious communities have included significant numbers of non-
believers.) Their condition is not, however, entirely different from
that of religious fundamentalists in a secular state. Another problem is more serious: it is very difficult to stop the religious majority from using state power across both communal boundaries and
distributive spheres. The first of these uses is obvious in Iran today,
where there is no recognition of communal autonomy, and I suspect that one could tell a long story of clerical corruption and
tyranny within the Islamic community itself.

Is the absence or ineffectiveness of democratic citizenship in Iran
morally problematic? Yes, because it blocks the full development
of complex equality and because it puts justice at risk—at greater
risk than it is in more differentiated societies. But it does not seem
to me that non-democratic societies are by virtue of that fact alone
unjust. If they were, how could we account for the debates about
justice that have gone on in so many of them? When the
Deuteronomist wrote that much-quoted line 'Justice, justice shalt
thou pursue', he was not calling for a democratic political movement. But he did have a coherent conception of justice, which connects in important ways to our own conception (and which we can
therefore recognize, even if it doesn't extend in the same way that

[7] On autonomy in medieval Islam, see S. D. Goitein, *A Mediterranean Society*,
ii. *The Community* (Berkeley, Calif.: Univ. of Calif. Press, 1971). On the idea of reciprocity as reiteration, see my 'Two Kinds of Universalism', *The Tanner Lectures
on Human Values* (Salt Lake City: Univ. of Utah Press, 1990), xi. 509–32.

ours does to political life). He was denouncing corrupt judges who bent the law in the interests of wealthy and powerful men, or who favoured Israelites over the 'strangers who dwelt in [their] midst'. These are certainly matters of justice, perhaps the most important matters.

THE DANGER OF COMPLEX INEQUALITY

In an actual Islamic republic, like Iran, without autonomous (non-Muslim) communities or separated spheres, distributive outcomes are likely to be patterned in a fairly common way. Pious Muslims, or people who give a good imitation of piety, will supplant other contenders and appear disproportionately among the powerful, the wealthy, and the well-placed, filling the ranks of the civil service and the professions. Obviously, this pattern does not falsify the prediction that I made at the start of this Response, for here the same people win out in every sphere *for the same reason*. The result is best called simple inequality; it is the result of dominance—in this case, a religious-political good, truth and power brought together by an act of revolutionary conquest, sweeps all other goods before it. The gender inequality described and criticized by Susan Okin, though it has a different history, is similarly patterned: patriarchy and male dominance are also examples of distributive simplicity.

Complex inequality, if it ever occurred, would look very different. Now we have to imagine separated spheres and autonomous distributive processes—and the same people winning out, and the same people losing out, again and again *for different reasons each time*. There is no injustice in the actual distributions, presumably, for all the available goods are distributed in accordance with their social meanings, to men and women who possess the appropriate qualities or who have performed in the appropriate ways. The problem is that one group of people possess all the qualities in the highest degree and are also the best performers; another group is more modestly qualified, its performances mediocre; and a third group has none of the appropriate qualities and consistently performs at a very low level. This last group constitutes a new underclass of excluded and dispossessed men and women who have, however, never been discriminated against; they have been fairly considered in every distributive process and everywhere rejected. They are citizens still, enfranchised (though they rarely vote and so are not courted by politicians), provided with a public education (but never intellectually engaged by any of the subjects taught), entitled to welfare (which doesn't, however, help them in any other sphere).

Is there really a significant class of people who fit this description, invisible today because many of its potential members are born into advantaged groups and shielded from distributive justice, who would be sorted out by genuinely autonomous processes? The answer has to be that we don't know; these processes are not yet in place, and they would have to work effectively over an extended period of time before we could say with assurance that their social product was complex inequality rather than the version of egalitarianism that I have described. A test for complexity: would the members of this underclass be as Elster writes (p. 97), 'like the mentally ill, more or less randomly distributed across all social groups'?

Clearly, the contemporary underclass bears no resemblance to this hypothetical and haphazard collection of people. Among ourselves, excluded men and women are not a random series of failed individuals, rejected one by one, sphere by sphere. They come, mostly, in groups with whose other members they share common experiences and, often enough, a family (racial, ethnic, gender) resemblance. Failure pursues them from sphere to sphere in the form of stereotyping, discrimination, and disregard, so that their condition is not in fact the product of a succession of autonomous decisions but of a single systemic decision or of an interconnected set. And for their children, exclusion is an inheritance; the qualities that supposedly produce it are now its products.[8]

All this is, again, simple inequality; we have not yet graduated to complexity. No doubt, the stereotyped results are achieved in subtle and complicated ways, and the political effort to alter, even overturn, those results is very difficult. But the condition is simple, and it tells us nothing about what would happen were we to distribute goods without the distortions currently produced by racism and sexism. Perhaps we would generate the same sort of

[8] I have taken the preceding paragraph from my essay 'Exclusion, Injustice, and the Democratic State', *Dissent* (Winter 1993), 55–64, where the argument of this section is developed at greater length.

underclass, the same hierarchical structures, differently inhabited; the people at each level, including the lowest, would be a random mix of blacks and whites, women and men—or perhaps not. The politics of complex equality is a wager on the anti-hierarchical effects of autonomous distributions. We are not, however, betting in the dark. Both history and everyday life, it seems to me, suggest a fairly radical scattering of talents and qualities across individuals. I wonder if people who imagine a radical concentration are not thinking too narrowly of themselves.

THE INJUSTICE OF CURRENT INTERNATIONAL DISTRIBUTIONS

Suppose that we achieve complex equality without affecting the gross inequalities of international society? Richard Arneson asks whether the internalist account of distributive justice gives us any reason at all to worry about these inequalities (p. 232) and Brian Barry insists that it obviously does not (p. 79). If the same individuals lose out again and again at home, it is even more true that the same countries lose out again and again abroad. But why is this so? If international inequalities have no *international* reason, as Arneson suggests ('they are not tainted even slightly by . . . relations of domination'), then indeed no injustice is involved. Consider the comparison between victims of earthquake and fire in this part of the world and men and women untouched by disaster in some other part. We should be 'morally troubled' if the second group doesn't help the first, but not because the comparison itself is troubling or the earthquake unjust. Arneson's inequality is very much like a natural disaster (though its explanation would presumably involve a mix of natural and social causes: climate, resources, political culture, and so on).

But if we tell a different story—of imperial wars; conquests, occupations, and interventions; the political control of trade, and so on—then we are likely at the end not only to be morally troubled but concerned specifically about the *injustice* of the resulting inequalities. We will be concerned because of our own belief, now widely shared, that political power in international society should be distributed in accordance with the principle of collective freedom and self-determination. How to identify the collective 'self' is still widely disputed, but it is clear enough that the British were not the appropriate determiners of Indian law and policy, nor the Americans of Vietnamese, nor the Russians of Lithuanian. And if these unjust determinations have deleterious social and economic consequences, then remedial measures are morally required. And these may well extend to far-reaching redistributions of wealth and resources.

But doesn't inequality itself, if it is accompanied by human suffering, require similar measures? I have already said so, but not as a matter of justice—justice is not the whole of morality—unless we can tell a story of engagement and responsibility. A number of writers have argued in recent years that evolving patterns of global proximity, knowledge, and interaction make us all responsible for one another.[9] The tendency is indeed clear, and this is the story that needs telling if the requirements of justice are to be expanded. But I am inclined to think that, for now at least, ordinary moral principles regarding humane treatment and mutual aid do more work than any specific account of distributive justice.

THE ROLE OF ORDINARY MORALITY

Several of the chapters in this book stress the role of ordinary morality in shaping distributive principles not only in international but also in domestic society. I concede the point, though I am unsure that morality works, as it were, from the outside, except when it serves as a minimalist constraint. Murder, torture, and enslavement are wrongful features of any distributive process—and they are wrong for reasons that have little to do with the meaning of social goods. We need a theory of human rights (or its functional equivalent in other cultures) to set the basic parameters within which distributions take place. The theory would derive, presumably, from a view of persons rather than of the things they make, and it would establish limits on how these persons may be treated. But even ideas similarly derived, when they affect the distribution of goods, work differently.

Consider, for example, the idea of 'personal responsibility' that figures in the arguments of Amy Gutmann and Jon Elster.

[9] See Charles R. Beitz, *Political Theory and International Relations* (Princeton, NJ: Princeton Univ. Press, 1979).

Personal (rather than national or kin group) responsibility is supposed to determine the jury's decision in a criminal court, and this
is because of what justice means in this setting. Health care, by
contrast, is not distributed in accordance with the same idea: doctors may not refuse to treat patients who are responsible for their
own diseases. They smoke too much, worry too much, work at
risky jobs, but their moral history doesn't matter when they appear
in the emergency room of the local hospital. They may be required
to pay higher insurance premiums: that has to do with our understanding of insurance. We may put a tax on cigarettes and use the
revenue to subsidize health care—but only after cigarettes have
ceased to be regarded as ordinary commodities. Similarly, welfare
benefits are distributed to people in trouble even if they are themselves the cause of the trouble (workers who are fired because, say,
of persistent lateness or carelessness still collect unemployment
insurance). But since the purpose of welfare is the reinstatement of
needy or excluded men and women in society and economy, benefits may be cut off when recipients wilfully refuse the means of reinstatement (new jobs, schooling, community service).

Ideas about personal responsibility play a part in all these distributive decisions, but their part is mediated, not direct. They
shape our understanding of particular goods; they don't serve as
general principles of distribution. They are reiterated in each
sphere, and so they might be called 'trans-sphere' principles, but
they are not transcendent, standing over and above all social
goods; as they are mediated, so they are modified and differentiated. This is the way ordinary morality commonly figures in arguments about justice, and it figures in this way whether its principles
are ahistorical and universal or particular to a time and place.
Personal responsibility can be described in either of these ways:
some such idea seems to be generated by every experience of social
interaction, but it can take different forms with reference to this or
that good in this or that place, with different consequences for distributive arguments.

I need only add that once we have finished with these arguments,
we are not morally finished. There are other judgements that we
may be called upon to make with regard to our society and its institutions (or with regard to other societies). Ideas about the good
life, republican virtue, divine law, self-sacrifice, and much else, lie
outside or beyond justice—which is not to say that men and

women possessed by one or another of these ideas should not join with their fellow citizens in arguing about the meaning of social goods. Entrance is free, though we may want to plead with some of them that they leave their conceptual baggage at the door.

THE IMPORTANCE OF EFFICIENCY

Efficiency is a moral principle implicated in all distributive decisions—and never discussed in *Spheres*. Jon Elster argues that we commonly believe ourselves bound to maximize the production and possession of whatever things we regard as goods. No criteria or procedures of distribution can stand, even if they are in line with the meaning of the good, if their result is that less of the good is produced and possessed overall. Hence the idea of a 'truncated utilitarianism', which requires us to 'maximize total welfare, subject to a floor constraint on individual welfare' (p. 94). Consider now how this might work.

Unemployment insurance and family assistance, let us say, provide the floor, while the labour market makes for maximization. It is certainly true that when we argue about the size of the benefits, we take into account the danger of market disincentives; and when we regulate the market (through minimum wage laws, for example), we are worrying that the floor may be inadequate. But this specific set of concerns depends on understandings we already have about jobs, markets, and welfare programmes. It doesn't appear in pre-bourgeois societies; medieval Christian and Jewish discussions of charitable obligations have a very different form. Maximizing productivity is not one of the goals they aim at.

Elster's fears about the exploitation of the welfare system by the able-bodied poor (an old concern) is best illustrated today by the American debate about how to help (or force) 'welfare mothers' into the labour market. One might well argue (against this policy goal) that caring for children at home is socially valuable work; taxpayers are not being exploited when they are asked to pay for it. Or, one might argue that work outside the home is necessary to the fulfilment of these women as individuals, perhaps also as citizens: we are not saving money but souls when we set time limits on the receipt of welfare. I don't see how considerations of efficiency can resolve disagreements of this sort; efficiency figures in the debates about family, work, and citizenship, but it comes into its own only after we know the meaning and value of the goods they involve. Until then, the maximization required by 'truncated utilitarianism' has no object. I am sure I shall regret this, but I'll say it anyway: efficiency (too) is relative to social meanings.

THE NEED FOR A HISTORICAL ACCOUNT

I am inclined to think that Michael Rustin is right to argue that the theory of complex equality needs, and lends itself to, a historical account of social differentiation. He is not suggesting that we repeat the progressist and Marxist mistake of valuing the future because it is, or will be, *there*. Indeed, on some accounts, we are moving toward a less differentiated society where numeral literacy and technical intelligence, and the education that provides or certifies them, will dominate over all other talents and goods. The point of a Rustin-like story would be to show how complex equality arises out of or fails because of actual social processes and conflicts. Its categories reflect real talk in the real world, and their use requires us to take sides in actual conflicts. Complex equality answers to questions asked with increasing urgency in the course of modern history.

Certainly, it seemed for a long time (and the case might still be made) that social differentiation was the decisive fact about modernity. It would be possible to give a historical account of each of the spheres along these lines: the liberation of the market from religious control (the just price, the ban on usury) and political control (mercantilism), the separation of workplace and household (the factory system), the walling off of church and state (religious toleration, autonomy of politics), the creation of independent schools and universities (academic freedom), the barring of kinship considerations (nepotism) from professional life and the civil service, the ban on the sale of offices and public services (simony, bribery), and so on. It is important to stress that none of these were absolute achievements; nor can they plausibly be described as a simple linear process. But they do hang together so as to constitute a recognizable way of life, within which men and women inhabit many different spheres, adapting themselves to different roles, observing different rules, exercising different talents, even fashioning different identities. Hence, at least, the possibility of complex equality.

Clearly, not everyone values this way of life or the version of egalitarianism it makes possible. Opposition takes a variety of forms: the desire for a great religious/political unification, the dream of a perfect meritocracy (satirized in Michael Young's social science fiction *Rise of the Meritocracy*,[10] which also provides an interesting, only partly invented, historical account), and the hope for a more straightforward egalitarianism (most explicitly advocated in this volume by Arneson). Perhaps one could give historical reasons for resisting these ideas, as Rustin seems to think, but one could probably also give historical reasons for defending them. Social differentiation generates real anxieties to which certain religious doctrines answer fairly well. Merit may well be the coming distributive principle, the goods that it best fits increasingly dominant over all others. And the local inequalities that differentiation allows are large enough and significant enough *right now* to make simple equality an entirely comprehensible choice. Complexity also has to be a choice, which is why I have treated its historical examples as exemplary rather than directional in character.

None the less, the history that Rustin would tell is the history of *our* way of life, and it can also be read as the gradual enactment of a set of values that we have good reasons to defend: freedom, individual autonomy, mutual respect, something like Miller's equality of status, and pluralism itself, which seems to me the condition of all the others. It is when we reflect on distributive justice in its largest sense, and on the values that we would like to see realized in all the spheres, that complex equality comes into its own.

[10] *The Rise of the Meritocracy, 1870–2033* (Harmondsworth: Penguin, 1961).

INDEX